The Book of Singapore's Firsts

Book of Singapore's Firsts
© Elizabeth Kay Gillis & Kevin YL Tan

Published by Singapore Heritage Society
177 River Valley Road #05-06
Singapore 179033
Email: info@singaporeheritage.com

www.singaporeheritage.com

No part of this publication my be reproduced, transmitted, or stored in a retrieval system, in any form, or by any means, without permission in writing from the publisher. This book is sold subject to the condition that it shall not, by way of trade or otherwise, be lent, hired out, resold, or otherwise circulated without the publisher's prior consent in any form of binding or cover other than that in which it is published, and without a similar condition being imposed on the subsequent purchaser.

ISBN 981-05-6185-7

Designed and typeset in Minion by Kevin YL Tan
Cover design by Chin Wei Woon

Printed by
Percetakan Warisan Sdn. Bhd.
No.65 Jalan 12/34A,
Kepong Entrepreneur's Park
52100 Kuala Lumpur

The Book of Singapore's Firsts

Kay Gillis & Kevin Tan

Singapore Heritage Society
2006

ACKNOWLEDGMENTS

A volume of this nature could not have been written and compiled without the help of a great many individuals. We are particularly grateful to Timothy Pwee of the National Reference Collection of the Lee Kong Chian Reference Library and Tim Yap Fuan of the National University of Singapore Library for their help and assistance in helping us locate resources and materials in the course of our research.

We would also like to thank Liu Wei Ho of the National Library Board for allowing us to read through her collection of Singapore 'Firsts' compiled in 1994; and to Mandakini Arora of AWARE who provided Kay with some useful information on the role of women and suggested some resources for our entries on nursing and health.

Thanks and gratitude to Rob and Marion Milliken who gave up part of their holiday in Singapore to bring a professional touch to many of the photographs we used in this book. We very much appreciate the advice and comments offered by our friend and distributor, Ian Pringle of APD Singapore Pte Ltd and Chin Wei Woon who designed the cover. Kay would also like to thank Yee Hok Seong for his help with transport and his willingness to give up a Sunday morning to trail after the photography team.

As always, we are grateful to our respective long-suffering families for putting up with our absences during the writing of this volume. Finally, we thank the Singapore Heritage Society's Executive Committee for their confidence in us and for facilitating the publication of this work.

Kay Gillis & Kevin Tan
July 2006

CONTENTS

1. A Capella — Automobile Club 1
2. Badminton Hall — Businessman of the Year 14
3. Cabaret Dances — Cyber Games Medallist 28
4. Debating Society — Dry Dock 54
5. Editor-in-Chief of the Straits Times — Eye Surgeon 60
6. Family Clinic — Frozen Embryo Babies 65
7. Gambier & Pepper Society — Government House 73
8. Harbour Board — Hydrofoil 78
9. Ice-cream Parlour — Iron Mill 87
10. Japanese Migrant — Jury Trials 91
11. Kidney Transplant — Knighthood 95
12. Land Lease — Lung Transplant 96
13. Malay Graduate of Nanyang University — Musical Society 103
14. National Anthem — Nursing Training 113
15. Observatory — Orchid Show 121
16. Pager — Pugilistic Competition 126
17. Quarantine Station — Queen's Medal 143
18. Race Course — Running Track, Tartan 144
19. Sailing Club — Synagogue 153
20. Tanker — Tuberculosis, Mobile Treatment Vans 170
21. Underground Shopping Mall — University 178
22. Vaccination Programme — Voting 181
23. War Memorial — Writer-in-Residence 183
24. X-Ray Machine — X-Ray Training 188
25. YMCA — YWCA 190
26. Zoo   191

List of Plates

1. Tomb of George Dromgold Coleman, Singapore's first architect.
2. Raffles Hotel, winner of the first URA Architectural Heritage Awards (1994).
3. Go Boon Kwan, founder of Ho Ho Biscuit Company (1898), Singapore's first biscuit factory.
4. Gate to Fort Canning Cemetery, designed by GD Coleman.
5. Fort Canning Cemetery, Singapore's first burial ground, circa 1907.
6. Cavanagh Bridge, Singapore's first steel suspended bridge (built in 1869).
7. Alexander Laurie Johnston, first President of the Singapore Chamber of Commerce (1837).
8. Benjamin Henry Sheares Bridge, Singapore's first viaduct and first bridge to be named after a former President of the Republic.
9. The Singapore-Johor Causeway, Singapore's first land bridge (1924).
10. Stamford Canal where the first Indian temple was reputedly built.
11. & 12. The Esplanade-Theatres on the Bay, Singapore's first purpose-built concert hall and performance complex. The Concert Hall was inaugurated in 2002.
13. Armenian Church, Singapore's first Armenian Church.
14. Old Portuguese Church of St Joseph's in Victoria Street.
15. Cathedral of the Good Shepherd, consecrated in 1846.
16. St Andrew's Cathedral, completed in 1861.
17. Convent of the Holy Infant Jesus, Singapore's first convent school, founded in 1852.
18. Dr Robert Little, Singapore's first coroner and one of the the first Nominated Unofficials.
19. Cheong Chun Tin, the first qualified dentist to establish a practice in Singapore.
20. Dr WRD Middleton, Singapore's first Municipal Health Officer.
21. Dr Lee Choo Neo, Singapore's first woman doctor.
22. & 23. The King Edward VII Medical College, Singapore's first medical school.
24. & 25. Tiong Bahru, Singapore's first public housing estate and 'satellite town' built by the Singapore Improvement Trust in 1936.
26. Thong Chai Medical Institute, the first free clinic in Singapore, founded in 1867.
27. Tan Kim Seng Fountain, the first public fountain.
28. Tan Kim Seng, philanthropist and organiser of Singapore's first Chinese Ball in 1852.

29. The second Pavilion at the Singapore Cricket Club.
30. The Old Race Course at what is now Farrer Park.
31. Caricature of Justice Sir John Tankerville Goldney, first President of the Singapore Golf Club, Singapore's first. The Club was established in June 1891.
32. The Old Golf House at Buffalo Road.
33. Singapore's first commercial digital radio service, SMART Radio, was launched on 19 November 1999.
34. Tombstone of Stephen Hallpike.
35. Members of Singapore's first literary society, the Chinese Philomathic Society, founded in 1896 .
36. The Botanic Gardens' first Director, Henry Nicholas Ridley.
37. Dr Nathaniel Wallich of the Royal Gardens in Calcutta.
38. Sir Peter Benson Maxwell, first Chief Justice of the Straits Settlements.
39. First page of the Second Charter of Justice establishing Singapore's first court, the Court of Judicature of Prince of Wales' Island, Singapore and Malacca.
40. Sir Song Ong Siang, Singapore's first local-born lawyer.
41. Sir Thomas Braddell, Singapore's first Attorney-General.
42. The Masonic Lodge on Coleman Street completed in 1879.
43. The Old Parliament House was Singapore's first court house.
44. William Henry Read, Singapore's first nominated European Unofficial (1867).
45. A view of one of Singapore's first markets, the Telok Ayer Market.
46. The present-day Telok Ayer Market designed by James MacRitchie, and completed in 1894.
47. The interior of today's Telok Ayer Market.
48. Ellenborough Market (on stilts), possibly Singapore's second market.
49. Whampoa's Ice House at Clarke Quay.
50. Whampoa Hoo Ah Kay, Singapore's first Chinese Unofficial member of the Legislative Council.
51. Dalhousie's Obelisk, Singapore's first gazetted National Monument.
52. The Raffles Library and Museum on Stamford Road.
53. Sungei Buloh Wetland Reserve, Singapore's first wetland park. It was opened in 2001.
54. St James Power Station, Singapore's first municipal power station. It was built in 1927.

55. St James Power Station, view of the engine room.
56. Capitol Building.
57. Flint Building, formerly occupied by Emmerson's Tiffin Room.
58. Criminal Investigation Department (CID) Headquarters in Robinson Road.
59. Singapore's first group of Queen's Scholars 1886-1887.
60. Thomas Dunman, Singapore's first Commissioner for Police.
61. Early picture of the Singapore Chinese Girls' School, Singapore's first English-medium school for girls (1899).
62. The Fu Tak Chi Temple on Telok Ayer Street.
63. The Old Parliament House, now the Arts House was Singapore's first Legislative Assembly building.
64. & 65. The Sri Mariamamam Temple, Singapore's first.
66. The first rickshaws were introduced in Singapore in 1880.
67. Charles Burton Buckley and the first 'auto-car' to be imported into Singapore.
68. Singapore's first car repair facility, established by two Australian brothers, CFF and TJB Wearne in 1906 in Orchard Road.
69. Singapore's first auto club on an outing at Tyersall, the estate belonging to the Sultan of Johore.
70. Advertisement of the Singapore's first bus company, the Singapore Traction Company (1925) depicting a trolley bus and an omnibus. The first trolley buses were introduced in 1927.
71. Twilight Kitchen was Singapore's first community film (2003). It starred Moses Lim and Zhang Wenxiang.
72. Dr Lim Boon Keng.
73. Early rubber plantation in Singapore.
74. The Prinsep Street Presbyterian Church.
75. Early scouts of the First Sands Troop (circa 1913).
76. The Cenotaph, Singapore's first war memorial.

Photo Credits

Plate Nos 1,2, 4, 6, 8, 11, 12, 13, 15, 16, 17, 24, 25, 26, 34, 42, 46, 47, 49, 51, 56, 62, 63, 64, 65, 66, 74 & 76 by kind courtesy of Rob and Marion Milliken of Comsight Pty Ltd, Australia.

Plate Nos 33, 53 & 71 courtesy of Kevin Tan

Plate No 27 courtesy of Kay Gillis

All other plates are in the public domain.

A Cappella

Singapore's first **Mandarin a cappella compact disc** album was *A Cappella Fanatix – Mandarin A Cappella,* jointly produced by Young Musicians' Society and Promote Mandarin Council in 2000.

The first **a cappella musical,** *No Strings Attached,* was written and produced by the five-man, one-woman a cappella group, Vocaluptuous under the direction of their musical director Juliette Lay. It was first performed in May 2000. The group also has the distinction of being nominated for their recording of Joyful/Joy to the World, by the international Contemporary A Cappella Society (CASA) for its 2002 Recording awards.

The first **a cappella festival** was the *Streats Explore A Cappella Festival* held between 28 February and 16 March 2003. The Festival featured groups like Neri Per Caso (from Italy), Ball in the House (USA), and Sam Rogers – The One Mouth Band (USA).

Academic Journal

Journal of the Indian Archipelago and Eastern Asia, 1847. The first academic journal published in Singapore was the *Journal of Indian Archipelago and Eastern Asia.* Volume 1 was published by the Mission Press in 1847. The monthly Journal lasted 9 years. Its objectives were to present as many papers as possible that were original or new to the English reader, and to make the *Journal* a work of reference on all subjects connected with the Archipelago.

The *Journal* was edited by James Richardson Logan. As he contributed many articles to the *Journal,* it was known locally as *Logan's Journal.* Interested British residents of the Straits Settlements promised to make their countrymen better acquainted with the Archipelago and its resources. Contributors' papers were given preference, then foreign publications in the Archipelago, papers that have already appeared in English but may have had a limited or an entirely local circulation were also published. Among the papers in the first issue was Logan's paper on 'The Present Condition of the Indian Archipelago' and Thomas Oxley's paper on 'Gutta Percha'.

One of the *Journal's* significant early articles (1848) was a two-part account of 'The Chinese in Singapore' by Seah Eu Chin. This was the **first account of Singapore's Chinese community** by a Chinese scholar. Articles in the Journal have contributed significantly to our knowledge of social conditions during this early period.

The second scholarly journal in English was the *Journal of the Straits Branch of the Royal Asiatic Society* which appeared in 1878. In 1922, its names was changed to *Journal of the Malayan Branch of the Royal Asiatic Society,* and subsequently, to the *Journal of the Malaysian Branch of the Royal Asiatic Society.* It remains in print today and is considered one of the most important academic journals in the region.

The **first Singapore Chinese scholarly journal** devoted to Chinese research about Southeast Asia did not appear until 1940.

This was the *Nanyang Xue Bao* or the *Journal of the South Seas Society*, edited by Xu Yunqiao. Xu came to Singapore from Shanghai in 1931 and taught in a number of Chinese schools for many years before joining the staff of the Chinese daily, *Sin Chew Jit Poh*. He and many of his colleagues from the paper helped found the journal. It continues in publication today.

Administration, Colonial

William Farquhar's Administration, 1819. The first members of the British administration in Singapore were appointed in 1819 by Lord Warren Hastings, Governor General of India. Major William Farquhar was appointed as Resident, and the other appointments were made from existing East India Company officials in Penang, Malacca or Bencoolen on the recommendation of Raffles. They were Lieutenant Henry Ralph, Assistant Engineer in Charge of Ordinance, Lieutenant Francis Crossley, Office-in-Charge of Pay and Stores, Lieutenant Low, temporary Cantonment Adjutant, Surgeon W Smith, Medical officer for Civil and Military Staff and Francis Bernard, Acting Master Attendant.

Advisory Council

1945–1946. The British returned to Singapore following the end of the Japanese Occupation in September 1945. Singapore was placed under the control of the British Military Administration (BMA). Lord Louis Mountbatten was Supreme Commander, while Sir Ralph Hone was appointed Chief Civil Affairs Officer (CCAO) for Malaya and Brigadier Patrick McKerron Deputy Chief Civil Affairs Officer (DCCAO) in charge of Singapore. In November 1945, Hone constituted an Advisory Council to which he appointed 17 officials and non-officials. These included prominent Singapore civic leaders like Tan Chin Tuan, Lee Kong Chian and Dr Abdul Samat. The Council was an informal body with no executive powers. It was not designed to be a Legislative Council but did include representatives of all ethnic communities, representing a wide spectrum of political and public opinion. Care was taken to include representatives of left-wing organisations. The first meeting was held on 14 November 1945 in the Legislative Council Chamber of the Colonial Secretariat. The Council lasted until April 1946 when the BMA came to an end. Among the crucial matters discussed by this Advisory Council was the subject of future legislative arrangements.

Between the end of the BMA and the inauguration of the new post-war constitutional arrangements, Governor Sir Franklin Gimson, was empowered to legislate with the help of the Governor's Singapore Advisory Council. This was a smaller body consisting of 14 members, 6 officials and 8 non-officials. The first and only **woman member** of these two Advisory Councils was Miss Lee Qiu of the New Democratic Youth Party. She was also a member of the Women's Association of the Malayan Communist Party and served as a Propaganda Officer in the Malayan Anti-Japanese Army during the Japanese Occupation. Following her stint on the Advisory Council, she worked as a primary school teacher in Jurong. In 1951, she fled to Tanjong Pinang and later made her way to Beijing. There has been no trace of her since.

Aerobatics Team

Osprey Reds 1973. Singapore's first aerobatic team – the *Osprey Reds* – was formed in March 1973. The team consisted of Lieutenants Jimmy

Lim and Harry Lim, Captains Stewart White and Timothy De Souza and its leader was Major Christopher Strong. The first **all-Singaporean aerobatic team** was the *Black Knights* which was formed a year later in 1974. The team consisted of Lieutenant Frank Singam, Captain Timothy De Souza, Lieutenant Harry Lim, Captain Michael Teo and was led by Lieutenant Jimmy Lim. All of the officer pilots came from the 140 Squadron of the Republic of Singapore Air Force.

Agricultural Society

Agricultural & Horticultural Society, 1836. On 24 May 1836, a public meeting was held at the Reading Room (located at what is today's Golden Shoe Car Park) to form the first Agricultural and Horticultural Society. The subscription to join was $2 quarterly and the meetings were held at 7.00 pm on the first Saturday of every month. The Governor was appointed President of the Society and Messrs Balestier, Montgomerie, Almeida, Brennand and Thomas Owen Crane were members of the committee. At the first meeting, Dr Thomas Oxley spoke on the objectives of the society. At the second meeting, Dr. Montgomerie spoke on the expense of clearing and draining the jungle to increase cultivation.

AIDS Cases

April 1983. Dr KV Ratnam discovered the first 3 AIDS cases at the Middle Road Hospital in April 1983. By the end of June 2005, 2,508 cases of HIV infection had been identified in Singapore. 957 of these were identified as asymptomatic carriers, 621 had full-blown AIDS and 930 patients had died. 2,217 of those infected with HIV were males and 291 were female. Patients are treated at the Communicable Diseases Centre at Tan Tock Seng Hospital. The organisation Action for Aids is a volunteer group working with patients identified with HIV infections and with AIDS. The organisation offers the only anonymous HIV testing facility in Singapore

Air Crash

17 February 1931. The first air force air crash happened at Seletar Air Force Base on 17 February 1931. At 11.00 am that morning, Flying Officer Davis and Corporal Boyce crashed into the sea off the Air Base at Seletar. Davis was flying a Hawker Horsley Bomber plane S1444. The accident happened 30 minutes after Davis took off. The plane dived from 5000 feet and crashed into the sea close to a small island about 2 miles (3.2 km) off Seletar jetty. Davis was found floating in the water and appeared to have been thrown out by the force of the crash. The body of Corporal Boyce was found among the wreckage of the plane. Boyce was serving in the Royal Air Force on a short term commission and came out to Singapore 4 months before the accident to join a new bomber squadron. He was buried in Bidadari Cemetery with full military honours on 19 February. Boyce was an orderly room corporal and was a passenger on the flight. He was buried at Bidadari Cemetery with full military honours on 18 February 1931.

The **first civilian air crash** took place on 13 March 1954. A London-based Qantas-BOAC Constellation aircraft from Sydney touched down on the new Kallang Airport. As it did so, it spun round and broke in two halves and exploded. Six members of the crew and one passenger managed to escape. Two crew members and 31 passengers were killed.

Air-Conditioned Buildings

Chinese Club, 1932. The first air-conditioning unit to be installed in Singapore was at the Chinese Club in 1932. It was a Carrier air-conditioner installed by Carrier's Singapore agents, United Engineers Limited. The first **air-conditioned cinema** was the *The Alhambra* in Beach Road. The Shaw Brothers purchased the cinema from the family of its owner Tan Cheng Kee (son of Tan Keong Saik), after Tan passed away. The first **centrally air-conditioned skyscraper** was the Bank of China Building completed in 1954. The 18-storey building was one of the first tower blocks in the region and was a forerunner of the high rise towers in the Central Business District. In the early 1950s, *Tai Thong Restaurant* became Singapore's first **Chinese restaurant** to be air-conditioned. The Elizabeth Grill at Raffles Hotel and the Adelphi Grill followed suit. All these establishments installed Carrier air-conditioners. Singapore's first **air-conditioned bus interchange** is *Toa Payoh Central Interchange*. It was declared open by Transport Minister Yeo Cheow Tong on 19 May 2002. The $16.5-million Interchange is integrated with the new HDB Centre (HDB Hub) and is also linked to Toa Payoh MRT Station.

Aircraft Carrier, Mooring

USS Kitty Hawk, 2001. *USS Kitty Hawk* (CV 63) was the first aircraft carrier ever to moor alongside Singapore. The Kitty Hawk is a conventionally-powered aircraft carrier built by the New York Shipbuilding Corporation at Camden, New Jersey and commissioned at the Philadelphia Naval Shipyard on 29 April 1961. It moored alongside Singapore at 4.00 pm on 23 March 2001 at the Republic of Singapore's new deep-draft vessel pier at Changi Naval Base. US Chief of Naval Operations, Admiral Vernon Clark and Singapore's Chief of Navy, Rear Admiral Lui Tuck Yew were present at the momentous occasion. The USS Kitty Hawk is loaded with 87 aircraft, 4 terrier missiles and is manned by a crew of 4,500 personnel. It has a standard displacement of 61,000 tons and a top speed of 33 knots.

Air Force

Singapore Air Defence Command, 1971. Singapore's first air force was the Singapore Air Defence Command which was set up on 15 September 1971. That same day, the Republic of Singapore Air Force took control of Tengah Air Base. The first squadron formed was the 120 Squadron. The first RSAF pilot to achieve 100 flying hours was Captain Michael Teo of 141 Squadron. He became Singapore's **first local Squadron Commander** in January 1975.

Air Force Base

Seletar Air Base, 1928. Plans to establish an airfield, flying boat and naval base in Singapore were formulated by the Royal Air Force (RAF) in 1921. By 1923 two sites in the northern part of the island were approved and eventually the site at Seletar was chosen. Seletar Air Base was completed in 1928. On 10 December 1928, the Royal Air Force (RAF) Far East Flight of four Supermarine Southampton seaplanes (flying boats) landed at the newly constructed airstrip. The flight was led by Group Captain Henry Meyrick Cave-Brown-Cave, who became the **first Station Commander** of RAF Seletar. The flight, which went through Egypt, India, Hong Kong, Japan and Australia, arrived in Singapore on 10 December 1928. The Flight flew a total of 27, 950 miles and became No 205 Squadron on 1 January 1929.

Cave-Brown-Cave (1887-1965) later became Officer Commanding of 205 Squadron at Seletar (1929), Officer Commanding, Far East Command, RAF Base Singapore (1930), and Air Vice-Marshall (1935). RAF Seletar served as a civil airport before the opening of Singapore's first civil airport at Kallang on 12 June 1937.

In 1932, RAF Tengah Air Base was opened. It was built to give cover to the Singapore Navy Base. In September 1971, RAF Tengah was handed over to the Singapore Air Defence Command (later renamed the Republic of Singapore Air Force) and renamed Tengah Air Base. The Flying Training School was set up Tengah Air Base in 1969. The first batch of 35 pilot trainees trained in 8 Cessna 172 H planes. From 1971to 1976, Tengah Air Base was home to the Five Power Defence forces of British, Australian and New Zealand pilots. In 2005, the Tengah base is home to 114, 140, 142, 143, 145 Squadrons flying F16 Fighting Falcons, EZC Hawkeyes, A4SU Super Skyhawks as well as logistic and maintenance support groups.

Air Force Training School

Flying Training School, Tengah Air Base, 1969. In January 1968, the British government announced its decision to withdraw all its forces by the end of 1971 instead of mid-1970s as originally planned. Shortly after the announcement, the first batch of Singaporean pilot trainees was recruited. The applicants underwent stringent medical and aptitude tests and interviews, and the successful candidates were sent to the United Kingdom for jet training.

An Air Command was established and designated the Singapore Air Defence Command (SADC) in September 1968. On 1 Aug 1969, Minister for the Interior and Defence, Lim Kim San, inaugurated the Flying Training School (FTS) in RAF Tengah (now Tengah Air Base).

The **first batch of 35 fighter pilot trainees** at the FTS trained in 8 Cessna 172H planes. They graduated in November 1970. Amongst this batch was 2LT Goh Yong Siang who rose to be Chief of Air Force on 1 Jul 1995.

see also *Republic of Singapore Air Force*

Airline, Commercial

Malayan Airways, 1947. Singapore's first commercial airline was Malayan Airways which was established May 1947. It operated a twin-engine Airspeed Consul between Singapore, Kuala Lumpur, Ipoh and Penang. By 1955 Malayan Airways had a fleet of Douglas DC-3s. When the Federation of Malaysia was formed in 1963, Malayan Airways became Malaysian Airways. Three years later, it was renamed Malaysia-Singapore Airlines (MSA), acknowledging the joint shareholding of the governments of Malaysia and Singapore. MSA ceased operations in October 1972 and two new airlines, Malaysia Airline System (now called Malaysia Airlines or MAS) and Singapore Airlines (SIA), were born.

Airline, Budget

Valueair, 2004. Singapore's first private budget airlines, Valueair was launched on 5 May 2004, flying the popular Singapore-Hong Kong route at a promotional rate of $174 for return tickets. Its original Chairman and acting Chief Executive Officer was Lim Chin Beng, formerly managing director of Singapore Airlines. In July 2005, Valueair merged with Jetstar Asia, a subsidiary of Qantas. Geoff Dixon took over as Chairman and Ken Ryan as CEO.

Air Plane, Landing

Race Course, 1911. In 1911, the **first flight demonstration** of an aeroplane took place at the Race Course at what is now Farrer Park. It was piloted by Belgian M Joseph Christiaens, and was Singapore's first step into aviation. The **first plane landed** in Singapore around 1912. It was a hydroplane which took off from the beach near the old Sea View Hotel off Meyer Road. In 1919, the **first overseas aircraft** landed at the Race Course from England en-route to Australia. It was a Vickers Vimy piloted by Captain Ross Smith. The plane landed on 4 December 1919 enroute from London to Darwin. Smith won the £10,000 offered in March 1919 by the Australian Government for the first flight made by an Australian from Britain to Australia in a British aircraft. Under the rules of the challenge, the flight had to be completed within 720 hours, and the take-off was to be made from Hounslow Aerodrome or Calshot Seaplane Station in England. Smith arrived in Darwin on 10 December 1919. The 1st Royal Air Force plane landed in Singapore on 20 April 1924.

Singapore's **first paying airplane customer** was in 1927 when newspaper tycoon W Van Lear Black touched down on Balestier Plain in a single-engine monoplane chartered from KLM in Europe. In 1929, the Seletar Air Base was completed. The government decided to allow the landing of commercial aircraft at Seletar Air Base. A Dutch aircraft (KLM Fokker F-7A) made the **first commercial landing** at Seletar on 11 February 1930, carrying eight passengers from Batavia (Jakarta). The first **scheduled service** to Singapore was operated by Imperial Airways. It left London on 9 December 1933. Kallang Airport was officially opened on 12 June 1937 and the first aircraft to land there was a flight of Hawker Ospreys off the aircraft carrier *HMS Hermes* on 21 November 1935. Kallang was replaced by Paya Lebar Airport (1955), and then Changi International Airport (1981). The first commercial airline to **land at Changi Airport** was a Singapore Airlines' Boeing 747, Flight SQ692 which landed on 12 May 1981 at 7.25 pm. The first airline to land at the Changi Airport's **Terminal 2** was Singapore Airlines' Flight SQ23 from Amsterdam and Zurich. It carried 317 passengers and landed on 22 November 1990 at 7:40 am.

The first plane flown by Singapore Airlines' predecessor, Malayan Airways, was a twin-engine Airspeed Consul which took off from Singapore, on 1 May 1947. Its **first stewardess** was Miss Rosemary Tay. The first Boeing airplane to land in Singapore was a Qantas Boeing 707 which landed at Paya Lebar Airport on 10 August 1959. Singapore Airlines introduced its **first non-smoking flight** in April 1988.

The **first Jumbo jet** flew into Paya Lebar Airport on 3 July 1971. The Pan American Airways Boeing 747 under the control of Captain IR Anderson, landed at 6.18 pm with 22 passengers on board. About 5000 people were at the airport to welcome the plane. The plane had taken about 20 hours to complete the flight from San Francisco via Honolulu, Guan, Manila and Saigon. This was the start of a new service between San Francisco and Singapore. Flights operated three times a week leaving San Francisco on Monday, Wednesday and Friday arriving in Singapore on Tuesday, Thursday and Sunday. The plane left the following day for San Francisco with 41 passengers on board, all American citizens.

Singapore-born Flight-Lieutenant Tan Kay Hai was the first Straits Chinese to fly with the Royal Air Force and to win the **Distinguished Flying Cross**. The **first pilot to land at the**

Paya Lebar Airport, was the First Officer Chan Soon Kin of Malayan Airways, who had up till then clocked 8,000 flying hours to his credit.

Airport or Airfield

Race Course, 1919. Singapore's **first airfield** was at Race Course Road, actually a field used for horse-racing (See *Race Course*). Singapore's **first airport** at Seletar operated as an air base from 1929 until the Kallang Basin swamps were reclaimed for Kallang Airport in 1937. The Kallang Airport was Singapore's **first civil airport**. The original runway was circular with the principal runway running East-West along what is now Stadium Road. The terminal building was renovated extensively in 1993 to house the headquarters of the People's Association.

Air Show

Singapore hosted its first international Air Show at the Paya Lebar Airport from 8 to 16 April 1961. The show included static displays, an exhibition and cultural programmes.

Alligator Incident

see *Crocodile*

Amusement park

New World, 1923. The New World was conceived and built by two Straits Chinese brothers Ong Boon Tat and Ong Peng Hock, sons of tycoon Ong Sam Leong. There is a general misconception that it was the initiative of the Shaw Brothers, Asia's movie moguls. When in their 30s, and while working in their father's company, Ong Sam Leong & Co., the Ong brothers decided to venture into the entertainment business, as part of a land speculation exercise. At the time, Boon Tat headed the company as Administrator to the Estate, while Peng Hock worked as the Attorney. The primary business of Ong Sam Leong & Co., listed in the 1922 *Singapore and Malaya Directory*, was 'Merchants, Estate & Property Owners'.

The second amusement park was Great World Amusement Park ('Tua Say Kai' in Hokkien) which started out as an aggregation of some 150 shacks in the 1920s. It was later developed by one of its landholders, Lee Choon Yung, into an amusement park aimed at lower-income families. Shortly before World War II, it was sold to Shaw Brothers. During the Japanese Occupation, it served as a camp for Australian Prisoners-of-War (POWs), and fell into disrepair after the war ended. Great World Amusement Park reopened in grand style in 1958 with four movie theatres – the smaller Atlantic and Canton cinemas, facing Zion Road, and the larger and more luxurious, Globe and Sky cinemas, looking out to Kim Seng Road. Great World Amusement Park closed at the end of March 1974 but the cinemas continued to play till 1978. Shaw sold it in 1979 to the Malaysian sugar magnate Robert Kuok who tore it down to build Great World City Shopping Centre (1997).

Anaesthetics, usage

1847. The first recorded administration of an ether anaesthetic was recorded in the *Singapore Free Press* in 1847. The ether was administered by Dr Robert Little on a boatman to enable a splinter to be removed from the latter's hand. This took place surprisingly soon after the first demonstrated use of ether as an anaesthetic in Boston in October 1846.

Animal Welfare Organisation

Society for the Prevention of Cruelty to Animals, 1876.
A Society for the Prevention of Cruelty to Animals was established in 1876 but was dissolved in 1902. Its residual funds, comprising some $9000, was used to build an Animals Infirmary. The responsibility for monitoring cruelty to animals was given to the Municipality. In 1921, there were 990 prosecutions for animal cruelty and 953 convictions. The Society was revived and became the Singapore branch of the Royal Society for the Prevention of Cruelty to Animals. In 1954, the Association was revived by Miss Lucia Bach and moved into its headquarters in Orchard Road. In 1959, when Singapore ceased to be a crown colony, the 'Royal' was dropped from the Society's name.

Aquarium, Public

Van Kleef Aquarium, 1955.
Singapore's first public aquarium was the Van Kleef Aquarium opened in September 1955. Located at the foot of Fort Canning Hill along River Valley Road, the aquarium was home to more than 6,000 aquatic creatures. The aquarium was named after KWB Van Kleef, a Dutch resident who donated $470,000 towards its construction. The aquarium was maintained by the Primary Production Department (now Agri-Food and Veterinary Authority of Singapore). The aquarium was most popular in the 1970s, with almost 400,000 visitors a year. In 1986, the aquarium underwent a $750,000 facelift. However, the revamped aquarium was not popular with visitors who complained about the lack of information on the creatures on display. In May 1991, Van Kleef Aquarium closed its doors for good.

Architect

George Dromgold Coleman, 1826.
The first architect in Singapore was George Dromgold Coleman who spent fifteen years in Singapore from 1826 to 1841. Coleman was born in Drogheda, County Louth, Ireland in 1795. Little is known about his academic background but he appears to have been an articled pupil with an established architect. In 1815, at the age of 19, Coleman went to Fort William (Calcutta) in India where he practiced architecture and where he built many houses for merchants. His association with John Palmer brought him to Java in 1820 where he built a cathedral. He stayed in Batavia for two years before traveling to Singapore in June 1822.

After Coleman arrived in Singapore, he waited four months for Raffles to return from Bencoolen in Sumatra. He must have been looking for work because while waiting, he designed a Residency House. Raffles was impressed with Coleman's design and immediately commissioned him to design a garrison church. Coleman was paid for both jobs and in January 1823, the Residency was built atop Bukit Larangan - Forbidden Hill - now called Fort Canning Hill. The building was constructed of timber with a thatched (attap) roof. The Residency was a bungalow with a 100-foot frontage and was 50 feet deep with rough plank walls, Venetian windows and was known named Government House. It stood at Fort Canning until it was reconstructed in 1859. Due to several delays, Coleman was not to build the garrison church for a decade. It was only in 1835 that construction of St Andrew's Church (later replaced by St Andrew's Cathedral) began.

On 9 June 1823, Raffles left Singapore for the last time. At the same time, Coleman returned to Batavia in Java, where he stayed for two-and-a-half years, where he became busy with extensive agricultural speculation. He built large embankments and reservoirs for irrigation of rice fields, surveying sugar plantations and developing schemes for buildings on sugar estates between 1824 and 1825. But when war broke out between the Dutch and the native Javanese in 1825, Coleman returned to Singapore. His first commission was a large Palladian house for David Napier. This was followed by a commission for a palatial brick residence for Java merchant John Argyle Maxwell; now the Old Parliament House (1827).

In 1829, Coleman was engaged to undertake a topographical survey of Singapore. He surveyed islands off the port, all the shoals and slopes and heights of hills along the coast in minute detail and the map he produced was the first comprehensive map of Singapore island and town. It was printed in Calcutta in 1836. In addition to his government duties, Coleman continued his architectural practice. He designed the Armenian Church of St Gregory the Illuminator in Hill Street (1835), and many warehouses and godowns including one for the philanthropist Tan Kim Seng. In 1835, together with William Napier (David Skene's younger brother) and Edward Boustead, Coleman set up The *Singapore Free Press and Mercantile Advertiser* (1835). Coleman used the Palladian style in many of his buildings. He also developed a 'colonial' style that had been modified to suit the tropical environment. His houses often had wide verandahs and louvred windows. He died in Singapore on 27 March 1844 after a brief illness and was buried in Fort Canning Cemetery.

Ho Kwong Yew is one of the first generation of **foreign-educated local architects** who returned to Singapore and set up the Architectural practice here. Ho was educated as a structural engineer and later became a registered Architect in Singapore. Because of his civil engineering background, his design was logical, sophisticated, but artistic. He employed new building technology and new building materials, especially reinforced concrete, because of its fluidity, easy to be moulded, and offered new possibilities of forms. As a charismatic local architect, he succeeded in getting lots of projects from both European and Chinese business clients. His 1930s Modern Style houses were always straightforward in character, logically proportioned, and freely designed; as a reflection of the new, liberal, optimistic attitudes towards life; the spirit of entrepreneurships of the 1930s. One of his masterpieces, the house in Haw Par Villa for the famous tycoon Aw Boon Haw was bombed by the Japanese in 1942, and Ho was himself was executed by the Japanese occupation army.

Ng Keng Siang was trained at the Bartlett School Architecture in London. He was the first Singaporean to become a **member of the Royal Institute of British Architects**. He designed the Asia Insurance Building. When it opened in 1954. it was the tallest building in Singapore. It was the first attempt to produce Regional modern architecture.

Architectural Heritage Awards

URA, 1994. In 1994 the Urban Redevelopment Authority (URA) gave its first Architectural Heritage Awards in 'recognition to monuments and buildings with preservation and conservation status in Singapore judged to have been well restored'. In 1994, these awards were called the Good Efforts Awards and were presented to 9 architects and owners. The winners in the National Monuments Category were: City Hall, Raffles Hotel and Empress Place Building.

Three awards were given to buildings in the early phase of conservation; No 24 Bukit Pasoh Road, No 83 Duxton Hill, and 9-35 Erskine Road. In the Three R category of Conservation (restoration, retention of character and repair) three awards were given to three residences in Emerald Hill: Nos. 41, 74 and 94. In 1995, the awards were named the Architectural Heritage Awards.

Architecture Graduates, Local

Singapore Polytechnic, 1964. The first batch of architecture students from the Singapore Polytechnic School of Architecture graduated in 1964. They were: Lee Seng Loong, Liew Beng Leong, Tay Kheng Soon, Teoh Ong Tuck and Wee Chwee Heng.

Area Licensing Scheme

1975. In 1975, the government introduced the Area Licensing Scheme to control traffic flow in the central business district area. It was applied to an area encompassing 725 hectares. Vehicles other than emergency vehicles or buses entering this Restricted Zone had to purchase and display an area license to enter.

In 1995, a pilot **Road Pricing Scheme** was introduced to deal with congestion on the East Coast Parkway. Cars were charged as they entered the central area under an overhead gantry. Payment was through a cash-card slotted into an 'in-vehicle unit' installed on the car's dashboard. In 1998, the **Electronic Road Pricing** was introduced. Different rates were charged for the use of popular routes at different times of the day.

Army Camp

Cantonment Road, 1819 & Tanglin Barracks, 1860. Military accommodations were built in early Singapore from the earliest times. The first such accommodation was at what is now Cantonment Road where barracks were built in 1819 to house the East India Company's Sepoy troops. Troops were 'cantoned' in this area till they moved in 1824 to the end of Silat Road. Because of the Sepoy cantonments in this area, it became known as Sepoy Lines. Other than the cantonments in this area, there were other cantonments of troops in Bras Basah Road.

The outbreak of the Crimea War encouraged the Indian government to give serious consideration to building a fort and an army camp. In 1857, Governor Edmund Blundell gave the military permission to purchase two pieces of land to establish a military post. The 210-acre site in Tanglin had been a nutmeg plantation owned by William Willan. It was bought at a cost of 5,500 rupees in 1860. Construction of the Tanglin Barracks commenced that same year. Captain Collyer of the Madras Engineers arrived in Singapore in 1858 to create a defence network in Singapore and it was he who supervised the building of Tanglin Barracks. The construction cost £30,000 and were large airy structures with wooden boards and an open verandah running along all four sides of the building. Unfortunately, Calcutta's refusal to commit troops to be stationed in Singapore meant that the barracks remained unoccupied after they were completed and soon fell into disrepair. By 1863, it was estimated that it would cost an additional £20,000 to renovate the barracks. Nothing was done till the transfer of power from the India Office to the Colonial office in 1867. By 1870, the Tanglin Barracks had been completely renovated and the 80th Foot Staffordshire Volunteers occupied the camp.

The camp consisted of barracks for the men, bungalows for the officers, a parade ground and a rifle range. There was also a cricket ground, a garrison church, a golf course and stables. Rudyard Kipling stayed at Tanglin Barracks when he visited Singapore in 1898. He wrote two poems during his stay there and these became part of his 'Barrack Room Ballads'. Between 1968 and 1988, the camp was used by the Defence Forces of the now independent Singapore.

Arts Centre, Contemporary

The Substation, 1990. The Substation is Singapore's first independent contemporary arts centre. It was founded by Kuo Pao Kun in September 1990 and occupies an old, disused electrical substation on Armenian Street. The centre has a black box theatre, a gallery, a dance studio and 2 multi-function classrooms. The Substation supports research and innovation in the arts, nurturing and challenging Singapore artists by providing an open space for experimentation, promoting interaction, facilitating critical dialogue in the arts and fostering regional and international arts networks.

Arts Festival, Singapore

1977. The first Singapore Arts Festival was launched on 24 April 1977 at the Victoria Theatre with a special Festival Showcase Night. It featured a special guest performance by the Pembroke Girls' Choir from Australia led by Colin Curtis and the Singapore Youth Orchestra led by guest conductor Yoshino Osawa. The performance included a rendition of the Grand March from Verdi's *Aida*. The premiere was held the following night on 25 April and was attended by Chai Chong Yii, Senior Minister for State (Education). The festival showcased local talent and awards were given to successful local entrants such as Les Petite Fleurs, the Rose Eberwien Dancers and the Phoenix Dance Troupe. There were band performances by the Maris Stella High School Orchestra and Singapore American School Concert Band. The festival was organized by the Young Musicians' Society and the Ministry of Education.

Arts Festival, London

2005. On 25 February 2005, the first Singapore Arts Festival opened in London. The Singapore season featured a variety of cultural and arts performances including the Singapore Dance Theatre and the T'ang Quartet. The opening show was titled *Insomnia* and was held at the Institute of Contemporary Art. Amongst the performances were 'The Continuum: Beyond the Killing Fields' featuring shadow puppets, music and dance and was performed in English and Khmer languages.

Art School or Academy

Nanyang Academy of Fine Arts (1938). In the early 1930's, a Japanese-trained Chinese artist, Huang Suiheng, founder of the Xiamen Art Academy, China, stopped by Singapore on his way back from France. During his short stay here, Huang observed that the strategic global position of Singapore, together with its tropical influence made it an attractive place to set up an institution for fine arts. On his return to China, he persuaded Lim Hak Tai, a teacher at the Xiamen Art Academy to establish an art school in Singapore. The outbreak of the

Sino-Japanese War drove Lim and a group of art teachers to Singapore. They visited Tan See Siang, a local businessman to discuss the idea of establishing a fine arts institution in Singapore. In 1938, the Nanyang Academy of Fine Arts was established in a shophouse in Geylang with 14 students. It later moved to a rented bungalow off River Valley Road. It moved 6 times in 67 years. By the 1970s the institution was operating at a loss despite an enrolment of about 180 students. In 1978, the school was in danger of closing. The Chinese community strongly responded to the proposed closure and a new management committee re-organised the institution. Its alumni include many Cultural Medallion winners such as Ng Eng Teng and Wee Beng Chong and is a veritable 'Who's Who' of the Singapore art world. Strong government financial backing and polytechnic level funding enabled the school to offer a wide variety of fine arts courses. In 2004, the school moved into new purpose-built premises in Bencoolen Street which cost S$110 million. The institution offers a wide variety of full-time Diploma courses and part-time Certificate courses in fashion, visual arts and performance, as well as several degree courses in collaboration with some British universities.

Asian Games Medallist

Neo Chwee Kok, 1951. Singapore's first Asian Games gold medal was won by Neo Chwee Kok ('Flying Fish') in the 1951 Asian Games in Delhi, when he won the 1500m freestyle swimming event. Neo (1931-1986) was also the **first Singapore swimmer to compete at the Olympics.** At the Delhi Games, Neo was the superstar of the pool, splashing his way to an astounding four-gold medal haul (400m, 800m, 1500m freestyle and 4x100m relay), aged only 21 and resting only 10 minutes between the 800m freestyle and 4x100m relay.

Ng Liang Chiang (1921-1992) won Singapore's **first track and field gold medal** for 110m hurdles at the Delhi Games. In 1974, Chee Swee Lee became the **first Singaporean woman gold medallist** at the Asian Games. She was only 19 years of age and won the 400 metres finals in a games record time of 55.08 seconds. The first Asian Games **team gold medal** was won by Singapore's men's 4x100m relay swim team at the Delhi Games. The team comprised Barry Mitchell, Lionel Chee, Wiebe Wolters and Neo Chwee Kok. It was and still is the only relay gold ever won by Singapore in the Asian Games series. In the 1954 Asian Games in Manila, the waterpolo team won Singapore's **first gold medal for team sport.** The champion team comprised: Kee Soon Bee (Captain), Tan Hwee Hock, Gan Eng Teck, Tan Eng Bock, Keith Mitchell, Oh Chwee Hock, Wiebe Wolters and Oh Kian Bin.

Asian Wall Street Journal, Asian Editor

Reginald Chua, 1997. The first Asian Editor of the *Asian Wall Street Journal* was Singaporean Reginald Chua, who was appointed in July 1997. Chua, who joined the *Journal* in 1993 as its Manila correspondent, opened its Hanoi bureau in 1995. In 1997, he was appointed deputy managing editor in Hong Kong.

Auctions and Auctioneers

Crane Brothers, 1827. In 1825, Thomas Owen Crane founded the first auction house in Singapore. In 1825, Crane left England with the intention of settling down in India. However, he was shipwrecked off the coast of Spain. He was able to swim ashore, and lived for a month on shoe leather, rats and shellfish. A vessel bound for Singapore rescued him and so he came to Singapore instead. Soon after he arrived, he founded a business called Thomas O. Crane. In 1842, his brother William came up from Australia to join him. The firm was then renamed Crane Brothers. They were land agents and auctioneers. William returned to England in 1857 and Thomas Crane continued in business as Thomas Crane & Co until he retired in 1861. In 1826, Thomas Crane married Marianne d'Almeida, the eldest daughter of Dr. Jose d'Almeida. They had fourteen children and lived for many years in their house in Geylang. He left Singapore in 1866 and died in London in 1867. He was a Justice of the Peace, Secretary of the Agricultural and Horticultural Society and one of the wardens of the first Freemason's Lodge. Thomas and his son Charles sang a duet 'Larboard Watch' at the first concert given by the Amateur Musical Society in 1865. His son Charles Crane continued to run the business until July 1899 when he left Singapore.

The **first Chinese auctioneer** was Yow Hi Ting. He was educated at Queen's College, Hongkong and came to Singapore and became involved in a variety of business ventures. He became a leader of the Cantonese community in Singapore.

Automobile Club

Singapore Automobile Club (1907). The Singapore Automobile Club met for the first time on 17 June 1907 outside the Singapore Club in Fullerton Square. It was a red letter day in the history of motoring in Singapore. The cars assembled in the square for a photo to be taken by GR Lambert and there were 30 cars of all descriptions, including HRH the Sultan of Johore's 50-horsepower Mercedes, the Governor Sir John Anderson and Miss Anderson in a red Gregoire. There were 4 Humbers, De Dions, 2 Darracqs, Oldsmobiles, Albion, Wolseley and Star automobiles. Charles Burton Buckley was there in his 'obsolete motoring machine' nicknamed the coffee machine. The members of the club then drove to the Seaview Hotel for refreshments. Mr. Lambert had found it difficult to line all the cars up in the square so it was decided that they would meet at Tyersall, the Sultan of Johore's residence, the following week to try again.

B

Badminon Hall

Singapore Badminton Hall, 1952. In 1948/49, the Malayan Team won the inaugural Thomas Cup Tournament held in London. The victory also won Malaya the right to host the next Thomas Cup Tournament, scheduled for 1952. As no suitable indoor hall in Malaya was available, the Singapore Badminton Association (SBA) decided to build one in Singapore. In 1951, the SBA's request for a piece of land at Guillemard Road to build a badminton stadium was granted with a 99-year lease (effective from 1 Jul 1951). The Singapore Badminton Hall (SBH) was completed in May 1952 but it was not ready for the second Thomas Cup Tournament which was held from 27 to 28 May that year. In any case, the tournament was held at the Happy World Stadium where the Malayan Team comprising: Wong Peng Soon, Ong Poh Lim and Ismail Marjan, successfully defended their title. The SBH was opened by Governor Sir John Nicoll on 7 June 1952.

Bakery

Whampoa's Bakery, 1830s. In 1830 Hoo Ah Kay ('Whampoa') (1816-1880) came to Singapore to assist his father who was a successful grocer and ship chandler. He started a bakery in Havelock Road to supply bread to visiting ships. It later moved to Club Street. In 1843, Messrs Elder & Whitlaw established the Singapore Bakery at the corner of Tanjong Pagar Road. It was situated near the military canton, and provided bread and biscuits for domestic and marine markets.

Ball, Chinese

Tan Kim Seng's Ball, 1852. In February 1852, local tycoon Tan Kim Seng entertained the European and Chinese communities to the first Chinese ball ever held in Singapore. It was held in his newly-completed godown in Battery Road, and the upper floor was converted into a ballroom and banquet hall for the occasion. Thomas Church, the Resident Councillor, proposed a toast to Tan's health. The food was reported to have been magnificent and included birds nest soups, ragout, kangaroo tails, fish of all kinds and a variety of pastries. French, German and Hungarian wines were served.

Ballet Company, Professional

Singapore Dance Theatre, 1988. The Singapore Dance Theatre (SDT) was formed as a professional ballet company in January 1988. It was an offshoot of the Ballet Group formed by the Ministry of Community Development in 1984 to introduce a Western component into the National Dance Company. The Company was founded by Goh Soo Khim and Anthony Then. They were also the artistic directors of the company. Goh had the distinction of being the **first Asian woman admitted to the Australian National Ballet School**. She graduated as its top student in 1966. The first Patron of the SDT was Second Deputy Prime Minister

Ong Teng Cheong and the first Chairman of the Board of Directors was Justice Lai Kew Chai. The new company aimed to develop a repertory of ballet dances with a distinctive Singaporean identity. The debut performance was held at the Victoria Theatre between the 12 June and 14 June during the 1988 Singapore Festival of Arts. It was called 'Beginnings' and included works by five foreign choreographers including Mark Ruhala from 'A Chorus Line' and Graeme Murphy from Australia. The seven pioneer dancers were Mario Esperanza, Ricardo Culalic, Jamaluddin Jalil, Donato Ferrer, Chantal Pestana, Ellie Lai and Elizabeth Thng. The works performed were Beginnings, Windsong, Chameleon Scarf, Sequenza VII and the Raymonda Pas de Dix.

Ballroom Dancing

1930s. Ballroom dancing started in Singapore in the 1930s. The **first dance studio** was Pohsan Dance Studio, set up in 1937 by Low Poh San. Low and his wife Jenny became Singapore Professional Ballroom Champions in 1946 and from 1950 to 1953. In the 1960s, Low's son and daughter, Sunny and Betty Low became the Singapore Rock and Roll and Cha Cha King and Queen. Sunny Low later formed the Sunny Low Dancers who performed regularly on Singapore television. The **first Singapore Dance Masters** was held at Raffles City on 26 February 2005. It was organised by the YMCA and the Alvyn Low Dance Centre.

Band Concert

1831. In June 1831, the Band of the 29th Madras Native Infantry gave the first public band concert in Singapore at the Esplanade along Connaught Drive. The Infantry had just arrived in Singapore and the band members gave the concert to celebrate the occasion. After the first concert, they gave a band performance every Saturday afternoon. The chains surrounding the bandstand were taken down and the carriages were driven in and stood in a circle around the bandstand to listen to the concert. The bandstand was on a mound where Raffles' statue was later placed in 1887.

Bank

Union Bank of Calcutta, 1840. The first bank in Singapore was the Union Bank of Calcutta, established on 1 December 1840. However, it suspended operations a few years later. The first foreign bank to set up a branch in Singapore was the Algemene Bank Nederland. This was in May 1858 and it was known as The Netherlands Trading Society. The **first Post Office Savings Bank** was opened in 1877.

The **first local Chinese bank**, the Kwong Yik Bank, was founded in 1903 by well-known Cantonese contractor and gambier planter, Wong Ah Fook. Wong Ah Fook was a native of Toishan in Kwangtung Province and came to Singapore when he was 16 yeas old. The name Kwong Yik means 'benefitting Cantonese people' and the shareholders were predominantly Cantonese. The **first local bank manager** of the Bank was Boey Lian Chin who later became a director of the bank. The Chinese bank fulfilled an important need in Singapore. Most banks were English banks but few Chinese businessmen could speak English and it was difficult for them to use banking facilities. The establishment of the Kwong Yik Bank was a boon to these businessmen. The bank got into difficulties in 1913 because of loans granted to its own directors. The bank was liquidated and the Government amended the Bank Ordinance to place tight restrictions on banks making advances to their own directors and officers.

Bar Top Dancing

31 July 2003. At midnight on 31 July 2003, the first legal bar top dancing took place simultaneously at three bars in Singapore: Coyote Ugly, Devils Bar and 37 The Bar. Up until 2003, dancing was only permitted in designated dancing areas. In November 2001, the National Crime Prevention Council set up an Advisory Panel on Licensing to look into various licensing procedures for nightspots including the issue of bar top dancing. The March 2003, the panel recommended that the restriction on bar top dancing be lifted. At a press conference held at the Ministry of Home Affairs Headquarters on 8 July, the Senior Police Commissioner, Soh Wai Wah, announced that the restriction would be lifted on 1 August 2003. He added that the safety of customers was the responsibility of the pub owners. Pubs and bars wishing to introduce bar top dancing were required to apply for a Live Entertainment Licence. This cost $140 per month for bars that could hold less than 200 people and $210 per month if the bar could hold more than 200 people. Also the bar tops had to specially strengthened with steel and concrete to withstand the weight of the clubbers. Railings had to be installed for the safety of the dancers. Three bars had received their licences by 31 July 2003. All three held special celebrations to mark the occasion. Coyote Ugly rained confetti down on the party-goers at midnight and Coyote Ugly's bar staff led the patrons in a ten minute dance on the bar top. 37 The Bar held an Arabian theme night and featured snake charmers and 37 belly dancers. Devils Bar provided 50 bottles of free champagne at midnight. Prime Minister Goh Chok Tong said in his 2003 National Rally Day speech that the introduction of bar top dancing signalled a shift in the mindset of Singaporeans from a strait-laced Victorian attitude to a more relaxed and open-minded approach.

Battalion, Military

1st Singapore Infantry Regiment (1 SIR), 1957. Singapore's very first battalion of regular soldiers, the First Singapore Infantry Regiment (1 SIR), was formed on 12 March 1957 against a backdrop of impending self-government. Recruitment began on 4 March 1957 at the British Army's Malayan Recruiting Centre at Bras Basah Road as well as the Government Exchange at Havelock Road and Chua Chu Kang Road. Only Singapore citizens and persons born and bred in Singapore were recruited. Out of a total of 1,420 applicants, only 237 were accepted for training. It was intended that 1 SIR together with another battalion would form part of a Regiment within a Brigade Group in the Singapore Military Forces. Getting 1 SIR fully established was slow. The British-run Malayan Basic Training Centre (MBTC) at Nee Soon could only train about 40 recruits per month as it was involved in training other locally enlisted personnel of the British Forces. The **first two recruits** were Harchand Singh (SMP No 100001) and Foong Fok Kay (100002).

Bicycle Club

1890. In 1890, the Singapore Cycling Club was formed with 23 members. The **first bicycle race** was held on 27 March 1891. The registration of bicycles was introduced on 1 October 1947, with 345,703 registered.

Bicycle Factory

Battery Road 1895. In 1895, Edward Lyon established himself as a bicycle manufacturer in Battery Road. The company was the forerunner of the Straits Cycle Company which later made Laju bicycles.

Bird Park

Jurong Bird Park (1971). The idea of a Bird Park was conceived by Deputy Prime Minister and Defence Minister, Dr Goh Keng Swee in 1968 after a visit to a bird park in Brazil. A 20.2 hectare site was allocated at Bukit Perepok in Jurong and work commenced in December 1968. On 3 January 1971, the Jurong Bird Park opened to the public. The project cost $3.5 million excluding the cost of the land. The park is designed to represent the natural habitats of the bird species and its collection consists of more than 9000 birds. It specialises in birds of the Southeast Asian region and showcases the region's exotic and endangered species. It fulfills an important breeding, research and educational role. Bird shows are held daily at the amphitheatre. One of the more spectacular features is the Waterfall Aviary. It was opened in 1971, closed for renovations in 1990 and reopened in 1994. It is the world's largest walk-in aviary with the highest man-made waterfall of 30 metres. It is landscaped to stimulate a tropical rainforest environment with 10,000 exotic plants and 1,800 birds from more than 80 African and South American species. The park was designed by 2 experts: John J Yealland, curator of birds at London Zoo and John Toovey, an aviary architect also from the London Zoo.

Biscuit Factory

Ho Ho Biscuit Company, 1898. The Ho Ho Biscuit Company was the first biscuit factory to be established in Singapore on 17 November 1898. It was a limited company promoted by Go Boon Kwan. The factory in Chin Swee Road used the latest English machinery and the flour was imported directly from Adelaide, Australia. The Company specialized in ship's biscuits or hard-tack biscuits and it won a diploma and a bronze medal for its biscuits. The factory supplied biscuits to countries in the region.

Blood Transfusion Service

1939. In 1939, the first Singapore Blood Transfusion Service (BTS) was established to provide the country with an emergency transfusion service in case of war. The main objective was to collect and to build up a reserve of blood plasma for war casualties. The base for the service was the Department of Physiology at the King Edward VII College of Medicine in Sepoy Lines. Professor Scott MacGregor, Professor of Physiology and the Principal of the Medical School, Dr GV Allen were instrumental in organising the transfusion service. There was no shortage of donors, and teams of volunteers were trained to register donors' blood type . By the end of 1940, several thousand blood donors had been registered. By the middle of February 1942 when the Japanese invaded Singapore, blood stocks were completely depleted.

In June 1946, a civilian blood transfusion service was re-established at the General Hospital under the supervision of the Department of Pathology with the assistance of two lady volunteers, Mrs Ong Tiang Wee and Mrs Gardener. The essential feature of the blood transfusion service was that blood would only be collected from voluntary donors. The British Armed Forces contributed heavily to the programme. In August 1953, the Blood Transfusion Service moved into a purpose-built centre at the General Hospital under the direction of Dr Carl Alexander Gibson-Hill.

Boarding House

Hallpike's Boarding House (1831). In 1831, Mr. and Mrs Stephen Hallpike started a boarding house in High Street. Hallpike had bought half the land owned by Morgan & Co. extending from the corner of High Street near the Court House (now Old Parliament House) to the bridge on the river side. The other half was bought by Seah Kim Swee of the Seah Eu Chin family. Hallpike ran a blacksmith's shop and shipyard at the back of the boarding house and his wife ran the boarding house. The lane that ran down to the river became known as Hallpike Lane. Hallpike died in Singapore in June 1844 at the age of 61, and his widow married his partner, JB Gordon in London in 1846.

Bodybuilding

Bodybuilding was first introduced in Singapore in the early 1940's when British military personnel working at the British Ordinance Department (BOD) began strength training to build a better physique. Singaporeans, intrigued by this new and mysterious activity, considered bodybuilding a privilege reserved for the members of the BOD. Curiosity grew rapidly and shortly, enough interest in bodybuilding was generated that the Strength & Health Club, considered Singapore's **first bodybuilding gym** opened its doors. The club attracted the country's top boxers, weightlifters, and within a short time, people began to train and become bodybuilders.

Up to the early 1960s, bodybuilding was governed by the Singapore Amateur Weightlifting Federation (SAWLF). In 1960, SAWLF sent representatives to Kuala Lumpur to compete in the Mr Asia competition. Ching Teng Soon won a Gold Medal in Class 1 Division while Abbas Hussein won a Silver in the Class 3 Division. In 1962, the Singapore Amateur Body Building Association was formed, and it organised the **first junior Mr Singapore** competition in 1963. There are no records of the outcome of this competition. In 1965, the Singapore Amateur Bodybuilding Association changed its name to the Singapore Amateur Bodybuilding Federation (SABBF). In 1969, the SABBF organised the International Federation of Bodybuilding Mr. Singapore at the Victoria Theatre. Rohmat Bin Juraimi became the **first Mr Singapore** and represented Singapore in the Mr Universe Contest in New York, USA where he was placed 6th in Class II. The **first Singaporean bodybuilder to win a gold medal** at the International Olympic Council sanctioned World Games Bodybuilding Championships was Azman Abdullah. He won a gold medal in the middleweight category in 1993. He also won a gold medal at the World Bodybuilding Championships, that same year. Azman, a 5-time Mr Singapore, 3-time Mr Asia, and SEA Games gold medallist in three consecutive Games (1989, 1991 & 1993) was voted Sportsman of the Year title for 1993 for the second time.

The first Singaporean to represent Singapore in the **Mr Universe competition** was Pang Lai Seng held in Montreal in May 1967. Pang was a 29 year-old engine driver who had won many bodybuilding titles including Mr Ironman in 1955 and 1956 and Mr Singapore and Mr Malaysia in 1963. He competed in Class 2 for those of 5 foot 5 inches and over.

Book – Locally Printed

Political and Commercial Considerations Relative to the Malayan Peninsula and the British Settlements in the Straits of Malacca, 1824. In 1822, just three years after Singapore was founded, the British set up Mission Press, its first printing and publishing office, with the aim of spreading evangelism. Operations began in the private residence of one of the missionaries, where Raffles Hotel now stands. In the course of time, the publishing programme became diversified. Mission Press published textbooks and matters pertaining to the government and to the commercial and mercantile community and, in 1824, John Anderson's *Political and Commercial Considerations Relative to the Malayan Peninsula and the British Settlements in the Straits of Malacca* was published. Judging by its learned content, this would qualify as the first scholarly book published on the island.

The **first book by a local author** was published in 1827. This was *A Vocabulary of the English, Bugis and Malayan Languages*, jointly authored by CH Thomsen and Munshi Abdullah bin Abdul Kadir (1778-1840). Mushi Abdullah was considered the 'Father of Modern Malay Literature'.

The **first Chinese book** published in Singapore was Sophia Martin's *Three Character Classics for Instruction of Females* (Xun Nu San Zi Jing) published in 1832. The publisher is not known. This Christian manual, written to teach girls and women about the importance of education and the fear of God was printed using the traditional woodcut method of printing. The book was written in three-character sentences, very much in the style of *San Zi Jing*, a traditional primer for Chinese children. Sophia Martin came to Singapore from Batavia for health reasons and she founded a Chinese boarding and day school in North Bridge Road in 1837. She married TW Whittle three years after arriving in Singapore and she left in 1857 to live in India. The book is now in the Harvard-Yenching Library at Harvard University.

The earliest surviving **Malay book** published in Singapore is *The Substance of Our Saviour's Sermon on the Mount*, published in 1829. The earliest Tamil literature was also religious in nature. The first **Tamil book** known to be published in Singapore was *Singai Nagar Anthathi*, a collection of verses written by SN Sathasiva Pandit, in praise of the deity at the Tank Road Chettiar's Temple. The *Tamil First Book of Lessons* by KT Mariathas Pillai was printed by the Jawi Peranakan Press in 1887 for students of the Anglo-Tamil School.

Book & Literature Prizes

1972. The National Book Development Council of Singapore was set up in February 1969 to promote reading, writing and publishing. In 1972, the Council inaugurated the Book Council Book Awards. The first two awards were made in 1976. The books chosen were *We Dream Too Long* by Goh Poh Song and *Son of a Mother* by Michael Soh. In May 1991 the **Singapore Literature Prize** was inaugurated to recognise quality creative writing in English. The first winner was *Fistful of Colours* by Suchen Christine Lim. In 2004, the prize was widened to include creative works by Singapore authors in the four official languages. The first winner of the **Malay prize** was

Mohamed Latiff Mohamed; the **Tamil prize**, Ma Elangkanan; and **Chinese prize**, Ying Pei An.

Book Shop

During the 19th century, English books were sold by subscription and later by advertisements in the local newspapers. Early Chinese bookshops were found everywhere in Singapore and traders would import books from China. The most famous of these early booksellers was Koh Yew Hean (publishers of the *Straits Chinese Magazine* from 1897–1907). Department stores such as John Little & Co also sold books and magazines. The first major bookshop was the Methodist Publishing House (MPH) at the corner of Stamford Road and Armenian Street. Originally known as the Mission Press, it subsequently became known as the Amelia Bishop Press (1893), then Methodist Publishing House (1906) and Malayan Publishing House (1927). Through a series of ownership changes, the company is now MPH and its flagship bookstore has moved from Stamford Road to Parkway Parade.

Botanic Gardens

Fort Canning (1822). Modern Singapore's founder, Sir Stamford Raffles, was a keen naturalist. He set up the first Botanic Garden on Government Hill at Fort Canning in 1822 mainly to introduce into cultivation, economic crops such as nutmeg, clove and cocoa. In August 1819, Raffles shipped over 100 nutmeg plants, 100 clove plants, 1000 nutmeg seeds, 350 clove seeds, 25 large nutmeg plants and 25 large clove plants from Bencoolen. He also sent a gardener, a Mr Dunn, in his vessel, the *Indiana*, to plant the seeds and plants that would form the basis of Singapore's spice plantation economy. The formation of this 'experimental' garden was part of a long tradition of developing botanical gardens in European colonies. In setting out the gardens, Raffles was strongly influenced by Dr Nathaniel Wallich of the Royal Gardens in Calcutta. A 19-hectare site bordered by Hill Street and Canning Rise was set aside for the Gardens. Raffles donated $1,000 towards the upkeep of the gardens and Dr William Montgomerie supervised it with 10 labourers and one foreman. Dr Montgomerie gave most of his attention to the spice garden. After Raffles left, the East India Company refused to pay for the Garden's upkeep and they were abandoned in June 1829 and the land parceled out for other purposes, including the building of the Armenian Church.

The second Botanic Gardens was founded at its present site in 1859 by the revived Agri-Horticultural Society. The new Gardens, bounded by Cluny Road, Tyersall Avenue and Holland Road was situated on a 23-hectare site. The land was originally owned by Hoo Ah Kay (Whampoa) and he agreed to swap his land in Tanglin for a plot on the Singapore River (present-day Clarke Quay) on which he later built an ice-house (see *Ice Factory*). In 1866, the Society bought another 100 hectares of land from the William Napier Estate. However, by 1874, the Society had gone into debt over the upkeep of the Gardens and the Government stepped in and took over its administration. From an ornamental garden with roads, terraces, a bandstand and even a small zoo, it has come a long way in evolving into a leading equatorial botanic garden of 52 hectares.

Botanic Gardens – Superintendent & Director

Henry James Murton (1853–1882). The Botanic Gardens' **first supervisor** was Henry James Murton. Born in Cornwall, England, Murton trained as a gardener at Kew Gardens from 1872 to 1873. In 1875, he became Superintendent of the Singapore Botanic Gardens. In 1880, he was dismissed and he went to Bangkok where he was appointed to the Royal Gardens there. Murton was the author of a *Catalogue of Plants Under Cultivation in the Botanic Gardens, Singapore Straits Settlements* (Singapore: Government Office, 1879). He had also prepared a manuscript on *Flora of Singapore*, but this manuscript appears to have been lost. He died in Bangkok in 1881 or 1882. The genus *Murtonia Craib* and some other species of plants were named in his honour.

The Botanic Gardens' **first Director** was Henry Nicholas Ridley, who was born in England on 10 December 1855. Like Murton before him, he was a former Kew gardener and arrived in Singapore in 1888 to take charge of the Botanic Gardens. Ridley, sometimes called 'Mad Ridley' for his idiosyncratic mannerisms and strong advocacy for rubber planting, led the Gardens for the next 23 years, retiring only in 1912. Ridley is regarded as the Father of the Rubber Industry and he devised a process to extract rubber without damaging the tree. Ridley died on 24 October 1956.

Bowling Alley, Private

American Club, 1955. The first private bowling alley in Singapore was built at the American Club in Claymore Hill in 1955. The idea for these alleys came from rubber magnate, Tan Eng Joo (nephew of Tan Lark Sye), who took a deep interest in the sport while studying at the Massachusetts Institute of Technology in the 1940s. Tan, who wanted to 'bring a part of American culture to Singapore', mooted the idea of including four bowling lanes at the American Club in Singapore, which he helped found. Tan later persuaded his friend, Jackie Oei Tjiong Le (b. 1918), son of Indonesian Chinese sugar tycoon Oei Tiong Ham to open Singapore's first public bowling alley.

Bowling Alley, Public

Jackie's Bowl, 1962. After helping establish the first private bowling alley at the American Club in 1955, Tan Eng Joo persuaded his friend, Jackie Oei Tjiong Le (b. 1918), son of Indonesian Chinese sugar tycoon Oei Tiong Ham to open Singapore's first public bowling alley. It was known as Jackie's Bowl and was located at the old Orchard Cinema complex in Grange Road. Envisioning a family-oriented bowling alley, Jackie Oei roped in Khoo Teck Puat and Loke Wan Tho as major shareholders in a bowling alley. Loke was then the head of well-established Cathay Organisation, which had an entertainment complex at Orchard Road. Loke leased prime space to the bowling alley at a relatively low rent and Jackie's Bowl Orchard opened in 1962. It quickly became a popular entertainment spot and Oei was proud of the fact that bowling alley once boasted one of the highest lineages in the world (ie number of games played per lane per day.) With the redevelopment of the Cathay site at Orchard into what is now Orchard Cineleisure in the 1980s, Jackie's Bowl Orchard was closed. Oei and his business associates also started Ocean Bowling Private Limited in 1964 and it ran Jackie's Bowl Katong at what is now Ocean Park, another

Cathay Organisation property. That bowling alley closed down at the end of 2004.

Bowling World Champion

Adelene Wee, 1985. Adelene Wee (b 1965), became Singapore's **first World Bowling Champion** when she won the Ladies' Masters title in the 1985 World Games in London, at age 20. She first shot into the limelight at 17 when she won the 1982 Singapore International Bowling Championships. Subsequently, she captured the Sukhumvit Open title in Thailand, breaking the world record for the 6-game series with a total of 1,280 pinfalls, the same year. For her outstanding achievements, she was 'crowned' both best 'Sportsgirl' and 'Sportswoman of the Year' in 1982. Adelene continued her winning streak winning golds in the doubles, all-events and masters at the 1983 Asian FIQ Youth Championships and in 1985, returned home with three gold medals in the singles, masters and team events. She reached her zenith by winning the gold medal at the World Games in 1985. This victory helped her win the 'Sportswoman of the Year' title, a second time. Over the next 10 years, Adelene continued to represent Singapore in various international events until her retirement from competition in 1995. Henry Tan Yoke See was the first to put Singapore in the world bowling map by winning the **highest single game** (298 pinfalls out of a possible 300) and bagging the individual silver medal at the World Games in Copenhagen in 1970.

Boxing, World Title Fight

Flyweight Title Fight, 1989. On 25 February 1989, the first World Boxing title fight to be held in Singapore was staged at the National Stadium Podium Block. The World Super Flyweight title fight was between Ellyas Pical of Indonesia and Mike Phelps of the United States. The International Boxing Federation organized the fight and the promoter was Dunoo Promotions. Ellyas Picul won the fight on points. The Referee was Lucien Joubert. Dunoo Promotions lost thousands of dollars as there was not a large turnout for the match. Only 760 tickets out of 18,000 were sold. The price of the tickets may have contributed to the low attendance. A ringside seat was $250 and a 1st class seat was $100. The **first ring death** occurred on 22 September 1934, at the New World Stadium, when 21-year-old Joe Thunderface from Pasadena, California, died in his fight with local boxer, Frankie Weber.

Boys' Brigade Company

First Company, Prinsep Street Presbyterian Church, 1930. The Boys' Brigade (BB) movement was founded in Glasgow in 1883. Its stated object was 'the advancement of Christ's kingdom among Boys and the promotion of habits of Obedience, Reverence, Discipline and Self-respect and all that tends towards a true Christian manliness'. The Brigade's motto is 'Sure & Stedfast'. The first Singapore Company started in quite a fortuitous way. Ex-Sergeant Quek Eng Moh, an old boy of the 1st Swatow Company of Swatow in China met James M Fraser on a road in Singapore one day in 1930. He recognized Fraser as a BB member as the latter had the BB buttonhole badge on. Quek told Fraser that the Swatow stalwarts wanted to have a BB Company in Singapore. On 12 January 1930, Fraser and the 1st Swatow Company Old Boys founded the 1st Singapore Company at Prinsep Street Presbyterian Church, with the approval of Rev William Murray. Fraser himself had been in the Aberdeen BB in Aberdeen and was an ex-officer of the 23rd London Company. By 1931, when it held its first annual inspection, it had 63 members and it was attended by a large crowd. By 1941, there were 7 companies. A contingent from Singapore attended the Silver Jubilee of the Boys' Brigade in England in 1954. The Boys' Brigade is a uniformed youth organisations within the schedule of the Ministry of Education extra-curricular activities and is represented annually at the Singapore Youth Festival. It is a registered society and is affiliated to the Singapore Council of Social Service and to the People's Association. The local headquarters are now located at Ganges Avenue.

Breakwater

Offshore Mole, 1914. The first breakwater or mole was completed 1914. The granite rubble structure created a second entrance to Singapore Harbour. It was one mile long (1.6 km) and provided shelter for some 40 coastal vessels during the northeast monsoon. On the landward side, Telok Ayer Basin (now, Telok Ayer Wharves) took form as a line of wharves for coastal vessels with an opening in the centre leading into a tidal basin for lighters.

Brick Kiln

Pillai's Kiln, 1819. Narayana Pillai, an Indian contractor from Penang accompanied Raffles on his first visit to the island in 1819. Pillai, a shrewd businessman, soon built Singapore's first brick kiln - in the vicinity of today's 'Little India'.

Bridges

1822. The first bridge across a river was built sometime in 1822 and demolished in 1843. It was built under the direction of Lieutenant Philip Jackson and was a drawbridge built of wood and joined North and South Bridge roads where Elgin Bridge now stands. It was rather narrow and had to be augmented by a ferry service. It was known as Presentment Bridge or Monkey Bridge. In 1843, this bridge was replaced by Thomson Bridge, a footbridge constructed by John Turnbull Thomson.

The **first steel suspended bridge** was Cavenagh Bridge. It was built in 1869 to link the civil district on the North Bank of the Singapore River with the Commercial District on the South Bank. Cavenagh Bridge is the oldest bridge still in its original design and it replaced a ferry that plied the river at 1 cent per ride. The bridge was designed by the Public Works Department and the cast iron pieces were made by P & W MacLellan in Scotland in 1868 and assembled here by convict labourers. The original design allowed for the bridge to be raised at high tide but that proved to be technically impossible. The fixed suspension bridge was not able to withstand the rapidly growing volume of vehicular traffic and when the Anderson bridge was opened to traffic in 1910, Cavenagh Bridge became a pedestrian bridge. The original notice placed on the bridge by the Police that prohibited its use to any vehicle with a laden weight of 3cwt still remains on the bridge.

Singapore's **first overhead pedestrian bridge** was opened on 7 April 1964. The bridge spanned Collyer Quay, allowing pedestrians to walk from Change Alley to Clifford Pier and vice-versa. The 34-metre light-gauge bridge is now part of the Change Alley Aerial Plaza. The

first suspended pedestrian bridge was built over the Geylang River in 1998 to connect the Indoor Stadium to Tanjong Rhu. The bridge is 120 metres and 3 metres wide and can accommodate 5,000 pedestrians per hour in both directions. The **first viaduct** (bridge carrying a highway or railroad over a valley, low ground, or road) is the Benjamin Sheares Bridge. It was officially opened in 1982. The bridge spans Marina Bay and links the Eastern and Western sections of the East Coast Parkway expressway. It is the **first bridge to be named after a former President**. It is 1.8 km long and was built by Sato Kogyo. Since 1992, the Singapore Armed Forces Recreation Association has organized the annual Sheares Bridge Run and Army Half Marathon. About 65,000 people take part. Part of the run involves crossing the full length of the bridge.

Bridge Club

Singapore Branch of Malayan Contract Bridge Association, 1962. In 1962, the Singapore branch of the Malayan Contract Bridge Association was formed, and its first meeting was held at the Adelphi Hotel in Coleman Street. After Singapore left Malaysia in 1965, it was decided that a Singapore association be formed. In July 1966, the Association changed its name to the Singapore Contract Bridge Association (SCBA). Bridge activities were held at a number of different venues, but it now has a permanent home at the Singapore Intellctual Games Centre in Bishan. The SCBA is recognised as a National Sporting body by the Singapore Sports Council and is responsible for selecting members of the National Bridge Teams. In 1987, the SCBA inaugurated the annual Singapore Inter-club Bridge League. This is now the largest and most popular bridge event in Singapore.

British Peer in House of Lords

Lord Michael Chan, 2001. Singapore-born Lord Michael Chan became the **first ethnic Chinese** to sit in the House of Lords in Britain. Lord Michael Chan Chew Koon was born in Singapore in 1940 and was educated at Raffles Institution. He studied medicine in Britain and returned to work as a paediatrician in Singapore. In 1974, he won a Heinz Fellowship to undertake research at the Great Ormond St. Children's Hospital. In 1976, he was appointed as Senior lecturer at the Liverpool School of Tropical Medicine. He was deeply involved in the welfare of the Chinese community in Britain and became Chairman of the Chinese in Britain Forum. In 2001, he was appointed Peer in recognition of his work with medicine and ethnic communities and became Baron of Oxton. He died on 21 January 2006 after a sudden illness.

British Resident

William Farquhar (1770-1839). The first Resident of Singapore was Colonel William Farquhar who was appointed by Raffles in 1819. Farquhar joined the Madras Engineers in 1790 at the age of 20 . He served in Malacca for 23 years. In 1803, he was appointed as Resident of Malacca and remained as Resident there until the Dutch returned in 1818. His time in Malacca provided Farquhar with valuable Malayan experience and he gained an intimate knowledge of politics in the Riau-Lingga region. He was known as the 'Rajah of Malacca' and commanded respect with a combination of grace and authority. He was accessible to all, was ready to hear complaints and judge disputes and he had a reputation for being impartial towards rich and poor. He spoke fluent Malay and married a girl from Malacca.

Farquhar negotiated a treaty in 1818 to safeguard British trade against the revival of Dutch trading privileges. He urged the East India Company to set up a base there to protect British trade in the Straits of Malacca. He was a close colleague of Raffles and had his complete trust. In December 1818, the Dutch annulled Farquhar's treaty and established a garrison in Riau and installed a Resident with authority over the Riau region including Johore and the nearby islands. In December 1818, Raffles dispatched Farquhar to the Carimon Islands to see if the islands would provide a suitable site for a trading post. Raffles was not due to sail with Farquhar but when Raffles was prevented from sailing to Aceh, Raffles sailed south to find Farquhar. They found that the Carimon Islands were rocky and unsuitable for a settlement. On 28 January 1819, the fleet of 8 ships anchored off St. John's Island near the mouth of the Singapore River. The following morning Raffles and Farquhar went ashore. The Temenggong trusted Farquhar and realised the material advantages of a British trading post in Singapore. On 6th February 1819, Raffles signed a formal agreement with Sultan Hussein and Temenggong Abdul Rahman to establish a trading post subject to a payment of $5000 per year to Sultan Hussein and $300 to Temenggong Abdul Rahman. The next day, Raffles appointed Farquhar as the first Resident of Singapore responsible to Raffles as Lieutenant Governor of Bencoolen. Apart from a brief visit by Raffles in May 1819, Farquhar ran the trading post for three years.

Under his leadership and direction, Singapore became a successful trading port. Farquhar sent to Malacca for settlers and suppliers and his reputation encouraged traders to come flocking to Singapore. Singapore's location and free trade policies encouraged the growth of trade. Within two and a half years, Singapore was able to attract 3000 trading vessels and the import/export trade was worth $8 million. Farquhar encouraged traders from all parts of the region and by 1821, Singapore became a cosmopolitan port of 5000 inhabitants including Bugis, Chinese, Indians, Armenians and Straits Chinese.

Raffles returned to Singapore in October 1822 and was delighted with the progress of the port. However, he disapproved of many of Farquhar's measures. He set aside the considerable achievements of Farquhar and removed him from office. Farquhar remained in Singapore for a few months before leaving for Scotland at the end of 1823. He was given a wonderful farewell by the people of Singapore who understood and appreciated Farquhar's considerable achievements better than did Raffles. He died in Scotland in 1839. Farquhar was Singapore's first resident but he was also perhaps the 'real founder'.

Bucket System, sanitation

Two-Pail System, 1913. In 1907 WJR Simpson presented the findings of a study he had made on sanitary conditions in Singapore: *First Survey of the Sanitary Conditions of Singapore*. There had been concern for some time about the high death rate from dysentery and cholera. Simpson, who had been a health officer in Fremantle and Calcutta, and was considered to be the 'first living expert on Imperial health'. He recommended that all town refuse be incinerated and dumping be prohibited. He also recommended the introduction of a

2-pail system of night-soil removal until the introduction of back lane facilities would allow for the introduction of a water carriage sewage system. There was strong resistance to the bucket system of night-soil removal, and voluntary removal of night-soil was a failure. It was not until the introduction of a Strategy of Organised Compulsory Night-soil Collection in 1913 that the bucket system began to be effective. It started with a pilot programme in Tanjong Katong. Night-soil coolies were employed to remove the nightsoil in that one area. By 1921, there were 6 compulsory areas. By 1940, nearly 20,000 households were participating in the bucket or 2-pail system of night-soil removal. Although households involved in the scheme paid a fixed rate whether it was collected or not, there was still strong resistance to the programme and housholds used every means to impede collection. Along with other important public health measures such as improved drainage, more fresh water and controls over the provision of adulterated milk, death rates began to plummet and Singapore became a safer and healthier place to live in. The bucket system was completely abolished in the late 1970s.

Bus

1920s. Motorized buses (or omnibuses as they were then called) began replacing the electric tramways as a form of public transport in the early 1920s. The rural and fringe areas were served by small Chinese bus companies, usually owned and managed by individuals. These bus companies had very few buses and thus operated very few routes. They were nicknamed 'mosquito buses' because of the way they weaved in and out of traffic. These 'mosquito buses' became increasingly popular, and by 1921, there were 147 of them. By 1927, the number had increased to 456 buses. The Singapore Traction Company introduced the first motorized buses in 1926 and it plied the route from Joo Chiat to Tanjong Pagar route. The **first double-decker bus**, operated by Singapore Bus Services, went into service in 1977. Service 86 took passengers from Tampines to Shenton Way. It was launched by Senior Minister of State Ong Teng Cheong. Each double-decker bus could seat 87 passengers. The **first air-conditioned bus** appeared on the roads in 1984.

Bus Company

See also Trolley Buses

Singapore Traction Company, 1926. In October 1925, the Shanghai Electric Construction Company Limited established the Singapore Traction Company (STC). STC was given a 30-year monopoly to run trolley buses and motor-buses (or omnibuses) within the town. Omnibuses were introduced in 1926 to supplement the trolley bus services. The STC needed to provide a service to the site of the new Naval Dockyard in Sembawang. It was too far for the trolley bus and the omnibus service took passengers for 14 miles (22.5 km) up Thomson Road from Raffles Quay to the 15th milestone, 5 miles (8 km) past Seletar Village. Buses were 1st class only and the fare ranged from 6 cents to 45 cents. By 1929, there were 90 trolley buses serving a total distance of 30.5 km.

Bus Interchange, Air-conditioned

Toa Payoh Interchange, 2002. The first air-conditioned bus interchange was opened in Toa Payoh in 2002. The interchange sits above the Toa Payoh MRT station and is adjacent to the HDB Hub. When it opened, members of the public criticized the authorities for the extravagance of this interchange.

Businessman of the Year

Michael Fam, 1986. The Businessman of the Year awards were first presented on 19 February 1986. A crystal trophy was presented to Michael Fam by Deputy Prime Minister Goh Chok Tong at the Shangri-la Hotel. The award was sponsored by Business Times and DHL. The panel of 12 judges was headed by Chandra Das, Chairman of the Trade Development Board. Fam was selected for his joint roles as Chairman of the Fraser & Neave group and the Mass Rapid Transit Corporation. Fam was also Chairman of the Singapore Press Holdings' management committee, Nanyang Technological Institute and Times Publishing Berhad. Fam also received a portrait of himself.

In conjunction with the award, an essay competition was held. The top prize of $2,500 went to Chan Wai Ming, a management consultant with Forbes Management Consultants, for his essay on what it takes to be a successful entrepreneur or executive in business.

The **first woman** to win the Businessman of the Year Award (now called the Singapore Business Awards) was Olivia Lum in March 2005. The panel of judges awarded her the prize for her work in developing her water treatment company, Hyflux into a major corporate player.

C

Cabaret Dances

New World Amusement Park, 1920s. The first cabaret dances in Singapore were held at New World Amusement Park in Kitchener Road. The Park had a huge dance floor where people came to dance. The cabarets were a major new attraction when the Park opened. Girls were either local or from Hongkong or the Philippines. There were strict rules governing the girls' behaviour during the dances and the girls were not allowed to drink too much and get rowdy or refuse to dance. They were also expected to dress well. However, cabaret dances were not designed only to attract men. People from all walks of life attended the cabarets to dance and enjoy the music. Cabarets typically opened around 7.00 pm and closed at midnight during the week, and 1.00 am on Saturday nights.

Cabinet

David Marshall's Cabinet, 1955. Following the **1955** general elections under the Rendel Constitution, the following Cabinet appointments were made by the Labour Front Coalition. Chief Minister and Minister for Commerce: David Saul Marshall; Minister for Communications and Works: Abdul Hamid bin Haji Jumat; Minister for Local Government and Housing: Francis Thomas; Minister for Health: Joseph Armand Braga; Minister for Labour and Welfare: Lim Yew Hock; and Minister for Education: Chew Swee Kee. The Official Ministers appointed by the Governor were: Chief Secretary: William Goode: Minister for Finance: TM Hart; and Attorney-General: EJ Davies. Speaker of the Assembly was George Oehlers. The Cabinet was presented to the people on 7 April 1955 at Empress Place.

After the **1959** elections, the first to be held for self-governing Singapore, a nine-member cabinet was appointed from the winning People's Action Party (PAP). The Cabinet comprised: Prime Minister: Lee Kuan Yew; Deputy Prime Minister: Toh Chin Chye; Ministers: Ong Eng Guan (National Development); Goh Keng Swee (Finance); Ong Pang Boon (Home Affairs); Kenneth M Byrne (Law & Labour); Ahmad Ibrahim (Health); Yong Nyuk Lin (Education); and S Rajaratnam (Culture).

Following Independence in **1965**, the following Cabinet PAP members were appointed; Prime Minister: Lee Kuan Yew; Deputy Prime Minister: Toh Chin Chye; EW Barker (Law & National Development); Goh Keng Swee (Defence); Jek Yeun Thong (Labour); Lim Kim San (Finance); Ong Pang Boon (Education); Othman Bin Wok (Culture and Social Affairs); S Rajaratnam (Culture); Yong Nyuk Lin (Health). AP Rajah was appointed Speaker of Parliament.

Cable Car

Mount Faber to Sentosa, 1974. The first cable car service to Sentosa was officially opened by Deputy Prime Minister Goh Keng Swee on 15 February 1974. It cost S$5.8 million and consisted of 43 cabins. The next day, more than 1000 people rode the cable cars. In 1999 the world's first glass bottomed cabins were installed.

Cable Broadcast Services

Rediffusion, 1949. Cable radio company Rediffusion was originally a British company (British Electric Traction) providing power cables for trams. When broadcasting began in earnest in the UK in 1922, the Company capitalized on their existing network of cables to run additional 'cable radio' wires between the same poles to carry radio signals using alternating current (AC) through the same cables as the direct current (DC) power to trams. In March 1928, Rediffusion (literally 'broadcasting again') was born. Rediffusion was introduced to Singapore in 1949, the company's first stake in broadcasting in the Far East. The combination of affordable subscriptions (S$5.00 a month), excellent local programming, entertaining disc-jockeys made service extremely popular and the business very successful. Before long, the ubiquitous Rediffusion box was found in almost every home, shop and office. Many well-known names in Singapore's entertainment industry were first featured on Rediffusion and many Singaporeans remember listening spellbound and transfixed to their boxes, listening to the likes of legendary Cantonese storyteller Lee Dai-Soh. In the 1970s, Rediffusion, like the radio, lost much of its popularity due to television. Today, Rediffusion continues to provide broadcasts to its customers (for just S$10.00 a month) but has also diversified into audio, visual and cable electronics services.

The **first cable television network** was launched on 2 February 1993 at the Singapore Polytechnic. The network, which linked up the Polytechnic campus was called *Spectel*. The **first public broadcast service** was launched in 1995 by Singapore Cable Vision (SCV). The Company was given a monopoly for cable television services for seven years in exchange for its linking up all Singapore homes with fibre optic cables. In July 2002, the company merged with telecommunications company, StarHub to form StarHub Cable Vision Ltd.

Cadets, Civil Service

Dudley Francis Amelius Hervey, 1867. The first cadet in the newly formed Straits Settlements Civil Service was Dudley Francis Amelius Hervey who was appointed in 1867, the year the administration of Singapore was transferred to the Colonial Office in London. Hervey had a long and varied career with the service, accompanying several expeditions including one to Acheen (Aceh). He went on political visits to Kedah, Pahang, Trengganu, Kelantan and Selangor in 1870. In 1883, he accompanied Sir Frederick Weld to Negri Sembilan to investiagte the feasibility of opening up the residential system there and he served as Resident Councillor of Malacca from 1882 till his retirement in 1893. The second cadet was Allan Skinner who arrived in the Straits Settlements in 1868. Skinner was Colonial Treasurer (1881–1887), and then Resident Councillor in Penang (1887-1897). Skinner was also **the first Inspector of Schools** and founder of the educational system in the Straits. He is particularly noted for helping to found the Straits Branch of the Royal Asiatic Society (now Malaysian Branch of the Royal Asiatic Society).

Cadet Corps

Army Cadet Corps, Raffles Institution, 1901. The history of the National Cadet Corps (NCC) can be traced back to the formation of the first Army Cadet Corps in Raffles

Institution on 15 May 1901. A second unit was formed in St Joseph's Institution the following year. The aim of the Army Corps was to prepare students for service in the Singapore Volunteer Corps (SVC), a military reserve for the Straits Settlements. The first two decades proved sluggish for the fledgling corps, but in the 1920s, it began an aggressive recruitment of members. Among the recruits at this time was Singapore's first President, Yusof Ishak, then a student at Raffles Institution. Yusof had the distinction of being the **first student cadet** to be commissioned as Cadet Lieutenant. The Army Corps grew by leaps and bounds throughout the 1930s and 40s, and by 1949, there were also the Sea Cadet Corps and Air Training Corps.

In the early years, the Corps was managed first by the Ministry of Education and then by the Ministry of Interior and Defence (MID). In 1969, the NCC HQ was formed, integrating the land, sea, air and Girls' units, together with NCC Police. When the Ministry of Interior and Defence split in 1970 into the Ministry of Defence and Ministry of Home Affairs, the police cadet corps element broke away to form the National Police Cadet Corps (NPCC). The Police Cadet Corps started out an experimental unit in Bartley Secondary School in 1959.

Camera – Locally Manufactured

Rollei (1970-1980). Rollei, the legendary German camera manufacturer established by Paul Franke and Reinhold Hedidecke in 1920 established a factory in Singapore in 1970 to cut costs. The name Rollei was first used in 1926 with a stereo camera called a 'Rolleioscop'. Rollei became famous for their Rolleiflex and Rolleicord twin-lens reflex cameras which they began manufacturing in 1929. In 1966, Rollei came up with their 35mm miniature camera and from 1966 to 1970, they were made in Germany. In 1970, production of this now 'cult' camera was moved to Singapore. However, the company declared bankruptcy in 1981 and after several changes of ownership, was bought up by Korean giant, Samsung. The factory, located in Bedok, Singapore, closed down. The Rollei 35 made in Singapore was a design icon. The idea was to have the smallest full-frame 35mm camera possible. To do this, designers did away with a rangefinder and made the camera scale-focus (requiring the user to estimate the distance between the camera and the intended subject). Furthermore, the shutter-speed, ISO dial and aperture dial are all located on the front of the camera while the rewind lever, frame counter and flash shoe are at the bottom of the camera.

Campaign

Anti-Spitting Campaign, 1958. The first national campaigns were launched in 1958, shortly after the People's Action Party took power in the City Council elections. Under the supervision of Ong Eng Guan, the first elected Mayor, the first campaign launched was the Anti-spitting campaign in August 1958. The Mayor suggested that the campaign was 'of tremendous importance because spitting is a habit which has entrenched itself for many years and if we succeed in this campaign, we shall succeed in every health campaign'. In the same year, an Anti-Litter Campaign and Kill Pests Campaign were also launched. The Speak Mandarin Campaign was launched by the then Prime Minister Lee Kuan Yew on 7 September 1979. It was the **first of the recurrent campaigns** along with the Courtesy Campaign launched in the same year.

Car Imported & Assembled

Charles Burton Buckley's car, 1896. The first 'auto-car' was imported into Singapore in 1896 by Katz Bros representing Benz et Cie. Katz Bros. referred to these cars as 'motor velocipedes'. The first car owner was the well-known local lawyer, Charles Burton Buckley (he of the *Anecdotal History of Singapore* fame). Buckley referred to the car as his 'coffee machine'. Registration of cars began in 1906. By 1908, there were 21 people driving cars, motor bikes and steam rollers.

In 1906, two Australian brothers, CFF and TJB Wearne, opened the first car repair shop in 1906. Wearne Brothers was located in Orchard Road. The firm supplied every kind of work associated with the motorcar industry. Their first garage measured 200 feet by 100 feet. They also provided storage for 25 cars and kept a supply of petrol. They were the sole agent for Star, Frick, Oldsmobile and Reo cars and trolleys. Later, they became the sole distributor of Ford and Morris cars.

The **first lady motorist** in Singapore was Mrs Dare, wife of GM Dare, who drove a 12 horsepower two-cylinder Star.

The **first Malay driver** was Hassan bin Mohamed, who was taught by Mrs Dare. Lim Peng Han, the fifth and youngest son of Dr Lim Boon Keng, was the **first local Chinese to race** in the British circuits at Donington and Brooklands between 1930 and 1934.

The **first car assembly plant** in Singapore was established by Ford in 1926. It was Ford's first assembly plant in the region and the only automotive assembly plant in Malaya.

Car, Solar Powered

Sunspeed 1, 1999. The first solar-powered car built in Singapore was *Sunspeed 1*, was built by students and staff of the Renewable Energy Department at Singapore Polytechnic in 1999. It was a 3-wheeled car and weighed 300 kg.

Cartoon, Chinese

1907. The first Chinese cartoon appeared in the *Chong Shing Yit Pao*, a revolutionary daily newspaper which began publication in 1907. The paper was printed by the Chong Shing Press and its offices were situated in Cross Street. In 1906, Sun Yat Sen came to Singapore and launched the *Tung Ming Hui*, a Chinese revolutionary organization that became the Kuomintang in 1912. Tan Chor Lam was elected chairman and Teo Eng Hock became its vice-chairman. The organization needed a mouthpiece and Tan and Teo set up a revolutionary press. The members contributed to the cost of the press, and Tan and Teo topped the list of donations with $400 each. On 20 August 1907, the newspaper was started. Most of the well-known revolutionaries wrote for the paper and Sun Yat Sen contributed some articles himself. It was almost certainly the first Chinese newspaper to carry pictures apart from advertisement blocks. It published a cartoon every day on its literary page. As the paper was staunchly anti-Manchu, the cartoons reflected this stance. They were described as crude but quite effective. The cartoonists drew their inspiration from cartoons published in *Min Pao*, a revolutionary periodical published in Japan which was the focus of these cartoons.

Causeway

Johor Causeway, 1924. On 28 June 1924 at 8.30 am, the first Causeway across the Johore Straits was officially opened by the Governor Sir Laurence Guillemard in front of a large and distinguished crowd. The Governor cut the ribbon across the roadway with a golden knife handed to him by the Sultan of Johore. The Band of the Johore Forces played and Singapore gunners fired a 17-gun salute. In his speech, Sir Laurence declared its completion as one of the greatest engineering works undertaken in the Far East. The causeway cost $17 million to build and took 5 years to complete. The cost was shared between the Federation of Malay States, the Straits Settlements and the State of Johore. The contract to build the Causeway was given to Messrs Topham, Jones and Railton and the Consulting Engineers were Messrs Coode, Fitzmaurice, Wilson and Mitchell. One of the major objectives of the project was to join the Johore railway to the Singapore railway. Since the completion of the Johore railway in 1909, the missing link was provided by a wagon ferry service and a passenger launch service. As Malayan prosperity increased, the railway traffic had increased and in 1921, 58,402 wagons had been conveyed across the Straits.

The causeway was a huge granite bank 3465 feet long and 60 feet wide. It accommodated a double railway track, a road 26 feet wide and a footway. It contained 1.5 million cubic yards of stone quarried at Bukit Timah and Pulau Ubin. The granite from Pulau Ubin was brought to the project site in 300-ton hopper barges towed by tugs and moored in position. When it was completed, the roadway was sealed with a 9 inch granite rubble closely packed and a 6 inch layer of granite metalling on top. As the causeway blocked shipping down the Straits, a lock was constructed at the Johore end. It was 170 feet wide and 32 feet long and allowed small craft to pass down the Straits. The use of the causeway by the railway was considered to be urgent, and the causeway was opened for goods trains in October 1923. On 27 January 1942, the Gordon Highlanders and Lim Bo Seng's Quarry Workers Union blasted a 60-foot gap in the Causeway after the British forces retreated to Singapore. It was mended a year later by the Japanese occupation forces and it has remained in use ever since.

Cellphone

See MOBILE PHONE

Cemeteries – Various

One burial **traditional Malay burial** ground in Singapore, located in Bukit Kasita in Kampung Bahru (near Keramat Bukit Kasita) is supposed to have been in continuous use for the last 400 years. The first **British Christian cemetery** was the cemetery on Government Hill or Fort Canning. When the British arrived, they appropriated the royal burial ground at Bukit Laraggan (Forbidden Hill, later renamed Fort Canning in 1859) and installed the first British Christian cemetery there. It was a small site of just 0.8 hectares (2 acres) and was used only from 1819 to 1822. It was quickly replaced by another slightly larger one on Fort Canning. As the Europeans settled in various parts of the island, they established churches. In keeping with their age-old practices, burials took place in the church yard, typically located just behind these churches. These church-yard cemeteries were more common in rural churches than those in town even though some burials did take place in the Cathedral of Good Shepherd in Victoria Street. Up to a decade ago, beautiful and elegant tombstones graced the well-manicured grounds of the Church of the Nativity of the Blessed Virgin Mary at the end of Upper Serangoon Road. These have since been exhumed. The last remaining **church-yard cem-**

etery is that of St Joseph's Church in Upper Bukit Timah Road. The cemetery is located at the back of this old village church and contains more than 100 visible tombs. Most of them are dilapidated and some appear to be very old, possibly dating from the 19th century. After Fort Canning, the next important Christian cemetery was the Bukit Timah Cemetery which opened in 1865 and closed in 1907.

The earliest recorded **Chinese cemetery** was the Qing Shan Ting (Cheng San Teng or 'Green Hill Pavilion'), a Cantonese/Hakka cemetery at the junction of South Bridge Road and Tanjong Pagar Road (east of Ann Siang Hill and west of Peck Seah Street). Interestingly, this cemetery was run by the Hok Tek Chin Temple or Fuk Tak Chi Temple (now converted into the Fuk Tak Chi Museum on 76 Telok Ayer Street). Qing Shan Ting cemetery reached its capacity in the 1830s and the temple acquired another burial ground in Havelock Road called Loke Yah Teng (Green Field Pavilion). In 1843 the Trustees of the Jewish synagogue in Singapore acquired a block of land on a 99 year lease in Orchard Road for the **first Jewish Cemetery**. By 1900, the cemetery was nearly full and the area was part of the expanding commercial district and a fresh plot of land was sought. In 1900, the Trustees purchased land in Thomson Road for $5000. In 1903, Manasseh Meyer bought adjoining land and donated it to the the Trustees just keeping the Meyer Plot as a private burial plot. The cemetery was extended in 1933 and again in 1937. In 1976, the community was offered land in Chua Chu Kang for a new cemetery. The Orchard Road Cemetery held 160 graves. The Thomson Road Cemetery held 705 graves.

Cenotaph

See *War Memorial*.

Census

1824. The first census was taken on 1 January 1824. The census on Singapore island revealed that the population then was 10,683 and was made up of 74 Europeans, 16 Armenians, 15 Arabs, 4,580 Malays, 3,317 Chinese, 756 Natives of India and 1,925 Bugis. While censuses were held before 1871, they were taken in a rather haphazard way often using untrained police personnel. There were censuses of this sort from 1824-1830 and from 1832-1834 and then in 1836, 1840, 1849 and 1860. The original documents concerning these censuses are no longer available and figures for this period can only be derived from secondary sources. **The first systematic census** was taken on 2 April 1871. Censuses were held every ten years up to 1931. The 1941 census was postponed until 1947 and there was a census in 1957. They have been held at regular intervals since then. The introduction of compulsory registration of births and deaths in 1872 improved the accuracy of the census. A reliable and accurate census paints a valuable picture of the trends and changes in the population of Singapore over time. It can show the rate of growth of the population, the composition and origin of its settlers, and the ratio between the sexes at various times in Singapore's history. The first **census of industrial production** covering all establishments employing 10 or more persons was conducted by the Department of Statistics in 1960.

Chamber of Commerce

Singapore Chamber of Commerce (1837). The first chamber of commerce, the Singapore Chamber of Commerce, was founded in 1837. Before 1837, merchants met on an *ad hoc* basis to oppose the introduction of various pieces of legislation proposed by the Indian government. It was proposed that they should set up a permanent organisation to promote their interests. A meeting of merchants was held on 8 February 1837 in the Singapore Reading Room off Commercial Square (now the site of the Golden Shoe car park) to establish the Singapore Chamber of Commerce to defend the rights and interests of the mercantile community in Singapore, to collect and classify mercantile information and to establish a court of arbitration to adjust commercial differences referred to it. It was open to all races and communities and the first committee included Europeans, Chinese, Eurasians and Arabs. The **first President** was Alexander Laurie Johnston. Johnston came to Singapore in 1819 and founded the firm AL Johnston & Co. The first Secretary of the Chamber of Commerce was EJ Gilman, a partner in the firm of Hamilton Gray. The earliest Chinese members were Tan Kim Seng from Kim Seng & Co, Seah Eu Chin and Whampoa Hoo Ah Kay.

The Chinese merchants withdrew their support of the Chamber during the latter half of the 19th century. The last Chinese member, Cheng Seng Chye & Co. of Boat Quay, left in 1860. The reasons for this are unclear. The Chamber played a critical role in the development of the rubber industry through its formation of a Rubber Association to 'improve the conditions governing the trade in plantation rubber in Singapore' and to conduct Auction Sales governed by regulations laid down by the Chamber of Commerce. The Chamber of Commerce Rubber Association was established in June 1911 and the first auction was held on the 12 September 1911 with eleven lots going for auction. The weekly auctions were held in the Exchange Building at the seaward end of Battery Road. In 1912, 599 tons of rubber were offered at the Singapore auctions. In 1918, over 52,000 tons were offered. The auctions helped to make Singapore the world centre of the rubber trade. The first meeting after the Japanese Occupation was held on 26 April 1946 at the Fullerton Building and EMF Fergusson of the Straits Trading Company was elected Chairman. In 1948, Fergusson was nominated by the Singapore Chamber of Commerce to represent the organisation in the Singapore Legislative Council. On 17 April 1964, the organisation voted to change its name to the Singapore International Chamber of Commerce. The **Chinese Chamber of Commerce** was formed in 1906 and its first President was Goh Siew Tin. The **Indian Chamber of Commerce** was formed in 1935, and its first President was Rajabali Jumabhoy.

Changi Quilt

Girl-Guide Quilt, 1942. The Changi quilts were a series of quilts each comprising 66 embroidered squares created and signed by women civilian internees in Changi Prison, Singapore, during the first 6 months of their captivity by the Japanese. The first of these was the Girl Guide quilt made for Elizabeth Ennis, leader and organizer of the Girl Guide group operating among the young internees at Changi. The guides secretly made the Girl Guide quilt for Ennis' birthday. They collected material and met secretly to make a beautiful patchwork quilt of hexagon rosettes with the name of each girl embroidered in the centre of the rosette she had made. When Ethel Mulvaney of the Canadian Red Cross saw the girls' quilt, she encouraged the women internees to make other quilts. Three more quilts were made. The internees collected unbleached calico rice, sugar and flour bags, and collected and traded material scraps and needles to make the quilts. Many of the squares had patriotic symbols or poignant reminders of their home country. One square had an embroidered picture of a brick wall and was embroidered with the words 'Changi Holiday Home'.

Making the quilts was designed to alleviate boredom, boost morale and pass information to their husbands who were interned in the military camps. Each woman tried to put something of herself into the embroidered square. One quilt was made for the Australian Red Cross and the back of the quilt bears the inscription, 'Presented by the women of Changi Internment Camp 1942 to the wounded Australian soldiers with our sympathy for their sufferings.' One quilt was made for wounded Japanese soldiers. This quilt included floral motifs and images of the Rising Sun and Mount Fuji. The Japanese allowed the quilts to be sent to the military hospital at Changi Barracks. The Australian and Japanese quilts are now in the Australian War Museum in Canberra while a third is held by the British Red Cross. The Girl Guide Quilt remained in Ennis' possession.

Chart

Ross' Chart, 1819. The first detailed chart of Singapore harbour was made in February 1819 by Captain Daniel Ross. His 'Report of a Survey of Singapoora Harbour, 7 February 1819' was published in the *Calcutta Journal or Political, Commercial and Literary Gazette*, 6 April 1819, at pages 59-60. Ross, commanding HEICS *Discovery* and Lieutenant John GF Crawford, commanding HEICS *Investigator* arrived from Macau in December 1818 to make a hydrographic survey of the Straits of Malacca. Sir Stamford Raffles invited the two men and their ships to accompany him to Singapore. After their arrival in Singapore, Ross immediately began to survey the surrounding waters. He completed the report on 7 February 1819. His report went into great detail of tidal movements, depths, and the prevailing winds in the harbour. Perhaps his most significant remarks were this:

> *Singapoora Harbour, situated four miles to the N.N.E. of St. John's Island, in what is commonly called Singapoora Straits, will afford a safe anchorage to ships in all seasons, and being clear of hidden danger, the approach to it is rendered easy by day or by night. Its position is also favourable for commanding the navigation of the Straits, the track which the ships pursue being distant about five miles; and it may be expected from its proximity to the Malayan Islands and China Seas, that in a short time numerous vessels would resort to it for commercial purposes.*

See also **Government Survey**.

Checkpoint

Seletar Airport, 1929. The first checkpoint was built at Seletar Airport in 1929. Until 1966, the immigration checkpoints were built to cater to air and sea-based arrivals only. The first sea-based checkpoint was built at East Wharf, Singapore Harbour Board. It moved to South Quay in 1961, to Finger Pier in 1975 and to the

World Trade Centre in 1992. From 1 July 1967, Singapore and Malaysian citizens needed travel documents to travel between Singapore and Malaysia. The Changi immigration post was set up in 1967 to clear passengers travelling to Penggarang in South Johor. A checkpoint was set up at the Railway Station in Keppel Road in 1966 and at the Customs Checkpoint at Woodlands in 1966 to clear passengers travelling by land.

Chettiar Temple

Tank Road (1855-1860). The first chettiar temple built in Singapore was the Chettiar's Temple in Tank Road built between 1855 and 1860. It was originally called the Sri Dhandayuthapam, or the Subramaniam Temple. The building was built by the Nattukottai Chettiars. It was renovated in 1961 and again in 1981. It is one of the most splendid of the Hindu temples in Singapore and is traditionally the location of the Naarathri Festival and the destination of the Thaipusam Festival. The temple is owned by the Trustees of the Nattukottai Chettiars Temple. The sculptures depicting Hindu deities were made by sculptors from the Mamallapuram School of Madras in Madras, India. The temple features a pair of 6 metre-high Kamalam-patterned rosewood doors.

Chief Justice

See *Judge*.

Chief Minister

David Saul Marshall (1955–1956). David Saul Marshall was born on 12 March 1908, the son of Saul Nassim Marshall, a trader who arrived in Singapore to seek his fortune. He was educated first at St Joseph's Institution and then at Raffles Institution. At school, he was a brilliant pupil and was a prime candidate for the coveted Queen's Scholarship. Unfortunately, Marshall worked so hard for the scholarship examinations that he collapsed on the eve of the examination and had to be sent to Switzerland to recuperate. Thereafter, he took up a series of odd jobs and finally left for England in September 1934. In 1937, he was called to the Bar at Middle Temple and in 1938, to the Singapore Bar. In Singapore, he started work at the prominent firm of Aitken & Ong Siang where he began building up an impressive reputation at the criminal bar. In the period World War II, Marshall concentrated on his legal career and was not active in local politics although he did sign up as a member of the Singapore Volunteer Corps when war was imminent. Just before the war Marshall resigned from Aitken & Ong Siang and joined Allen & Gledhill.

During the War, Marshall was detained as a civilian internee. When he resumed practice at Allen & Gledhill when Singapore was liberated, becoming its first Asian partner in 1949. In 1950, he resigned from Allen & Gledhill to pursue his lifelong ambition to study medicine but had a change of mind and rejoined the legal profession in the firm of Battenberg & Talma.

In February, an old friend Gerald de Cruz visited Marshall with the aim of recruiting him into the newly-formed Malayan Democratic Union (MDU). Marshall turned de Cruz down as he was anxious to rebuild his legal career. Marshall then dedicated his non-working hours to his own Jewish community, and served as president of the Jewish Welfare

Board from 1946 to 1951. In June 1947, he was elected as a committee member of the Singapore Association of which Sir Roland Braddell was president. Later, in November 1949, Marshall drifted into membership of the Progressive Party. In March 1950, he was elected to the Party's committee. Earlier that year, John Laycock suggested that Marshall should stand for Municipal Commissioner but Marshall felt unready for the task. A year later, Marshall again turned Laycock down when the latter suggested that he stood as candidate for the South Ward.

As a prominent lawyer and social figure, Marshall was much sought after by the various groups seeking to form political parties following the convening of the Rendel Constitutional Commission. Soon, Marshall drifted apart from the PP and gravitated towards men like Lim Yew Hock and Francis Thomas who inaugurated the Singapore Socialist Party (SSP) in April 1954. Marshall turned down the presidency of the SSP when it was offered to him, but later accepted when the SSP merged with the Singapore Labour Party to form the Labour Front.

When the Labour Front shocked everyone by taking the majority of seats in the 1955 general elections, Marshall became Singapore's first Chief Minister. Marshall's political career was brief. In the 14 months that he was Chief Minister, he pushed relentlessly for an end to colonial rule and independence for Singapore. As a result of he confrontation with Governor Sir John Nicoll, Marshall succeeded in precipitating all-Party constitutional talks in London in 1956. After failing to secure independence for Singapore, Marshall returned to Singapore and resigned as Chief Minister on 7 June 1956. Less than a year later, he resigned from the Labour Front. Lim Yew Hock succeeded him as Chief Minister.

In 1961, Marshall stood as a Workers' Party candidate for the Anson by-election and won by the slimmest of margins. Marshall proved a formidable speaker and opposition member but his political views were out of the ordinary person's depth. He lost his seat in the 1963 election when he stood as an independent candidate. Marshall retired from politics after his defeat at the 1963 general elections. He continued to be the pre-eminent criminal lawyer and in 1978 was appointed Singapore's ambassador to France. It was his chance to serve Singapore once more, and the former political foe of the PAP and Lee Kuan Yew proved himself to be one of Singapore's best emissaries. He retired in 1990 at the age of 82. In December 1994, the National University of Singapore conferred on him an honorary Doctor of Laws. He died on 12 December 1995 at the age of 87.

Chinese Consul

Whampoa Hoo Ah Kay, 1877. The first Chinese Consul appointed to Singapore was Whampoa Hoo Ah Kay, who was appointed in 1877. He was also Consul for Russia and Japan. He was born in Whampoa near Canton (Guandong) in 1816 and came to Singapore in 1830 at the age of 14 to help his father in business. His father established the firm of Whampoa & Company and it was the provisioner and ship chandler to the British Navy. The company had its premises in Telok Ayer Street. Whampoa extended his father's business and he became one of Singapore's leading merchants and traders. He was Honorary Treasurer of Tan Tock Seng Hospital (1844) and in 1869, **became the first Asian appointed to the Legislative Council**. Hoo was also an extraordinary member of the Executive Council, and an honorary magistrate (1872). In 1876, Hoo was awarded a

Companion of the Order of St Michael and St George (CMG) for his public services. He died on 27 March 1880 and his remains were taken back to China.

Chinese Protector

William Pickering (1877–1888). The colonial government established the Chinese Protectorate in 1877 to deal with two serious problems confronting the Chinese community in Singapore: (a) the serious abuses of the labour trade, in particular the credit ticket system; and (b) control of the secret societies. A report into the trade recommended the appointment of a Protector of Immigrants to look after the welfare of new arrivals and protect them from kidnapping and other abuses.

In 1877, the government established a Chinese Protectorate to deal with all matters concerning the Chinese in Singapore. **The first protector** was William Alexander Pickering (1840–1907). Pickering joined the British Navy in 1856 and apprenticed for the next four years on the *Lady McDonald*, travelling to many ports in Burma, Siam, China and Malaya. In 1862, Pickering got a job in the Imperial Maritime Customs office in Fuzhou and studied the local dialect and written language while working as a tidewaiter. After only five months, his superiors took notice of him, especially his language abilities and this encouraged him to hire a native Mandarin instructor to teach him the language. Within a year of working in the Customs Office, Pickering obtained a grant to continue his language studies. In 1863, he accompanied the Commissioner of Customs for Formosa to the island and helped establish customs houses in some southern port cities. There, he took the opportunity to study the local dialect and visit aborigines in the interior. In 1865, he was placed in charge of customs in Anping in the port of Taiwanfu. Two years later, Pickering accepted an offer to take charge of the Taiwanfu branch of the British firm of McPhail and Compant (later Elles & Company).

In 1870, Pickering fell ill with dysentery and fever and was invalided home to England where he was placed on twelve months' home leave. While in England, Pickering was appointed Chinese Interpreter to the Government of the Straits Settlements (1871). Pickering's extraordinary language abilities and his intimate knowledge of many Chinese dialects made him a great asset and he was expected to supervise cadets studying Chinese. One of the first cadets to take up the study of Chinese was Francis Powell, who later replaced Pickering as Protector of Chinese. In April 1877, Dr Nicholas Dennys was appointed Assistant Protector. Dennys was also well qualified for the post with many years experience in China and excellent proficiency in Cantonese.

Under the Chinese Immigrants Ordinance and a Crimping Ordinance, Pickering was authorised to license recruiting agents and agencies involved in the 'coolie trade'. The larger task was to supervise disembarkation of all immigrants arriving from China. He and his men boarded all incoming ships to explain to the men that an indebted man was expected to work for his passage money, and that a contract must be signed and honoured. There must be no restraint or confinement. If the newcomers had friends or family who could pay the passage money, this was actively encouraged and the men concerned were declared debt free. A system of control was slowly imposed over the rapidly increasing trade. Control over the transit trade was much more challenging and it was nearly four years before the situation improved.

Pickering also tackled the problem of controlling the secret societies. The key points of his plan were to collect information about the societies, to make use of the headmen to preserve law and order and to assist in secret societies disputes that had the potential to develop into gang warfare. This was only partially effective. The arrival of Governor Clementi Smith signalled a major change in policy. The Governor, an accomplished Chinese speaker, was determined to get rid of the toothless legislation controlling secret societies. He introduced new legislation to suppress dangerous societies and register benevolent societies. Pickering fought against this but a year after Pickering retired in 1888, the law was passed. The Protector was also expected to supervise Chinese women and girls. This was done through the Contagious Diseases Ordinance of 1870. To help deal with the problem, Pickering founded the Po Leung Kuk or 'Office to protect virtue' which was administered by a committee of prominent Chinese. Pickering also embarked on a personal crusade against gambling and this made him very unpopular. In July 1887, there was an attack on his life by Chua Ah Sioh, a member of one of the leading societies. Pickering never fully recovered from the attack and retired in 1888. Under his leadership, the Protectorate became a success and provided a valuable link between the government and the Chinese community. Disturbances became more infrequent and many undesirable labour practices were slowly eliminated. Pickering died in 1907.

Chinese Temple

Fuk Tak Chi Temple, 1820. The first Chinese temple was the Fuk Tak Chi Temple in Telok Ayer Street. The name means the Temple of Prosperity and Virtue. The temple belonged to the Shenist sect which combines elements of Buddhism and Confucianism. It had been built of attap and wood in 1820 and sat on the shoreline facing the sea. A brick temple was erected on the site in 1824. Its doors were painted with protective door gods and its benefactors included the Cantonese and Hakka communities and its main deity is Tua Peh Kong. It is now part of the Far East Square development built in 2000.

Chocolate Factory

Van Houten Chocolate Factory, 1965. The first chocolate factory in Singapore opened in Tanglin Halt in May 1965. The chocolate factory was a joint venture between CJ Van Houten & Zoon of Holland and Sheng Huo Enterprises Ltd. with a paid up capital of $2 million. The factory produced cocoa and chocolate products to meet local and overseas demands. The cocoa beans used in the factory came from Sabah, Trengganu and Ghana and the packaging was manufactured locally. The latest machines were imported from Italy, Germany and Switzerland and Van Houten provided much of the technical advice. Within a year, the factory began exporting its produce to Burma, Thailand, Hong Kong, South Vietnam and Cambodia. The factory employed 150 workers. In 1997, the factory was sold to Barry Callebaut (Singapore) Pte. Ltd, a company with its headquarters in Switzerland. Barry Callebaut is a merger of two leading chocolate companies, the Belgian Callebaut company, established in 1850 and the British Cacao Barry company, established in 1842. In 2005, the Singapore factory produced 18,000 tonnes of chocolate.

Cholera Epidemic

1841–1842. The first recorded cholera epidemic was in 1841–1842. The epidemic was caused mainly by poor water supply, unsanitary living conditions and unsatisfactory sewage disposal. Many epidemics followed. The one in 1873 was particularly severe, registering a mortality rate of 41% – 357 deaths from 857 cases.

Christmas Beach Party

Sentosa, 1993. The first public Christmas beach party was held at Sentosa's central beach on Christmas Eve 1993. The setting was idyllic but a heavy downpour kept the crowds away. About 1,600 attended the event. There was non-stop music and videos of live concerts were shown on 3 large screens. The event was called the 'Beach Bash' and cost $30 per person.

Christmas light-up

13 December 1984. The first Christmas light-up along Orchard Road commenced on 13 December 1984 when Minister of State for Trade and Industry, Dr Wong Kwei Cheong turned on the first Christmas lights along Orchard and Scotts Roads. Wong, who was also Chairman of the Singapore Tourist Promotion Board, presided over the ceremony which took place in the foyer of the Dynasty Hotel (now the Marriott Hotel) at 7.30 pm that evening. The 'Illuminative Decorations' consisted of 10,000 lights and stretched down Orchard Road from the Ming Court Hotel (now Orchard Parade Hotel) right to the Istana gates. On the Scotts Road end, the lights ran from the Dynasty Hotel to Goodwood Park Hotel. The light-up was organized by the Singapore Tourist Promotion Board, the Singapore Hotel Association, the National Association of Travel Agents of Singapore and the Singapore Retail Merchants Association. Since then, the Orchard Road Christmas light-up has been an annual highlight of the Christmas season.

Christmas Street Party

Orchard Road, 1988. The first Christmas street party was held on 24 December 1988 on Orchard Road. At 7.00 pm that evening, the stretch of Orchard Road from Scotts Road to the junction of Killiney Road was closed to traffic for 6 hours. An estimated 60,000 people went down to Orchard Road to join in the festivities. The mood was described as 'mellow'. A week later, the same stretch of road was closed for a street party to celebrate New Year's Eve.

Churches

Roman Catholic Church, 1833. The first church in Singapore was a Roman Catholic church made of wood and attap at the site of what is now the Singapore Art Museum. Costing just $700 to build, it measured 20 meters by 10 meters. Before this church was built, the Catholics used to attend mass at Denis McSwiney's house. This church soon outgrew its congregation and a new church was commissioned by Father Jean-Marie Beurel. This was the Cathedral of the Good Shepherd. The church's foundation stone was laid in June 1843 by John Conolly, a resident and merchant. The first design for the church was prepared by John Turnbull Thomson but it was thought too expensive. A second design by Denis McSwiney was accepted and construction cost $18,355.22. The church was consecrated on 6 June 1846. Charles Dyce added the tower and spire in 1847, and when the Church became a

Cathedral, a special consecration service was held in 1897. On 28 June 1973, the Cathedral was gazetted a National Monument.

The **first Anglican church** was St Andrew's Church. Even though land had been set aside for the construction of an Anglican church in Raffles' Town Plan of 1822, it was not till 1835 that the foundation stone of the Anglican Church of St Andrew's was laid. The building was designed by George Dromgold Coleman and cost $11,000 to built. It was completed in 1837 and JT Thomson added a tower and spire later on. Unfortunately the building was struck by lighting twice and was condemned as being unsafe. In 1852, it was torn down and a new church – the present St Andrew's Cathedral (completed 1861) – was built in its place.

Singapore's oldest church, the Armenian Church of St Gregory the Illuminator in Hill Street was also Singapore **first Armenian church**. It was designed by George D Coleman and completed in 1835 at the cost of over $5,000. The church was consecrated on 26 March 1836, the anniversary of St Gregory The church is regarded as one of Coleman's masterpieces, with its elegant symmetrical classical style with projecting square porticos and a semi-circular chancel and altar. An English architect, Maddock, added the tower and spire in 1847. It has been gazetted as a national monument.

Singapore's **first Methodist church** was built in 1886 on land granted by the Government in Coleman Street. The church was opened in 1887 and remained in continuous use till 1909 when the building was taken over by the Anglo-Chinese School (now National Archives of Singapore). A new church, the Wesley Methodist Church was built in Fort Canning. It was opened on Christmas Day 1908 and dedicated on 4 February 1909.

The **first Portuguese church** was the Church of St Joseph on Victoria Street built in 1853. It was built on the site of the first Portuguese mission founded by Father Francisco da Silva e Maia in 1825. The church was completely rebuilt between 1906 and 1912. The current building was designed by the renowned firm of Swan and Maclaren.

The Prinsep Street Presbyterian Church, originally known as the Malay Chapel was Singapore's **first Presbyterian church**. Built in 1842 on the site of an attap shed that had been used as a Mission Chapel, the congregation comprised mainly Malay-speaking Straits Chinese.

Cinema

Paris Cinema, 1903. Singapore's first cinema was the Paris Cinema built in 1903 by an Indian jewellery company at Victoria Street. There were four shows a day at 6.00 pm, 7.00 pm, 8.00 pm, and 9.00 pm. The cinema attracted huge crowds and there were two admission prices: 10 cents or 50 cents. The **first air-conditioned cinema**, Cathay Cinema opened in 1939. It was also the first cinema to reopen after World War II. It opened on Sunday, 23 September 1945, with a grand film titled *Desert Victory*.

The **first and only drive-in** cinema was the Jurong Drive-In which opened on 14 July 1971. The cinema, located at Yuan Ching Road, next to the Japanese Gardens had just one screen measuring 47 ft by 110 ft (14.3 m x 33.5 m) was owned and operated by the Cathay Organisation Pte Ltd. Occupying 5.6 hectares of land, the drive-in could accommodate 899 cars and 300 walk-in patrons. It was the first of its kind in Singapore and Malaysia and the largest in Southeast Asia. Minister of Culture

Jek Yeun Thong was the guest-of-honour at the cinema's opening when it screened the gala charity film premiere, *Doctor in Trouble*. The Drive-In was based on the O'Halloran Hill cinema in Adelaide, Australia. There were special car speaker systems with adjustable volumes linking the sound-track to individual cars. The screen was elevated 25 feet above ground and tilted at an angle of six-and-a-half degrees. Watching a film at the Drive-In was like watching an enormous television screen in the total privacy of a small circle box. First-run English language features were intended for the Drive-in. The film *The Big Boss* which starred the late movie legend Bruce Lee, grossed an all-time high of S$12,000 for a single show on its opening night at the Drive-In. The cinema closed 30 September 1985.

The **first Omnimax** theatre or cinema was Omnitheatre at the Singapore Science Centre. Built in 1987 at the cost of $18 million, it can screen Omnimax movies and it contained a Planetarium Star Field Projector to allow the screening of Planetarium shows. It has a 23 metre tilted dome screen that is 5 storeys high and a 1570 screen format and can seat 276 people. The **first digital cinema** was Orchard Cineplex. Opened on 16 October 2003, the digital cinema launch attracted 350 industry partners and media representatives. The opening featured the screening of Disney's *Finding Nemo* in digital format.

Circumnavigation, Singapore Island

2 to 11 August 1825. Resident Crawfurd set out to complete a circumnavigation of the island of Singapore on 2 August 1825. The Bengal government instructed him to complete the circumnavigation to take formal possession of Singapore under the terms of the Treaty signed in 1824. He set sail in the 380-ton ship *Malabar* at 6.00 am and went Eastward towards Johore Hill, arriving the following morning. Thereafter, the ship went to Pulau Ubin and Crawfurd hoisted the British flag there and fired a 21-gun salute. It took Crawfurd four days to navigate the West Straits and then went to the Carimon Islands, Rabbit and Coney Islands. They returned to the harbour in Singapore and landed at daybreak ten days after their departure.

Civil Defence Public Spirited Citizen Award

Ng Joo Hong, 1989. The first ever Civil Defence Public Spirited Citizen Award was presented to Ng Joo Hong on 30 October 1989. Ng saved a 5 year-old boy caught in a fire in Bedok. The ex-combat engineer with the Singapore Armed Forces perched precariously on a 7th storey window ledge to grab the boy who was desperately holding onto a washing pole holder. He received a plaque and a commendation.

Clan Association Assembly Hall

Ning Yeung Wui Kuan, 1822. The Ning Yeung Wui Kuan, an association for men from Toi San (Taishan) District (located about 130km southwest of Guandong) built an assembly hall at the corner of South Bridge Road and Hokkien Street. It was built by Tsao Ah Chee (Chao Yazhi), a Chinese carpenter from Penang, who came to Singapore with the first settlers in January 1819. Tradition has it that Tsao built the flagpole at the mouth of Rochore (also spelt 'Rochor') River for the Union Jack to be hoisted. The hall was removed in 1847 and then again in 1875. In 1894, the clan association changed its name to Ning Yeung

Wui Koon. The building was demolished in September 1964.

Clinic – Free

Thong Chai Medical Institute, 1867. The Thong Chai Yee Say (medical institute) was established by a group of migrants from China in 1867 to provide free medical consultation and herbal medicine to all people, irrespective of race, religion and status. The name 'Thong Chai' was derived from the Chinese word *Tong*, meaning 'the same', symbolizing same or equal treatment for all; *Ji*, meaning 'to help or relieve' others. The Institute started out at a rented shop house 31 Upper Pickering Street. When Sir Cecil Clementi Smith, Governor of the Straits Settlement heard what Thong Chai was doing, he granted the Institute an 8,380 sq ft piece of land at Lot 13349, Kampong Melaka (No 3 Wayang Street to No 67 New Market Street) to the Institute to build its own premises. This building was completed in 1892. It was officially opened by Sir Cecil on 14 November 1892 and renamed Thong Chai Medical Institute. In 1960, the management wanted to demolish its Wayang Street premises to construct a bigger building. However, the traditional Chinese architecture-style building was gazetted as a conserved building in 1963, and as a National Monument in 1973. The Rebuilding Sub-committee then obtained an option to purchase a site for Thong Chai's new building at Chin Swee Road. In 1975, the 10-storey Thong Chai Building was completed and the medical institute moved into the building in May 1976. It was declared open by Prime Minister Lee Kuan Yew on 25 November 1976.

Clock, public

Old Court House Clock, 1845. Thomas Church, the Resident Councillor of Singapore for 19 years, gave a clock to the old St. Andrew's Church. When the church was struck by lightning in 1845, the clock was removed and placed on the fa ade of the Old Court House, facing High Street. The clock was made by Barraud and Lund of Cornhill, London. The dial measured 4 feet 6 inches in diameter and the bell was 20 inches in diameter. The bell bore the date 1839. The bell was later moved to the tower of the Police offices. It is not known what became of the clock when the Old Court House underwent renovations in 1873.

Coach of the Year

1970. The first Coach of the Year Award was instituted by the Singapore National Olympic Council in 1970. That year, the award went to three coaches: Tan Eng Yoon, for Athletics, Chan Ah Kow for Swimming, and Ang Teck Bee for Judo. Chan won the Coach of the Year an unprecedented three times (1970, 1971 and 1972), while Ang won the Award again in 1976. Chan's record was only equaled 30 years later by Sheik Alau'ddin bin Yacob Marican, when he won the Coach of the Year Award for Silat in 2000, 2002, and 2003.

Coffee Roasting Factory

Jurong, 1962. The first coffee roasting factory was set up in Jalan Rajawali in Jurong in 1962 by Werner Ernst Huber of the Anglo-Swiss Trading Company. Huber operated the factory – originally a modest zinc shed – under his subsidiary company, Boncafe Ltd. The coffee beans are imported from Celebes, Bali, Timor and Sumatra and blended and roasted in Singapore. The roasting was done using a Probat Werke coffee roaster made at Emmerich in Germany. The coffee was designed to appeal to all groups in Singapore. Production was now approximately 30,000 lb. per month and the factory employs about 100 workers.

Coins and Currency

Straits Settlements currency, 1826. Singapore did not have a dominant native currency until the Straits Settlements was formed in 1826. During this time, the main currencies in use were the Spanish Dollar, Dutch Doits and the Singapore merchant tokens (cockerel token coins inscribed with the denomination 'Satu Keping' or one Keping). In 1862, a new issue of one-cent, half-cent and quarter-cent coins was made for use in the Straits Settlements. They bore the inscription 'India Straits'. In 1867, the Straits Settlements were transferred to the Colonial Office in London, and the first series of coins bearing the inscription 'Straits Settlement', were issued in 1871. The first 5 cent, 10 cent and 20 cent pieces were issued on 18 May 1872.

The first bank notes issued were in denominations of $5 and $100. They were issued in May 1849 by the Oriental Bank. Singapore first issued its own currency notes in 1967. The first polymer bank note was a $25 note issued on 9 August 1990 to commemorate 25 years of independence. It was designed by Singaporean artist, Chua Mia Tee.

Cold Storage Provision

Singapore Cold Storage, 1905. In June 1903, the *Straits Times* carried an advertisement calling for subscribers to a new company called Singapore Cold Storage. This company would be the first in Singapore to 'provide cold storage' and introduce, store and distribute 'frozen beef, mutton, lamb, game, fresh butter, fruit and other Australian food supplies and products'. For people living in Singapore, this opened a new era of food provision and management. The company was registered on 8 June 1903 and opened its offices in Battery Road under the supervision of the manager, HWH Stevens. It bought land at Borneo Wharf down in Keppel Harbour and built a cold store consisting of two insulated rooms, each capable of storing 200 tons of frozen meat. The cold rooms were completed in February 1905. The **first consignment of frozen foods** was delivered to Singapore on the *Guthrie* on 24 March 1905. The consignment contained 225 tons of beef, 71 tons of mutton, 15 tons of lamb, 15 tons of fresh butter, 25 cases of milk and 14 tons of poultry and sundry goods and was valued at $188,000. The goods were transported from the ship to the new cold store by train. The company opened its first retail outlets at Orchard Road and Keppel Harbour on 30 March 1905.

Colonial Governor

Sir Harry St George Ord (1867–1873). The first Governor of the Straits Settlements was Colonel Sir Harry St George Ord who occupied the office from 1867-1873. Ord was born in 1819 and was commissioned as an officer in the Royal Engineers in 1837. He served in the Crimean War from 1854 and 1855 and thereafter transferred to the Colonial Service. In 1856, he was sent to the Gold Coast, and subsequently became Lieutenant-Governor of Dominica (1857) and Governor of Bermuda (1861-1866). He became Governor of the Straits Settlements in 1867 and he left in 1873. He later became

Governor of Western Australia in 1877. He was an unpopular governor as he was masterful and overbearing. He was described as being extravagant in his views of what was due to the dignity of his office. He did not seek advice and did not accept it when it was offered. However he was financially competent and succeeded in putting the Settlements on a sound footing. He was a Governor during a time of material progress driven by the opening of the Suez Canal in 1869. Ord was forbidden to extend the British Administration into the Malay States and was told his role was not one of 'intervention in native affairs'. He was succeeded by Sir Andrew Clarke who was considered to be more in tune with the business community and was more willing to 'dance to the bagpipes of Singapore', a reference to the power of the Scottish businessmen who dominated trade in Singapore at that time.

Commercial Air Flight

See AIR PLANE

Commonwealth Games Gold Medal

Tan Howe Liang & Tan Ser Cher, 1958. The first persons to clinch gold for Singapore at the 6th British Empire and Commonwealth Games were two weightlifters: Tan Howe Liang and Tan Ser Cher. They won lightweight and featherweight gold medals at the 1958 Cardiff Games respectively. Tan Ser Cher lifted a total weight of 685 lbs to clinch the gold in the featherweight division. Tan Howe Liang established a world record in the Jerk (lightweight division) with a lift of 347 lbs to win the gold medal. He later went on to win a silver medal at the Olympic Games in Rome in 1960. The only other person Commonwealth gold medallist and the **first woman gold medallist** was badminton player Li Li who won the 2002 women's badminton singles title at the age of just 19. Li Li was also Singapore's youngest Commonwealth Games gold medallist when she clinched the Women's Badminton Singles title at the 17th Games in Manchester in 2002. Li began formal badminton training at eight, and joined the national badminton squad when she was 14. Five years later, she was ranked among the top women's singles in the 2002 Commonwealth Games.

Commonwealth Heads of Government Meeting (CHOGM)

CHOGM 1971. The first Commonwealth Heads of Government Meeting (CHOGM) was held in Singapore in January 1971. Originally started as the Colonial Conferences in 1887, these meetings became known as the Imperial Conferences from 1911 to 1937. From 1944 to the early 1960s, the Commonwealth Prime Ministers Meetings were held almost annually in London. At Singapore, the term Commonwealth Heads of Government Meeting (CHOGM) was adopted to encompass both Presidents and Prime Ministers. Since then, CHOGMs have taken place on a biennial basis. The Singapore meeting was chaired by Prime Minister Lee Kuan Yew. This was the first such meeting outside the United Kingdom and the Declaration of Principles of the Commonwealth were adopted at this conference.

Community Centres

Serangoon & Siglap Community Centres, 1953. The first community centres were opened in Singapore in Serangoon and Siglap in May 1953. In 1946, the Colonial Office wanted to set up agencies to foster community development in the colonies. In Singapore, the Department of Social Welfare was given the task of setting up community centres to encourage participation in grassroots activities and to promote grassroots leadership. Some centres were purpose-built and some utilised existing structures such as children's centres. Large purpose-built centres such as Bukit Panjang (1955) and Buona Vista (1956) cost about $150,000 and offered a range of activities. The smaller ones such as Changi Point (1958) cost about $26,000. Local initiatives led to the building of the one in Yio Chu Kang in 1956. By the end of the 1950s, the centres were virtually autonomous and there was a tendency for them to be controlled by those grassroots leaders with political aspirations. After 1959, the centres came under centralised authority. The People's Association was set up by the People's Action Party in July 1960 to control the community centres, and the centres were revitalized to bridge the gap between the leaders and the people and to mobilize support for the ruling party. Facilities were expanded to provide a wider range of activities. They are still widely used today.

Computerised Wharf Documentation

1967. In 1967, the Port of Singapore Authority introduced the first computerised integrated documentation and billing system. In 1973, the **first online computerised** Container Handling Information System was introduced about a year after the new container terminal at Tanjong Pagar was opened. This was replaced in 1989 by PORTNET which allows freight forwarders and shipping lines, haulers and consignees to communicate electronically not only with the port authority but also with other government agencies such as Customs and the Trade Development Board.

Concert, Orchestral

Amateur Music Society Orchestra Concert, 1865. On 28 December 1865, the orchestra of the Amateur Musical Society gave a concert in the Upper Room of the Town Hall (now Victoria Concert Hall). The leader of the orchestra was a Mr Fenton, organist of St. Andrew's Cathedral. The programme consisted of a wide variety of choral and instrumental pieces including the Francois Adrien Boieldieu's *Overture to the Caliph of Baghdad*, Haydn's 1st Quintet and Locke's *Music for Macbeth*. *The Straits Times* wrote that the concert was a success from start to finish.

The first concert given by a **visiting professional orchestra** was that of the Radio Batavia Philharmonic Orchestra on 6 November 1949 at the Victoria Memorial Hall. The concert was given on the opening night of the 1st Singapore Festival of Music. The 19-member orchestra played Bach's *Third Suite in D Major*, Brahms' *First Symphony* and Beethoven's *Fourth Piano Concerto* with French pianist Jacques Genty. The concert was sponsored by the Straits Times Press Ltd, the Singapore Music Circle and Radio Malaya. The orchestra played to 3,200 school children at the Happy World Stadium on the 8 November 1949.

The **Singapore Symphony Orchestra gave its inaugural concert** on 24 January 1979 at the Singapore Conference Hall under the baton of Choo Hoey. The Orchestra played Rossini's *Overture to the Barber of Seville*, Schubert's *Unfinished Symphony* and Beethoven's *Emperor Concerto* with Singaporean pianist Ong Lip Tat, Ives' *Unanswered Question* and the traditional Chinese piece, *Dance of the Yao People*.

Concert Hall, Purpose-Built

Esplanade-Theatres on the Bay, 2002. While concerts have been staged in Singapore since the early 19th century, Singapore never had a dedicated, purpose-built concert hall till 2002. Oftentimes, concerts were staged in multi-purpose halls or auditoria, such as the old Town Hall (now Victoria Concert Hall), Capitol Theatre (at which the great violinist Jascha Heifetz played), Kallang Theatre (modified from an old cinema), or even the Singapore Indoor Stadium. The first purpose built concert hall in Singapore is the Esplanade-Theatres on the Bay complex completed in October 2002. The concert hall seats 1600 and has an orchestra pit that seats 100 musicians and choir stalls to seat 200. The acoustics were designed by acoustic expert 'Professor' Russell Johnson of Artec Consultants Inc, USA. The concert hall has a 12-metre organ with 4,889 pipes built and installed by Orgelbau Klais of Bonn. The concert hall is part of the Esplanade-Theatres on the Bay complex designed by DP Architects Pte. Ltd and Michael Wilford & Partners, and built by Penta-Ocean Construction Pte Ltd. (Japan).

The Concert Hall was inaugurated on 11 October 2002 with a Singapore Symphony Orchestra concert. The Orchestra played *Fanfare (3')* by local violinist-composer Er Yenn Chwen, Bach's *Concerto for Two Violins and Orchestra in D Minor, BWV 1043* featuring two guest soloists: Singapore-born Kam Ning; and American-born Korean Sarah Chang. The finale was Beethoven's *Symphony No 9 in D Minor*. The official opening was on 12 October 2002 and the Esplanade Opening Festival ran from 13 October to 3 November 2002.

Concorde Flight/Landing

7 June 1972. The first Concorde flew into Singapore on 7 June 1972. The Anglo-French Concorde Prototype 002 arrived at Paya Lebar Airport at 5.30 pm on a flight from Bangkok under the command of Chief Pilot, Brian Trubshaw. The Concorde was developed jointly by British Aircraft Corporation and Aerospatiale of France at a cost of soem S$2.3 billion. More than 7,000 people were at the airport to watch the Concorde land in Singapore for the first time.

While in Singapore, the Concorde made three demonstration flights of two hours each. The first flight was for Communications Minister Yong Nyuk Lin and Senior Cabinet Ministers. The second flight was for senior civil servants of the Department of Civil Aviation and the third flight was for representatives of regional airlines such as Thai International and Garuda. The Concorde flew on to Australia and returned to Singapore on 24 June for a one-day stopover. On 26 October 1977, British Airways (BA) and Singapore Airlines (SIA) announced an agreement for a thrice-weekly Concorde service between London and Singapore via Bahrain. On 9 December 1977, BA and SIA started a service between London Heathrow Airport and Paya Lebar Airport, Singapore via Bahrain, bringing the travel time to only 9 hours. However, the service was withdraw on 13 December 1977 after just 3 return flights, because the Malaysian Government complained of the supersonic boom over the Straits of Malacca. On 24 January 1979 the service resumed with new routings to avoid Malaysia. The service was terminated 1 November 1980, mainly because of falling traffic on the route, which was reportedly losing around £2 million a year.

Condominium

Beverley Mai, 1974. The first condominium was Beverley Mai in Tomlinson Road built in 1974. The Beverley Mai was designed by Seow, Lee Heah & Partners and completed by Timothy Seow & Partners. It was the first apartment block in Singapore to incorporate shared common facilities such as a swimming pool. The Beverley Mai consisted of 48 maisonettes, 2 deluxe apartments and 2 two –storey luxury penthouses. The site consists of two separate vehicular and pedestrian zones. This development was followed soon after by Futura Apartments (1976), Ardmore Park Apartments (1978) and Pandan Valley Condominium (1979).

Constitution

Order-in-Council, 1867. When the British obtained the right to establish a trading post in Singapore in 1819, it was done under the auspices of the East India Company, a company established by Royal Charter in 1600. The power to make law for Singapore lay with the Company and in that respect, Singapore had no real Constitution to speak of. In 1858, the East India Company was abolished and the Straits Settlements (including Singapore), came under the new Indian Government. The Crown took over the direct administration of the territories formerly administered by the Company but this did not have an immediate effect upon the legal system of the Straits Settlements.

On the 10 August 1866, the Government of the Straits Settlements Act was passed to provide for the separation of the Straits Settlements from the Government of India. The Order was made on the 28 December 1866 and on 1 April 1867 the Statute came into operation. By Letters Patent dated 4 February 1867, the Straits Settlements was granted a colonial constitution. Legislative authority in the Colony was vested in the Legislative Council which had 'full Power and Authority to establish such Laws, Institutions, and Ordinances, and to constitute such Courts and Officers … for the Administration of Justice and for the Raising and Expenditure of the Public Revenue, as might be deemed necessary for … Peace, Order, and good Government…' The Council was to comprise the Governor and 'such Public Officers … as shall be Designated, and such other Persons … as shall be Named for that Purpose' by royal instructions and 'such other Persons as may from time to time be Provisionally Appointed'. There were two classes of members in the Council, the Official Members and the Unofficial Members, with Officials taking precedence over the Unofficials. The number of the Official Members always exceeded that of the Unofficial Members and gave the Governor who also possessed a casting vote, effective control over the Council.

In 1867, the Council consisted of the Governor, the Chief Justice, the Officer Commanding the Troops, the Lieutenant-Governor of Penang, the Colonial Secretary, the Attorney-General, the Colonial Engineer and four unofficial Europeans. By 1871, the Lieutenant-Governor of Malacca, the Judge of Penang, the Treasurer, the Auditor-General and two more unofficial members were added to the Council.

Containers, Cargo

1967. In 1967, the first containers began to arrive at the Port of Singapore. In the second half of 1967, 1,300 loaded and 1,800 empty containers arrived. The number of containers being discharged in Singapore increased very rapidly after 1967. Companies shipping containers at that time were Maersk, Ben, Blue Funnel and Glen Lines. By 1970, nearly 9,000 containers were unloaded in Singapore. By 1982, the Tanjong Pagar container terminal had loaded one million containers for the first time. In the same year, Singapore became the busiest port in terms of shipping tonnage. By 2000, 17.4 million containers were handled by the Port of Singapore Authority.

Container Ship

Ottawasan Maru, 1972. On 18th February 1972, the first container ship sailed into Singapore waters. The vessel, *Ottawasan Maru* sailed into Sembawang port. The vessel had a capacity of 256 35-foot containers and operated only on the Far East run between Hong Kong, Taiwan and Singapore. The Japanese vessel was under charter to Sea-Land Service, a container vessel pioneer in the United States of America. The vessel called at Singapore to unload container transport equipment used to carry containers from factory to port and vice versa.

Container terminal

West Wharf, 1968. The first containers began arriving in Singapore in late 1967 when construction of Singapore's first purpose-built container terminal was underway. The growth in container traffic grew so rapidly that the Port of Singapore Authority (PSA) had to construct a temporary container yard in 1968 to centralise and handle containers discharged in Singapore. The temporary Container Yard was 58,000 square feet (5,388 square metres) and the freight Station was 30,000 square feet (2,788 square metres). It was located in the West Wharf area at Godown 55A. In 1972, the **first container berth** opened at Tanjong Pagar Terminal (East Lagoon) making Singapore the first port in Southeast Asia to accommodate container vessels. The $137 million terminal was officially opened on 23 June 1972 by Minister of Communications, Yong Nyuk Lin. The new berth could handle third-generation ships and was equipped with two 6-storey container cranes. The **first ship to use the terminal** was the all-container vessel *Nihon* of the ScanDutch Line under the command of Captain Berggren. The ship was welcomed to the new terminal by the bagpipe band from the PSA and three PSA tugs greeted the *Nihon* with water sprays. In 1974, the second container berth was opened and by 1982, there were 7 container berths at Tanjong Pagar terminal.

Contractor

Narayana Pillai. Singapore's first building contractor was Narayana Pillai, an Indian who worked as a clerk in the British East India Company in Penang. He came to Singapore with Raffles on the latter's second voyage in June 1819. He set up a brick kiln and opened a cloth shop. He was later appointed chief of the Indian community in Singapore and founded the Sri Mariamman temple. The original temple was built near the Stamford Canal but later moved to Temple Street in 1823.

Coroner

Dr Robert Little, 1848. Dr Robert Little arrived in Singapore in 1840 aboard the vessel *Gulnare* to join his two uncles who were working in Singapore. The first, Dr Alexander Martin came to Singapore with Raffles and was a surgeon and Senior Sworn Clerk at the Court of

Judicature. The other, Dr MJ Martin, ran a medical practice at the Dispensary in Commercial Square. Between 1840 and 1847, Dr MJ Martin and Little were partners in Martin & Little, Surgeons. After his uncle retired, he worked on his own. In 1859, Little took a new partner, Dr. Robertson and their practice was called Little & Robertson until he retired in 1892. Initially, Little lived at the Dispensary. In 1843 he moved to *Annanbank* in River Valley Road, and in 1845, to *Bonnygrass* on Institution Hill where he lived until he left Singapore. Little was one of the founders of the Presbyterian Church in Singapore and the Raffles Library (1844) and in 1848 he was appointed Coroner. He enrolled as a Volunteer during the 1854 riots and was appointed Legislative Councillor in 1867. Little was keenly interested in the *Journal of the Indian Archipelago* (or *Logan's Journal*) and wrote an important article on Opium for the first issue. He died in London in 1888. His two brothers, Martin and John, founded John Little & Company in 1853 (see DEPARTMENT STORE). The three brothers spent their working lives in Singapore.

Council of Ministers

See CABINET

Court

Resident's Court, 1823. The only body of 'laws' operational in Singapore were a set of Regulations promulgated by Sir Stamford Raffles in 1823. These regulations, which were most certainly illegal, provided for the establishment of a Magistracy, the appointment of 12 magistrates, and the establishment of a Resident's Court and a Magistrate's Court. From 1823 to 1827, Raffles' Regulations were the only laws in operation, and the Resident's Court and Magistrate's Court he established were the only courts on the island. It was not till 20 March 1827 that the long-awaited Charter of Justice (dated 27 November 1826) arrived. This Charter extended the jurisdiction of the Recorder's Court in Penang to the settlements of Malacca and Singapore. This Court was henceforth known as the Court of Judicature of the Prince of Wales' Island, Singapore and Malacca. It had the same jurisdiction and authority as the Court of King's Bench, and the High Courts of the Chancery, Common Pleas and the Exchequer in England. The Charter charged the Court to 'give and pass Judgement and Sentence according to Justice and Right' and in criminal proceedings, the court was required 'to administer criminal Justice in such or the like Manner and Form, or as nearly as the Condition and Circumstances of the Place and the Persons will admit of, as our Courts of Oyer and Terminer and Gaol Delivery in … England' but with 'due attention being had to the several Religions, Manners and Usages of the native Inhabitants.' The Court was presided over by a Recorder based in Penang who would travel on circuit to Malacca and Singapore and he was assisted by the Resident Councillors and the Governor.

Court House

Old Parliament House, 1827. Singapore's first official Court House was built by George Dromgold Coleman as a residence for the Scottish merchant John Argyle Maxwell. Construction on Maxwell's magnificent house began in 1826 and was completed by June 1827. Interestingly, Maxwell did not live in the house but rented it to the Government on a 15-year lease and in 1829 sold it to two other merchants, George Larpent and John Cockerell. Maxwell himself left Singapore in 1828 and left the management of the property to Armstrong & Company. In 1841, the house was again sold, this time to Thomas Church, the Resident Councillor who bought the building on the Government's behalf for 15,600 Spanish dollars. From the very beginning in 1827, the building was used as a Court House. The creation of the Court of Judicature that year required the government to find an appropriate building to house the court. Court sessions were held in the front portion of the building on the High Street side and in the central room of the first floor. The side-rooms were used by the Resident Councillor and other officials, while the Land Office occupied the ground floor.

Eventually, the front portion of the building was used by the Government as public offices. From then on, the building was popularly referred to as the Court House. The Court of Judicature functioned in this building from 1827 to 1839. During this period, the Recorder was based in Penang and only traveled to Singapore occasionally to hear cases. By 1839, the building became overcrowded with government offices and the Court House moved to a nearby building that sat on the site of the Old Attorney-General's Chambers on High Street. Maxwell's House again served as a court house, this time the home of the Straits Settlements Supreme Court from 1875 to 1939.

The **first purpose-built court house** in Singapore was at Empress Place (now the Asian Civilizations Museum). This building was constructed between 1864 and 1865 and served as the court house for only ten years, from 1865 to 1875. In 1953, the building, that housed the Social Welfare Department from 1945 to 1953 was renovated to accommodate the new Legislative Assembly. It was known as Assembly House from 1955 to 1965 when it was renamed Parliament House. Since 2004, the building has been used as an Arts Centre and is now known as the Arts House @ the Old Parliament.

Credit Bureau

30 April 2002. Singapore's first credit bureau was established on 30 April 2002 by the Association of Banks in Singapore (ABS). This was in line with the Monetary Authority of Singapore's direction to enhance Singapore's risk management capability. The credit bureau is intended to provide information on the credit repayment trends of individual customers.

Crematorium and Columbarium

Mount Vernon Crematorium and Columbarium, 1962. Singapore's first crematorium and columbarium was opened in 1962 at Mount Vernon. From a single crematorium in 1962, it soon grew to three cremators with three attached service halls to keep up with increasing demands. The Mount Vernon Crematorium was closed on 30 June 2004 and from 1 July 2004, all cremations were held at the new Mandai Crematorium and Columbarium Complex (MCC). Many thought that the closure of the crematorium at Mount Vernon was a prelude to its eventual demolition and the removal of the columbarium to either Choa Chu Kang, Mandai or Yishun. However, the Columbarium at Mount Vernon remains open and the Government has made no announcement as to whether the columbarium site will be needed for redevelopment although the date 2007 has been mentioned.

Cricket Club

Cricket Club, 1852. It has been recorded that cricket was first played on the Padang in 1837. In a letter to the *Straits Times*, the writer, who signed off as 'Z' complained that young men were playing cricket on the Padang near the New Church (on what is now St. Andrew's Cathedral). Games were often held with unconventional numbers of players, due to the shortage of available players. Informal matches were often held against crew of visiting ships. In April 1843, Admiral Sir Henry Keppel's anti-pirate gunboat *HMS Dido* arrived in Singapore and matches were held with the crew.

In October 1852, a meeting was held to discuss the formation of a cricket club. There is evidence to suggest that a Cricket Club was formed at that time. The moving force behind the club in the early years was the Armstrong family. There were no facilities for a long time and players used to store their cricket gear at the Masonic Lodge in Coleman Street. Refreshments were provided by the Hotel de l'Europe, located just across the Padang and a drink waiter would bring trays of drinks over to the players. Sometime in the 1860s, the first simple wooden pavilion was built. In 1877, a second pavilion was built. It was single storey bungalow with a wrought-iron pillared verandah. In 1884, the third pavilion was built on the central Padang site that the Club still occupies. It formed the basis of the structure that exists today. Women were not admitted into the club until 1938.

The first official cricket match was played at the Padang on 14 October 1852 between a 'Picked Eleven' and 'The Club' with 6 on one side and 9 on the other. 'The Club' won after making scores of 14 and 12 in the 2 innings. A week later, there was 'A Scratch Match between Sixteen Gentlemen'. In 1853, the Club managed to raise two sides of eleven players for the first time. The teams were usually a mixed side of merchants and officers stationed in Singapore.

Criminal Investigation Branch

1884. In 1884, the first detective branch of the Singapore Police Force was established. For the first time, the detective force was organised as a separate unit under the leadership of Inspectors Holmyard and Richards. Richards was often referred to as the 'Father of the Detective Force'. In 1899 Chief Inspector Perrett of the Metropolitan Police Force in London was appointed to Singapore as head of the Criminal Investigation Branch. It was a new appointment and he was given great powers. In 1901 Perrett set up a Criminal Registration Department and in 1903, the use of fingerprints was introduced. Perrett was appointed Assistant Superintendent of the Force in 1907. The success of the fingerprint branch was credited to one Sergeant Flak. In 1904, the **first Chinese Sub-Inspector** Tay Kim Swee was appointed to the Department.

Criminal Session

1828. The first Criminal Sessions were held in 1828. The Governor of Singapore and the Resident Councillor presided. There were 27 indictments including 6 for murder. Two of these were convicted.

See also GRAND JURY

Crocodile attack

Rochore River, 1819. The first recorded crocodile attack was in 1819. Charles Burton Buckley, in his *Anecdotal History of Singapore*, states that a crocodile took one of Major William Farquhar's dogs at the Rochore River. The crocodile was estimated to be 18 feet long.

Cultural Medallion

1979. The Cultural Medallion award was instituted in 1979 as an initiative of the then acting Minister for Culture, Ong Teng Cheong. The purpose of the award is to acknowledge the 'exceptional artistic talent and achievement' of artists in Singapore'. The Cultural Medallion is now the highest arts award in Singapore. In 1979, the winners were: Bani Bin Buang - Theatre (1929-1997); Choo Huey (b 1934) – Music; David Lim Kim San (b 1933) – Music; Edwin Nadason Thumboo (b 1933) – Literature; Madhavi Krishnan (b 1941) – Dance; and Wee Beng Chong (b 1938) - Visual Art. The **first woman** Cultural Medallion winner was Ms Madhavi Krishnan who won the award in 1980 for services to Indian dance.

Currency Issue

See *Coins And Currency*

Cyber Games medallist

Wilson Chia, 2005. On 19 November 2005, Wilson Chia became the first Singaporean to win a medal at the World Cyber Games. In September 2005, he won the Singapore National *Dead or Alive Ultimate* title and this earned him a place in the World Cyber Games Team Singapore. Chia made it to to the Grand Final of the cyber game *Dead or Alive Ultimate* but was defeated by Japanese player Tomoyuki Inui. Wilson won the silver medal and US$10,000 in prize money. Chia was a 24-year old multimedia and information technology graduate from Nanyang Polytechnic.

D

Debating Society

Singapore Debating Society, 1876. The first debating society, the Singapore Debating Society began in 1876 and carried on for the next 20 years. Among its members were many distinguished members of Singapore's European community, including Jonas Daniel Vaughan, Charles Burton Buckley, Messrs Knight,. Shelford, and Newton and Dr. Galloway. Members of the Legislative Council often took part in the debates. The meetings often took the form of a parliamentary debate. The meetings were held fortnightly in the Masonic Hall in Coleman Street.

The **first Chinese debating society** was formed in May 1882. The Celestial Reasoning Association held its first meeting at dinner at the house of the Chinese Consul, Tso Ping Lung. The gentlemen attending wore long coats as mark of respect to their host. The dining room was 'profusely and appropriately' decorated with evergreens. The Consul became President of the society. He first proposed a toast to the Prosperity of the Association. He then proposed the health of the Emperor of China. He submitted three topics as 'fit and proper' topics for the first debate. The topic selected was 'whether the use of the cane is necessary to the efficient training of children in schools here'. The objective of the association was to improve the standard of English among the members and generally to encourage learning and morality. Meetings were held fortnightly. Low Cheng Geok and Khoo Boon Lim were among the members. The society became defunct by 1889.

Dentist

Monsieur Poiron, 1835. Singapore's early dental practitioners were all itinerant dentists. They often travelled from india to Batavia and to Singapore. They advertised in the local newspaper and then usually rented houses on a short time basis or even practised in hotel rooms or boarding houses. Their most lucrative business was the construction of dentures. The first evidence of a dentist practising in Singapore was an advertisement in *The Singapore Chronicle* in June 1835. Monsieur Poiron from Paris advertised that he intended to exercise his profession during his stay in the port. The **first reference to orthodontics** was in 1850 when a K Newbolt offered to 'regulate children's teeth'. His charges were 'in accordance to the time required to complete the arrangement. The **first qualified dentist to set up practice** in Singapore was Dr Cheong Chun Tin who had been trained in America. He was in practice in Singapore in 1869. He died in 1898 and was succeeded by his two sons, Chin Nam and Chin Heng who practiced under the name of Cheong Brothers. Chun Tin Road and Cheong Chin Nam Road in Upper Bukit Timah Road are named after these early dentists. The **first woman dentist** was M Fambon who practiced in Victoria Street in 1912.

Dental Health Clinic

Dental Outpatient Unit, 1933. In March 1933, the first students of the Dental School based at the General Hospital graduated. The Dental School opened a Dental Outpatient Unit that expanded greatly due to overwhelming demand. In July 1937, the new Dental Clinic Building was completed. The building was used for both treatment and training and was known as the Dental School and Clinic.

Dental Health Programme

'Brushing Teeth' Campaign, 1969. In February 1969, the Government's first dental health campaign called 'Brushing Teeth' began in 600 primary schools. The campaign was an attempt to raise dental health standards among the young. It began at Telok Ayer Primary School where 500 six to nine year olds lined up and squatted over the school drain to show Health Minister Chua Sian Chin, the correct way to brush their teeth. The schoolchildren used a 25-cent locally made toothbrush which was inscribed with 'Use me after food'. They also carried a mug inscribed with 'Clean teeth never decay'. The campaign was introduced in Singapore after a dental report described the deplorable condition of the teeth of National Servicemen. In conjunction with the campaign, a Dental Health Exhibition called 'Keep Your Teeth Clean' was held at the Victoria Concert Hall in March 1969 as part of Dental Health Week. 25,000 apples donated by the Australian Apple and Pear Board were given away at the exhibition. The tooth brushing campaign was sustained throughout 1969 and by the end of the year, a total of 367,735 primary school children in 439 schools were brushing their teeth daily after their recess break under the supervision of their teachers.

Dental Training

Dental School, 1926. In 1922, the question of opening a Dental School as part of the King Edward VII College of Medicine was first mooted. The dental school offered its first four-year course in dental surgery in June 1926. There were no applicants. In November 1929, the **first Professor of Dental Surgery**, Professor Edgar Kingsley Tratman was appointed. The course was extended to five years and fees were $650 for the course. Graduates would be awarded a Licentiate in dental Surgery (LDS). A Temporary teaching clinic was opened in 1930 in the General Hospital. The **first graduate to receive the LDS** was Teo Lam Chye. **The first woman graduate** of the Dental School was Khoo Chik Lee, who received her LDS in 1937. By August 1938, 21 students had graduated. In 1938, a new Dental School was completed at the General Hospital. As it offered a dental Outpatient service, it was called the Dental School and Clinic.

The Singapore Dental Association was formed in 1965 and Dr Lau Kieng Hong was its first President. When the University of Malaya was established in 1949, the Dental School became a Department within the Faculty of Medicine and the LDS became the Bachelor of Dental Surgery (BDS) degree. In June 1950, the **first four recipients of the BDS** were Cheong Mow Lum, Chow Wai Nam, Mrs KT John and Lee Ek Chong.

The Malayan Dental Association was established in 1938 with Professor EK Tratman as its first President.

Department Store

Little, Cursetjee & Co, 1845. The firm of Little, Cursetjee & Co (precursor of John Little & Co) was founded by John M Little and Cursetjee

Frommurze in 1845. John Little was one of the three famous Little brothers who arrived in Singapore from Scotland in the early 1840s. The most prominent of these was Dr Robert Little, who was, among other things, the island's first coroner, Justice of the Peace, Honorary Secretary of Tan Tock Seng Hospital, Municipal Commissioner and Legislative Councillor. John Little's other brother was Martin, of which little is known. John Little started out as an employee of F Martin (possibly a relative of the Littles) in April 1844. In 1845, Mr Martin announced his retirement from business and the sale of his entire 'Stock-in-Trade on 30th June last, to Messrs Little, Cursetjee & Co, who will in future carry on the same business on the premises occupied by him from that date'. From 1 July 1845 Little and Cursetjee (a well-known Parsee merchant) started business in Singapore as Auctioneers and Commission Agents.

The business of Little, Cursetjee & Co. was rather extensive. Besides operating a retail business they were also auctioneers for properties ranging from a 200-acre spice plantation to valuable household furniture of Singapore residents. The partnership was quite successful and there were indications that the shop was already a landmark in Singapore by this time. According to Walter Makepeace, the store was the town's centre of gossip and a place where important meetings took place. Little, Cursetjee & Co., and later Little and Co. played an important social role. It was the modern day equivalent of a Central Box Office and tickets for plays, musicals and suchlike could be purchased from them. The partnership lasted till it was dissolved on 30 June 1853. On 1 July 1853, Martin Little was made a partner of John Little and the firm of John Little & Co. was born and the firm continued operations in its old premises. Cursetjee went on to set up his own business under the style of Cursetjee & Co. In 1894 John Little and Co. Ltd was registered by Harwood and Stephenson, London, with a capital of £75,000 pounds in £20 shares. The objective was to carry on business as exporters, importers and general storekeepers. Eventually, all three Little brothers returned to England. John Little himself died in April 1894.

Desalination Plant

Tuas, 2005. Singapore's first desalination plant opened on 13 September 2005 at Tuas. In 2003, the Public Utilities Board (PUB) awarded a 20-year 'design-build-own-operate' contract for the plant to SingSpring, a joint venture between Hyflux (70%) and the Ondeo Group (30%). In June 2003, Hylflux bought out its partners and became sole owner of SingSpring. The contract was to supply over 110,000 cubic metres of product water using seawater reverse osmosis. This would meet about 10% of Singapore's demand for water. The cost of the project was S$200 million. On 16 January 2004, Minister for the Environment Lim Swee Say attended the groundbreaking ceremony of the desalination plant. Prime Minister Lee Hsien Loong officially opened the first desalination plant on 13 September 2005. Singapore uses 1.14 billion litres per day and desalination is now a vital part of the 4 National Taps strategy to supply water to Singapore. The other three taps are the reservoirs and catchment areas in Singapore, water piped supplied by Malaysia and recycled water supplied by the NEWater facilities.

Dialysis Unit

Singapore General Hospital, 1969. In 1969, Dr Khoo Oon Teik and a group of volunteers organised a film premier to raise funds to establish Singapore's first kidney dialysis unit. It was located in the attic of the Singapore General Hospital (SGH). On 7 April 1969 (World Health Day), the National Kidney Foundation (NKF) was officially inaugurated. President Yusof Ishak became the Foundation's **first Patron**. The NKF opened its **first dialysis centre** with 10 dialysis machines at the Kwong Wai Shiu Hospital in Balestier Road in September 1982. It cost $1 million to refurnish the place and set it up with dialysis equipment. The NKF headquarters was also moved to a section of the hospital.

Digital Radio Broadcast, Commercial

SMART Radio, 1999. Singapore launched its first commercial digital radio service, SMART Radio, on 19 November 1999. This made Singapore the first country in Southeast Asia to provide commercial digital radio services. Currently, SMART Radio is operated by MediaCorp Radio and carries seven audio services (six new Digital Audio Broadcast (DAB) - only stations and one existing FM station) and two subscription radio services on Rediffusion. In addition to audio services, MediaCorp Radio is also transmitting lifestyle, traffic and stock market information in text form. Singapore adopted the Eureka-147 DAB system which the International Telecommunication Union recommended for worldwide adoption.

Diplomat

Ko Teck Kin, 1965. The first ambassador appointed after Singapore became independent in 1965 was Ko Teck Kin who was Singapore's **first High Commissioner to Malaysia**. Ko, a prominent rubber tycoon and banker, was born in Longxi District, Fujian Province, China in 1906. He came to Singapore from Palembang, Sumatra in 1945. From 1958 to 1965, Ko was President of the Singapore Chinese Chamber of Commerce. He fell ill within a year of his appointment to Kuala Lumpur and died in 1966.

Director Of Education

See **Inspector Of Schools**

Directory

A General Directory of the Habitable Globe and an Epitome of the Universe, 1846. In 1846, Robert Carr Woods, founding editor of the Straits Times, published the Singapore's first directory, which went by the rather grand title of A General Directory of the Habitable Globe and an Epitome of the Universe. The part relating to Singapore was only a few pages long and contained a report on the Indian Acts that were in force in Singapore and Government regulations. The Straits Times Directories were published yearly after 1846. Woods came to Singapore in 1845 at the age of 29 and was appointed by Catchick Moses to launch and edit the *Straits Times* to provide opposition to the only newspaper then in print, the *Singapore Free Press*. In 1846, Catchick Moses left Singapore and handed the press over to Woods. In 1860, Woods sold the *Straits Times* to Wynter & Co., and practised law. In 1861, he became a partner in the law firm of Rodyk & Davidson. In 1905, the Straits Times revived the *Straits Times Annual Directory*. The annual directory became an important reference manual. In 1935, the annual directories were again revived. The annual directories were revived again in 1950 following the end of the Japanese Occupation.

Disease, Named After Singaporean Discoverer

Tay Syndrome, 1971. The first doctor to have a disease named after him was Dr Tay Chong Hai (b. 1933) who discovered a rare genetic disorder characterized by brittle, banded 'tiger stripe' hair and red, scaly and dry skin caused by a deficiency in sulfur. Tay described the disease in Volume 104 of the medical journal, *Archives of Dermatology* in 1971 and in 1975, it was known as Tay Syndrome in dermatology textbooks. In March 2005, Tay was honoured with a lifetime achievement award by President SR Nathan at a gala dinner organized by the National Arthritis Foundation which he helped establish in 1984 and of which he was chairman for 14 years.

Doctor

Dr Thomas Prendergast, 1819. Singapore's first Government doctor was Sub-assistant Surgeon Thomas Prendergast. He accompanied Raffles to Singapore in 1819. The **first doctor in private practice** was Dr Alexander Martin. The first locally trained doctors graduated from the then Straits and Federated Malay States Government Medical School (later renamed King Edward VII College of Medicine in 1912) in May 1910. Seven licentiates received their Diplomas in Medicine, Surgery and Midwifery that year. They were: Chen Su Lan, Edwin W De Cruz, Wilfred F Carnegy, J Granapragasam, SR Krishnan, JS Lee and MW Chill. The most prominent was Dr Chen Su Lan, physician, anti-opium campaigner, philanthropist and social reformed. Chen founded the Anti-opium Clinic in Kampong Java Road in 1929, and the Chen Su Lan Methodist Children's Home in Serangoon Gardens perpetuates his name. He died in 1972, aged 87 years. The second was Dr Edwin De Cruz, a medical officer with Malayan Medical Service who served in Malacca, Singapore and Penang. De Cruz worked as a Senior Surgeon in Singapore and also lectured at the medical school. He died in 1974, aged 86. Dr Wilfred Carnegy was in the Government Medical Service for over 6 years and later became a ship surgeon before setting up a private practice. The **first Malay graduate** of the Straits and Federated Malay States Government Medical School was Dr Abdul Latiff bin Abdul Razak who graduated in August 1911. He was the **first Malay doctor in Malaya**. The **first woman doctor** was Dr Lee Choo Neo who qualified from the King Edward VII Medical College in 1919.

Drawbridge

See **Bridges**

Dry Dock

Dock No 1, 1859. There were several unsuccessful attempts to build a dry dock for ship repairs in Singapore. William Montgomerie, Charles R Prinsep and Jacob Clunis each applied for land to build a dry dock in 1834, 1838 and 1846 respectively. Clunis managed to obtain a lease of a block of land on Pulau Brani and registered a company in the name of Pulau Brani Dock Company. However, the Admiralty acquired his land in 1853 and the scheme fell through. In 1855, William Paterson of Paterson Simon & Co. and William Weymiss formed a dock company, the Patent Slip & Dock Company. Their first attempt to build a dry dock under the direction of Captain Cloughton, a former opium schooner commander, at Pantei Chermin in Keppel Harbour failed. The pit was abandoned and for years after that, was referred to as 'Cloughton's Hole'. The second attempt was more successful. The dry dock was Dock No.1 and was completed in 1859. In 1870, Dock No. 2 was completed. To provide more capital for its railway and tramway investments, the company went public in 1875 under the name of New Harbour Dock Company. Their main competitors were the Tanjong Pagar Dock Company, who built its first dock, the Victoria Dock in 1868 and its second dock, Albert Dock in 1877. After 1881, the docks and wharves were managed jointly by the two companies. In 1899, the New Harbour Dock Company merged with the Tanjong Pagar Dock Company to give the Tanjong Pagar Dock Company complete monopoly over all wharf facilities except for P&O Company's wharf at Tebing Tinggi. In 1905, the Government acquired the Tanjong Pagar Dock Company, signaling the end of nearly 50 years of private enterprise in the Singapore port.

E

Editor-in Chief of The Straits Times, Local

Leslie Hoffman, 1956. Born in Penang in 1915, Leslie Hoffman was educated at St Xavier's School in Penang. On leaving school, he joined the *Malaya Tribune* and by 1941, he was editorial chair of the *Morning Tribune*, the morning tabloid of the Tribune Group. During the Japanese Occupation, Hoffman was detained. While in detention, a fellow inmate offered him a job at the *Straits Times* once the war was over. Hoffman joined the *Straits Times* in 1945 working through the ranks to become senior sub-editor. In April 1956, he was appointed Editor-in-Chief of the newspaper, the first Asian to head the press. Hoffman retired from the press in 1970 when he reached the age of 55 and migrated to Australia. There, he lectured at the Royal Melbourne Institute of Technology's School of Journalism and later became Dean of the school. He retired from that post in 1985. Hoffman died on 11 June 1987 in Melbourne while waiting to board a plane for Darwin.

Elections, Political

Legislative Council elections, 1948. Singapore's first election for the Legislative Council was held on 20 March 1948. A total of 13,458 of the 22,395 registered electors turned up at the polls. Fifteen candidates stood for six seats and the successful candidates were: Sardon bin Haji Zubir (Independent or Ind) won the seat for Rural East; SC Goho (Ind), Rural West; Mohammed Javad bin Namazie (Ind) and John Laycock (Progressive Party or PP), two seats in Municipal North East; and CC Tan and A Mallal (both PP), two seats in Municipal South West.

The **first election for the Municipal Commission** was held on 2 April 1949. A total of 18 seats were contested in 6 wards, while members for the remaining 27 seats were appointed by the Government. The successful elected candidates were: City Ward – Mohammed Kassim bin Oli Mohamed (PP), Sandy Gurunathan Pillay (PP) and Hassan Ali bin Jivabhai (Ind); East Ward – Goh Hood Kiat (Ind), Frank C James (PP) and D Syed Hassan bin Aljunied (PP); South Ward – AP Rajah (PP), Dr Abdul bin Samat (PP) and Duncan Robertson (PP); West Ward – Cuthbert Frances Joseph Ess (PP), Gaw Sien Khian (PP) and Mrs Phyllis Eu Cheng Li (PP); North Ward – Patrick Joseph Johnson (Labour Party), Parkirisamy Vayloo (PP) and Chong Thutt Pitt (PP); Rochore Ward – Dr Pandarapillai Thillainathan (Ind), SA bin Mohammed Ali (PP) and Ahmad bin Mohammed Ibrahim (Ind). In 1951, the Municipal Commission was renamed the City Council.

The election for the first fully-elected City Council headed by a Mayor was held on 21 December 1957. Thirty-two seats were contested but only 165,404 voters or 32.8% of the total number of registered voters turned up at the polls. The People's Action Party (PAP) worked with the ruling Labour Front to field candidates in the various constituencies to avoid splitting the vote. The PAP won all but one of the seats it contested. It led a coalition with UMNO to form the majority in the

Council. The PAP's Ong Eng Guan became the Council's and **Singapore's first Mayor**.

The **first presidential election** was held on 29 August 1993. Ong Teng Cheong, a former Deputy Prime Minister, PAP Chairman and long-time trade union leader and politician defeated retired banker and former Accountant-General Chua Kim Yeow to become Singapore's first elected President. When Ong's term ended in 1999, the sole candidate, SR Nathan was declared Singapore's elected president.

Electric Tram

See **Tram**

Electricity

1906. Electricity was first introduced to Singapore on March 6, 1906. The power was provided by the power station built by the Singapore Electric Tramways Company. The Municipality laid a system of mains for street and domestic lighting all over Singapore and the work was completed under the supervision of Municipal Electrical Engineer J Mackail. The electric lights were first demonstrated when they were used to illuminate the Birthday Ball at the newly completed Victoria Memorial Hall. The Armenian Church of Saint Gregory on Hill Street was the **first church to be supplied with electricity**, when electric fans and lights were installed in 1909. Raffles Hotel was the **first hotel to have electric lights** and fans. Raffles Hotel started a massive renovation programme that started in July 1897. One of the major innovations was the 'double electric light installation'. The electricity was provided by two dynamos, each capable of lighting 800 16-candle incandescent lights as well as 5 2000-candle power arc lights. These lights illuminated the hotel's entrance from the road and the stables and outbuildings. Electric fans cooled the Dining Hall and private dining rooms and were available on request in all bedrooms. The entire hotel was lit by electricity. Although electric fans provided ventilation, the 'punkah wallahs' remained a familiar sight until the 1920s.

One of the **first private houses to have electric lights** was Tyersall Palace, built by the Sultan of Johore in 1892. The palace, situated on 67 acres of land, was opened in December 1892 to celebrate the Sultan receiving the Order of the Double Dragon from the Emperor of China. The power for the electric lights was provided by a generator installed within the grounds.

English Channel, Swim Crossing

Thum Ping Tjin, 2005. The first Singaporean to swim across the English Channel is Thum Ping Tjin. He swum across the 35 km stretch of water on 6 August 2005. It took him 12 hours and 24 minutes. Thum represented Singapore at the Atlanta Olympics and was voted Sportsboy of the Year in 1996. A graduate of Harvard University, Thum won a Rhodes Scholarship in 2002 and studied History and Politics at Oxford University. On the completion of his studies, he returned to Singapore to teach at Anglo-Chinese (Independent) School. His swim raised funds for the Methodist schools in Singapore. In 2006, he returned to Oxford to pursue a DPhil in Commonwealth History.

Entrepreneur, Woman

Hajjah Fatimah, 1800s. The first woman entrepreneur was Hajjah Fatimah. No records of her dates of birth or death exist but she was already very famous in Singapore by the 1840s. Fatimah was born in Malacca into a wealthy Malay family. She married a Bugis prince from Celebes (Sulawesi) but was widowed at a young age. She carried on a large, lucrative trade and owned many sea-going vessels. Fatimah had connections with several rajas from the Celebes, her husband's homeland, and these also helped to enhance her business. She had a house in Java Road in Kampong Glam where glam trees, used to make medicinal oil and for caulking boats were grown. Her house was torched by robbers on two occasions and Fatimah decided to finance the building of a mosque in its stead. This is the famous Hajjah Fatimah Mosque. The mosque was built some time between 1845 and 1846. Its minaret and ancillary buildings were probably constructed by John Turnbull Thomson. The main mosque was rebuilt in the 1930s by Malay artisans trained by the French contractor, Bossard Mopin, according to the designs of the local architectural firm of Chung and Wong. Fatimah's daughter, Raja Siti, married Syed Ahmad bin Abdul Rahman Alsagoff, a wealthy trader who owned several sailing vessels and steamers. Hajjah Fatimah passed away at the age of 98. Her tombstone and that of her daughter's are placed side-by-side in a special chamber within the Hajjah Fatimah Mosque, while that of Syed Ahmad bin Abdul Rahman Alsagoff can be found at the rear of the mosque.

Escalators, Public

Orchard Cinema Complex, 1965. The first public escalators were installed in 1965 at the Orchard Cinema complex in Grange Road. It was the first building in Singapore to have an escalator. In 1997, the complex was replaced by the Cineleisure Orchard complex.

European-Chinese Joint Company

Straits Steamship Company, 1890. The first joint European-Chinese company was the Straits Steamship Company set up on 20 January 1890. The company was registered in Singapore and had a capital of $10 million in $1 shares. The shares were all taken by local shareholders. The company was started by Tan Keong Saik, Tan Jiak Kim, Lee Cheng Yan – all prominent Straits Chinese community leaders – and Theodore Cornelius Bogaardt. The company began with five ships. Three of them – the SS Malacca, SS Billiton, and SS Hye Leong – were provided by Kim Seng & Co, Tan Jiak Kim's family concern. Bogaardt provided two ships –the SS Sappho and the SS Will o' the Wisp. They were all single decked schooner rigged vessels with small engines. The Company struggled during its first ten years but within 18 years it became the most successful local shipping company. Its early success was closely connected to the tin industry and the company shipped all the tin from Malaya to the smelter in Singapore run by the Straits Trading Company.

European Mercantile Company

AL Johnston & Company, 1820. The first European mercantile firm in Singapore was AL Johnston & Company established by Alexander Laurie Johnston. Johnston came to Singapore in 1819 and started the trading company in 1820. It was an agency house and represented Baring Brothers, the Sarawak Government and the Banque de Indo-Chine. Johnston's company was located at Battery Road and he lived on the premises. Johnston's was the first house on the Western bank of the Singapore River and had steps leading down to the river. It was known locally as Tanjong Tangkap as traders believed that he caught ('tankap') the captains of the vessels as they came up the river. His close friend, Raffles often sought his advice on all matters relating to the settlement. In 1822, Johnston was one of the three 'gentlemen' appointed to a committee to oversee the laying out of Singapore Town. He was one of the first Magistrates to be appointed and later became a Trustee of Raffles Institution and the first Chairman of the Chamber of Commerce. Johnston's Pier (now demolished) was named after him. He left Singapore in 1841 and died in Scotland in 1850.

Exchange, Four-Tier

Upper Serangoon Road, 2002. The first four-tier traffic exchange came into operation in February 2002. The exchange was at the junction of Upper Serangoon Road and Beatty Road and stretched from Yio Chu Kang Road to Upper Aljunied Road. It was designed to ease congestion in the Hougang, Sengkang and Punggol districts.

Executive Council, Asian Member

Mohammed Eunos bin Abdullah, 1930. The first Asian member of the Straits Settlements Executive Council was Mohammed Eunos bin Abdullah (1876-1934). He was appointed in 1930. Eunos was considered the 'father of Malay journalism'. He was educated at the Malay School at Kampong Glam and at Raffles Institution. He took a job in the Master Attendant's office and later became Harbour Master in Muar, Johore. In 1907, he was invited by Walter Makepeace, owner of the *Singapore Free Press* to edit a Malay edition of the paper, the *Utusan Melayu*. Under Eunos, it developed a distinct personality of its own. It provided local news chosen with urban Malay interests in mind and provided intelligent comment on the main issues of the day. It was occasionally mildly critical of the government. The newspaper became an important teaching medium in Malay schools. Eunos gradually took on the role of Advisor to the Singapore government in Malay Affairs. In 1922, Eunos was appointed a Municipal Commissioner, the first Malay to be appointed to this post, and in 1924, he became the first Malay member of the Straits Settlements Legislative Council. He was active in social and welfare organisations and was a Justice of the Peace. He was co-founder and President of the Kesatuan Melayu Singapura or Singapore Malay Union. Eunos was appointed the editor of a new daily paper *Lembaga Melayu*. For ten years, the paper represented the voice of moderate progressive Malay opinion. In 1930, Eunos was nominated to the Executive Council, the first Asian to sit on the Executive Council. He remained a member until he died in December 1933. He was replaced by Tan Cheng Lock.

Exhibition, At United Nations

Chng Seok Tin, 2005. The first Singaporean artist to have her works exhibited at the United Nations headquarters in New York City was Chng Seok Tin. Chng, who is almost blind, is well-known for her paintings, print-making, sculptures and writings. She has held about 20 solo exhibitions and was named Her World's Woman of the Year in 2001. Thirty-five pieces of Chng's works were displayed from 23 to 27 May 2005.

Expressway

Pan Island Expressway, 1982. Singapore's first expressway was the Pan Island Expressway. It became fully operational on 11 June 1982. The expressway was built in stages from 1970. The first stage was the Toa Payoh Southern Access Interchange. The completion of the flyovers across Paya Lebar Road and Aljunied Road marked the final stage of the project. The Pan Island Expressway stretches about 35 km from Changi to Jurong. The project used 20 contractors, most of them local.

Eye Centre

Singapore National Eye Clinic, 1990. The idea of a national eye clinic was first mooted in 1981 when the Singapore Eye Foundation was established. In February 1989 the pro-tem Eye Centre Planning Committee recommended that a National Eye Institute be established as soon as possible. The Institute was given a piece of land on the site of the original Accident and Emergency surgical unit at Singapore General Hospital. The first Medical Director was Dr Arthur Lim. The Deputy Director was Dr Ang Chong Lye. The **first Matron** appointed was Esther Lim Jit Wah and the first CEO was Ms Charity Wai. On 15 October 1990, the Singapore National Eye Clinic opened for business. In just over a year, 39,000 patients had attended the clinic and 2000 operations had been performed. The mission of the Eye Centre was to offer the highest possible standard of expertise in ophthalmology to the people of Singapore. In November the Hospital Eye Donation programme was introduced to encourage the donation of corneas for transplants. In January 1997, the Singapore Eye Institute opened to find better ways of treating common local sight problems. In January 1999, Lim stepped down as Director and was replaced by Associate Professor Vivian Balakrishnan.

Eye Surgeon, Local

Dr Tan Soo Hock, 1931. Singapore's first local eye surgeon was Dr Tan Soo Hock, who set up Singapore's first and only private hospital for Ophthalmology in 1931. Tan, who received his medical training in England, worked in London's Harley Street for several years before returning to Singapore in 1931 to open the Eye Hospital in Balestier Road. Tan, who was also a founder-member of the Labour Party was an ardent violinist and a sailing enthusiast. All his four children are doctors. He worked till the day he died, on 2 June 1986, at the age of 87.

F

Family Clinic

See **Polyclinics**

Family Planning Organisation, Voluntary

Singapore Family Planning Association, 1949-1966. The Singapore Family Planning Association (FPA) was formed on 22 July 1949, when a group of doctors, social workers and other interested people met to form a private family planning group. Its objectives were to provide family planning services to the population of Singapore to help them avoid unplanned childbirth with a view to improving the welfare of the family and the health of mothers. The FPA relied heavily on trained volunteers. Progress was slow in the early years due to a 'compound of ignorance, superstition, tradition, illiteracy and prejudice'. The FPA received considerable financial support during the Labour Front years (1955-1959).

In 1960, the People's Action Party funded a 3-month campaign that stimulated considerable interest in the issue of family planning. Clinic attendance rose by 16% following that campaign. It also removed some of conservatism and suspicion that made family planning work so challenging. By 1963 Singapore's birth rate dropped from 5.1% (1956) to 2.5%. This was an outstanding result and the FPA must take much of the credit for this achievement. However, members of the volunteer organisation struggled to cope with the increased demands on their time and resources, and were anxious for the government to play a larger role in family planning. Three years later in 1966, the government formed the Singapore Family Planning and Population Board (SFPPB) to take over the valuable work of the Singapore Family Planning Association.

Family Planning Clinic

Victory Dispensary, 1949. The Singapore Family Planning Association opened Singapore's first family planning clinic on 4 November 1949 at the Victory Dispensary at 316 South Bridge Road. Drs Goh Kok Kee and Tow Siew Ai were in attendance. Mrs SM Barnwell was the nurse on duty. Mrs Lim Kok Ann and Mrs Thevathasan acted as clerks. The clinic gave advice on family planning to married women and was open from 4.00 pm to 7.00 pm on Fridays. Two weeks later, two more clinics opened at the Queens Dispensary at 671 Geylang Road and the Union Dispensary at 347 North Bridge Road. The Queens Dispensary was opened for advice on family planning from 4.00 pm to 7.00 pm on Mondays and the Union Dispensary opened from 4.00 pm to 7.00 pm on Wednesdays. Three municipal clinics also offered family planning advice from 11.00 am to 1.00 pm at: Prinsep Street (Wednesdays), Joo Chiat Road (Thursdays) and Kreta Ayer Road (Fridays).

Family Planning Programme, Government

1965. The Singapore Family Planning Board came into operation in 1966. In March 1965, the government set up a Review Committee to look at the family planning situation in Singapore and to determine the level of government involvement required. The committee submitted a unanimous report to the Minister of Health in June 1965. In September 1965, the government presented the *White Paper on Family Planning* to the Legislative Assembly. The White Paper stated that the government accepted full responsibility for clinical work, research and publicity in the field of Family Planning in Singapore. It also introduced the first 5-Year Plan 'to liberate our women from the burden of bearing and raising an unnecessarily large number of children and as a consequence to increase human happiness for all'. As a result of the White Paper, a Family Planning and Population Board was set up under the Chairmanship of the Deputy Director of Medical Services (Health) Dr K Kanagaratnam. The Board took over the work of family planning in Singapore. A comprehensive programme of incentives and disincentives was introduced for larger families. Measures included paid maternity leave for the first two confinements, steep increases in fees at government hospitals for the third baby and lower priority for public housing for larger families. Voluntary sterilization was encouraged and abortion was liberalized under the Abortion Act of 1969. The birth rate had already fallen significantly before the programme came into effect. However, there was an accelerated decline in the birth rate during the first 5-Year Plan due to improved techniques of information dissemination and the provision of contraceptive supplies.

Fast-food Restaurant

A&W Restaurant, 1966. The first fast-food restaurant was the A & W Family Restaurant along Dunearn Road which opened in 1966. The American fast-food chain introduced hamburgers, hot dogs or 'Coney Dogs' and most importantly, its trademarked Root Beer to Singapore. Thousands flocked to the fast-food outlet to experience American food served in an air-conditioned environment. The chain was started in Lodi, California in 1919 by Roy Allen who sold his first frosty mug of root beer after purchasing the unique formula (comprising herbs, spices, barks and berries) from a pharmacist in Arizona. In 1922, Allen took in Frank Wright as his partner and the two of them combined their initials 'A' for Allen and 'W' for Wright and formally named the beverage A&W Root Beer. The first overseas branch of A&W was opened in Guam in 1963. It soon spread to the Philippines and eventually to Singapore in 1966. Fast food giant McDonald's opened its first branch at Liat Towers in October 1979. It proved to be so popular that it set a world record for serving the world's highest volume of hamburgers in a single day.

Facsimile (Fax) Transmission

1976. Telecom introduced the first facsimile (fax) machine into Singapore in 1976.

Film

Laila Majnun, 1933. The first film made in Singapore was a Malay language film, *Laila Majnun*. It was made in 1933 and was produced by the Bombay Chemical Company which supplied projector ear-horns for theatres in Malaya. The film, based loosely on the story of Romeo and Juliet, was a middle-Eastern love story with Islamic overtones. It was produced by KRS Chisty and directed by BS Rajhans and starred Bangsawan (Malay opera) actors, musicians and set designers. The success of

Laila Majnun prompted the Shaw Brothers to bring in film production equipment and a Chinese director to make Malay Films in 1937. Between 1938 and 1942, Shaw Brothers produced 8 Malay films: *Mutiara, Bermadu, Hanchor Hatt, Topeng Shaitan, Ibu Tiri, Terang Bulan di Malaya, Tiga Kekasih* and *Mata Hantu*. The **first local film to be produced in post-independence Singapore** was *The Last Blood* by a Singapore-based film company, Movie Impact. Its world premier was on 13 December 1990 at Prince Cinema on Beach Road. The **first Singapore film to be shown at the Cannes Film Festival** was Eric Khoo's film *12 Storeys* which was shown at the 1997 festival. The **first Tamil movie** made in Singapore was *Ulagam Sutrum Valiban* (Globe Trotting Youth) starring the great Indian actor MG Ramachandran (MGR). It was filmed on location in Singapore in 1973 and included sequences shot in Haw Par Villa and the Seaview Hotel. The **first full-length English comedy** ever shot locally was Michael Chiang's *Army Daze* directed by Ong Keng Sen which was released in 1996.

Film Censorship

1949. Film censorship was introduced in 1949. All films shown in public were submitted to Board of Film Censors of the Colony of Singapore. If a film was banned, the Board furnished the owner reasons for the ban in writing, and the owner was entitled to appeal to a statutory Committee of Appeal. The censorship guidelines were greatly influenced by the Emergency Regulations introduced in 1948, and objectionable scenes were those that included excessive violence, excessive gunplay and sabotage.

Film Festival

International Film Festival, 1987. Singapore's first International Film Festival was staged in 1987 and is now regarded as one of the best film festivals in Asia, attracting film makers and critics from around the world. The festival was conceived by Geoffrey Malone, an Australian permanent resident living in Singapore. In 1991, the film festival introduced the Silver Screens awards. The Singapore International Film Festival became the first Asian film festival to give awards for Asian feature films and Singapore short films.

Film School

Ngee Ann Polytechnic, 1993. In 1993, Singapore's first film school was opened at Ngee Ann Polytechnic. In July that year, the Ngee Ann Polytechnic offered a Diploma in Film, Sound and Video. This course later evolved and led to the establishment of a separate Department designed to respond to the need for creative and technical manpower in the emerging film, video and audio post-production industries in Singapore. Its first intake saw 40 students enrolling in the course and its first 33 graduates obtained their diplomas in June 1996. In 1995, the Department of Film, Sound & Video merged with the Department of Mass Communications to form the School of Film and Media Studies (FMS). Today, the School offers diploma courses in mass communications, film, sound and video, Chinese studies and an advanced diploma in film production.

Film Studio

Malay Film Productions, 1937. In 1937, the Shaw Brothers built Singapore's first film studio at No 8 Jalan Ampas, off Baliestier Road. Between 1938 and 1942, the studio produced eight Malay films. Unfortunately no footage of these films has survived. During the Japanese Occupation, the Japanese used the studio to make propaganda movies. In 1947, the Shaw Brothers re-opened the studios to make Malay films again. Between 1950 and 1967, they produced 250 films of heroism, fantasy and romance with thrilling story lines and majestic costumes. The films were strongly influenced by Indian films and many of the directors were Indian such as BS Rajhans. The studio's most famous star was P Ramlee, a gifted actor, composer, singer, musician and director. All his films made money for the studio. His most famous film is the self-directed *Penarik Beca* which won him many awards. In 1964, P Ramlee left to work in Kuala Lumpur as that had become the centre of the Malay filmmaking industry. By 1967, competition from television and Hollywood forced the closure of the Malay Film Productions studio. Shaw's rival, Cathay, set up Cathay Keris Studio in Ocean Park, East Coast to produce Malay films in 1953. Cathay Keris closed down in 1966.

Film, Community

Twilight Kitchen, 2003. Singapore's first community film, *Twilight Kitchen*, was released with screenings held from 17 July to 31 July 2003 at the Jade and Century cinemas. *Twilight Kitchen* is a heart-warming story about hope amidst a realistic and materialistic society and revolves around an ex-convict attempting to eke out a living. The movie, directed by Li Shi Xiong, starred Moses Lim and Zhang Wenxiang. In its second opening weekend (25–27 July 2003), it came within the top 10 grossing movies in Singapore. Preview of the movie, held on 12 July at Palm Valley, Botanic Gardens attracted close to 2,000 ex-convicts who were present to give their support to the film. *Twilight Kitchen* was jointly presented by CARE network, NCADA and Gateway Entertainment

Film, Full-length Animated

Sing to the Dawn, 2006. *Sing to the Dawn* will be Singapore's first full-length animated feature. The movies is based on a children's book by Ho Minfong of the same title. The story is about a young Thai village girl named Dawn who battles prejudices in her attempt to advance her education in the city. Directed by Frank Saperstein, *Sing to the Dawn* will use 2-dimensional cartoons fused with new technologies in 3-dimensional animation to save costs and ensure flexibility. Animation began in mid-2005 and the whole process is expected to take about 18 months and cost S$2.5 million.

Fire Brigade

1869. The first Singapore Fire Brigade was a voluntary fire brigade started in April 1869. Officers of the Police Force and Army were put in charge. In 1886, the idea of a professional fire-fighting force was first discussed, and in 1888, the Singapore Fire Brigade was established. The senior officers were British and the firemen were usually Malays. In 1905, Captain Montague Pett was appointed the first Superintendent of the Singapore Fire Brigade. He was the first professional fireman posted to Singapore and is often known as the 'Father of the Singapore Fire Brigade'. During the Japanese Occupation, 27 professional firemen were left to man the Central Fire Station in Hill Street. In November 1942, they were interned and replaced by a Japanese force. The other 62 firemen were marched to Changi Prison, including the then Superintendent, John Angus. Angus returned to the Service after the War and remained in Singapore as Superintendent of the Fire Brigade till 1960. He was awarded the Defence Medal in 1945 for bravery during the War. An Auxiliary Fire Service was started in March 1939 with 210 volunteers from the Government, the municipality and business community.

Fire Engine

1884. The first fire engine was a horse-drawn steam fire engine that arrived in Singapore in 1884. The engine could raise pressure quickly and was able to produce powerful jets of water. However, the cost of keeping four horses was expensive and the horses tired easily. It was not very maneuverable in the narrows streets of the central district and was soon replaced by the Merryweather Steam Fire Engine (nicknamed 'Fire King'). The 400-gallon steam engine was deployed in July 1906. Two additional fire engines were purchased in 1907. In 1927, these engines were replaced by petrol-driven fire engines.

Fire Ladder

Wheel Escape Ladder, 1908. The first Wheel Escape Ladder was introduced in 1908. The ladder could be extended up to 50 feet (15.24 metres) which allowed it to easily reach a two-storey building. The ladder could support the weight of four adults. A second ladder was purchased in 1911.

Fire Station, Purpose-built

Cross Street Fire Station, 1891. The first purpose-built fire station in Singapore was the Cross Street Fire Station. It was located opposite the site of the present Multi-Storey Car Park and came into operation in January 1891. The Beach Road Fire Station began operations in 1893 while the Central Fire Station on Hill Street was opened on 1 August 1909.

First Aid Courses

General Hospital, 1884. In 1884, there was a public demand for first-aid courses and some classes were held at the General Hospital. In 1935, Dr John Sutton Webster, a specialist radiologist at the General Hospital organized, with a few public-spirit friends and doctors, a series of first-aid lectures for the public. The **first headquarters** for Webster was a singular desk in the Radiology Department of the General Hospital. Those who attended Webster's lectures were recruited to form the first division of the St John's Ambulance Brigade in September 1938. When Webster retired and left Singapore in 1939, the Brigade foundered. It was decided that if all the past efforts was not to be wasted, a senior Government official of the Medical Services should head the Organisation. After some months of persuasion, the Director of Medical Services was persuaded to assume responsibility as Director of the St John's Ambulance Association.

First Lady

Puan Nor Aishah, 1965–1970. Puan Noor Aishah was born in Kuala Lumpur in 1933 and educated in Penang. In 1955, she married Yusof bin Ishak, then Managing Director of the Malay Jawi newspaper, *Utusan Melayu*. He became First Lady in 1965 when Yusof Ishak, then Yang di-Pertuan Negara (Head of State) of Singapore, became independent Singapore's first President. She and Yusof had three children, Orkid Kamariah, Imran, and Zuriana.

Flag Raising

The British flag – Union Jack – was raised for the first time in Singapore on 6 February 1819. The Singapore flag was raised for the first time on 3 December 1959, during the launch of 'Loyalty Week', after the installation of the Yang di-Pertuan Negara (Head of State), Yusof bin Ishak. The flag is halved horizontally: red over white with the crescent moon and five stars in a circle, all in white. The colour red symbolizes universal brotherhood and equality of men while the white symbolizes pervading and everlasting purity and virtue. The crescent represents a young country on its ascent, and the five starts represent the ideals of: democracy, peace, progress, justice and equality. On 30 Nov 1959, the Singapore State Arms and Flag and National Anthem Ordinance, 1959 was passed to regulate the use, display of the State Arms and State Flag and the performance of the National Anthem.

Floods, Island-wide

1855. In 1855, there were heavy floods all over Singapore island. It rained without stopping from 7.00 am on 30 November till 4.00 am on 2 December. The Serangoon district became a vast lake and communication in the area was by sampan.

Flour Mill

Prima Flour Mill, 1963. Singapore's first flourmill was opened in 1963 by Prima Limited. The founder of the flourmill was Cheng Tsang-man, a trader from Indonesia. He was attracted to invest in the project by the government industrialisation programme that offered generous tax incentives. The flourmill was officially opened on 18 August 1963 by Finance Minister, Dr Goh Keng Swee. It had a daily milling capacity of 230 tonnes of wheat grain and a silo capacity of 20,000 tonnes. Production was mainly for the domestic market. By 1965, the daily milling capacity was increased to 700 tonnes by the addition of two mills. In 1977, the Prima Tower Revolving Restaurant was opened for business. It became the world's only restaurant located on top of a wheat silo.

Flower Show

1861. The first recorded Flower and Fruit Show was held by the Agri-horticultural Society on 27th July 1861 at 5pm on the Esplanade. The Governor, Colonel Orfeur Cavenagh was present and a large number of Officials and residents. The show was seen as a step towards encouraging and promoting the much needed cultivation of fruit, vegetables, plants and flowers in the Settlements. *The Straits Times* wrote that such cultivation afforded a 'rational and beneficial amusement and recreation to the care worn, money making and business absorbed residents of Singapore'. The Judges for the Show were Messrs Jose d'Almeida, G Angus and D Aitken.

Flying Club

Singapore Flying Club, 1928. In April 1928 the Singapore Flying Club was formed with 90 ordinary members. Its premises were in Tanjong Pagar near Keppel Harbour and its first plane was a DH 60 Cirrus Moth Seaplane. In 1929, 7 pilots obtained their 'A' licenses. The Club changed its name to the Royal Singapore Flying Club in 1931 and in 1937, it moved to the new Kallang Airport. After World War II, it was re-formed in 1947 and called Republic of Singapore Flying Club.

Flyover

Toa Payoh Flyover, 1970. The first flyover in Singapore was built at Toa Payoh and was completed in May 1970 at the cost of $3.2 million. It spanned Thomson Road and was intended to relieve congestion at the Thomson Road/Jalan Toa Payoh/Whitley Road junction.

Food Control

1916. In 1916, Singapore suffered a shortage of food because of the limited number of ships available due to World War 1. A Food Control Committee was set up in May 1916 under the leadership of the Colonial Secretary, Frederick Seton James. In May 1919, Mr. Peel of the Malay States Civil Service was appointed as the first Food Controller. The committee set the price of Nestles Milkmaid Condensed Milk at $22 per case, but decided that it was not necessary to fix the price of other food goods at that time. In 1918, the failure of the rice crop in India and the partial failure of the crops in Siam and Malaya led to a serious shortage of rice in Singapore and Malaya. This was aggravated by heavy speculation in the Siam Rice Market. In May 1919, the Colonial Government took over the entire control of rice. A Control Scheme was introduced in July 1st 1919. The entire stock of rice was taken over and no stocks were permitted to be imported. The rice was sold to consumers at the price of 75 cents per gantang. The Government paid $6,900,000 in compensation to rice dealers. By selling rice at less than cost price, the Government lost about $6 million and the loss was shared equally between the Straits Settlements and the Federated Malay States and State of Johore. In February 1921, rice stocks improved. Food control was eased and trading operations gradually returned to normal. The total cost to the Government of rice control measures was almost $42 million. A Food Control Bill was introduced in November 1921. This bill allowed Food Control to be introduced in the future for 21 days following the declaration of a State of Emergency.

Food, Frozen

See **Cold Storage Provision.**

Football Association

Singapore Amateur Football Association, 1892. It is not known when football was first played in Singapore. Matches took place between visiting merchant ships and local selections at the old Fraser & Neave football ground. Records show that the first match was played in 1889 by British engineers at a Tank Road pitch. However, a governing body was only formed on 29 August 1892, and it was known as the Singapore Amateur Football Association (SAFA). It is the oldest football association in Asia. That same year, the Association Challenge Cup was played for the first time in Singapore. The Royal Engineers took the inaugural trophy.

Subsequent winners included Lincolns, Royal Artillery, Fusiliers, Singapore Cricket Club and Harlequins. In 1904, the first football league, the Singapore Football League, was instituted. The first league title went to the First Battalion, Manchester Regiment.

See also **Malaysia Cup** and **Tiger Cup**

Fort

Fort Canning, 1857. In 1857, the Government realised that Singapore town was lightly defended against either insurrection or attack from outside. To bolster its defences, the military acquired Government Hill and erected fortifications around it and installed seven 68-pound guns. Two years later, the hill was renamed Fort Canning after Viscount George Canning, Governor-General of India from 1857 to 1862. The Fort was never used in hostilities and was eventually demolished in 1907. Part of a gateway and the original fortifications survived and were restored in 1993.

Fountain

Tan Kim Seng Fountain, 1882. The first public fountain was built in 1882 to commemorate Tan Kim Seng's generous donation towards the construction of a fresh water supply system for Singapore. It was placed in Fullerton Sqaure near Johnston's Pier. It was opened by the president of the Municipal Council Thomas Scott in the presence of Tan Kim Seng's son, Tan Beng Swee. It was built by Andrew Handyside and Co. and the fountain bears the inscription ' This fountain is erected by the Municipal Commissioners in commemoration of Mr. Tan Kim Seng's donation towards the cost of the Singapore Waterworks'. In 1925, it was moved to the Esplanade next to the Cenotaph.

In 1994, it was fully restored. All broken and missing parts including the water spout, were replaced. A more efficient pumping system was installed and the fountain is now well lit.

Free Trade Agreement

Singapore–New Zealand, 2001. On 1 January 2001, Singapore's first free Trade Agreement came into force. The agreement had been entered into between Singapore and New Zealand. It was first mooted in July 1999 when New Zealand Trade Minister Lockwood Smith and Singapore Minister for Trade and Industry George Yeo agreed to explore bilateral ties between the two countries. In September 1999, Prime Minister Goh Chok Tong and New Zealand Prime Minister Jenny Shipley signed a memorandum of understanding. The first round of negotiations began in October 1999 in Singaapore. Following six further rounds of negotiations, an agreement was initialed by officials in Singapore in August 2000. In November 2000, Prime Minister Helen Clark of New Zealand and Prime Minister Goh Chok Tong of Singapore signed the FTA in Singapore. It was ratified by the Singapore Cabinet on 15 December 2000, and the New Zealand Cabinet three days later.

Frozen Embryo Babies

1987. Singapore's first frozen embryo babies, a set of twins, were born at the National University Hospital in 1987. The twins, a boy and a girl, were delivered by caesarian section. This was not only a first for Singapore but a first in Asia as well. The procedure was pioneered by Professor SS Ratnam of the National University Hospital.

G

Gambier And Pepper Society

1902. In 1902, the first Gambier and Pepper Society was formed to promote and protect the important gambier and pepper trade between Johore and Singapore, with Tan Joo Tiam as its first President. Tan was one of the leading gambier and pepper planters in Johore. His estates produced about 1000 piculs of gambier and 3000 piculs of pepper each month.

Gamelan Group, Professional

Gamelan Asmaradana, 2002. Gamelan Asmarandana is Singapore's first professional gamelan company. It was founded by Joyce Teo in 2002 who is its Artistic Director. The ensemble gave its first performance in October 2002 at the Opening Festival of the Esplanade-Theatres on the Bay. It comprises music teachers and other professionals, most of whom have had more than 10 years' experience playing the gamelan and other forms of music. Since 2002, it has been Ensemble-in-Residence at the LaSalle-SIA College of the Arts. Its Artistic Director, Joyce Teo is the first qualified gamelan music teacher in Singapore, specializing in Javanese and Sundanese gamelan. Since 1992, she has conducted recitals, talks and workshops for various organizations.

Gardens Open To Public, Private

Whampoa's Garden, 1840s. Whampoa Hoo Ah Kay created a garden that became a public resort. He bought a piece of land on Serangoon Road in 1840 and built a bungalow. The extensive gardens included an orange plantation, a fruit orchard and a Chinese garden laid out by gardeners from China. Plants from all around the world were displayed together with the luxuriant tropical foliage. There was a pond containing water lilies of all colours and a magnificent lotus, donated by William Henry Read. There was a menagerie full of animals and a collection of birds in the aviary. Whampoa's Gardens, or Nam-sang-Fa-un in Cantonese were a retreat for the members of the Chinese community especially at Chinese New Year when they would flock to visit the garden. When he died, the property was bought by Seah Liang Seah who renamed it 'Bendemeer'.

Gardener

Mr Dunn, 1819. The first gardener to arrive in Singapore was a Mr Dunn who arrived in 1819. He came with a recommendation from Raffles. He had a supply of spice plants and seeds that were planted at Government Hill (now Fort Canning).

Gasworks

Singapore Gas Company, Kallang, 1862. Singapore's first gas company, the Singapore Gas Company was established in 1861. It built its first gasworks in Kallang in 1862 using coal as feedstock. The Company continued in existence till 1900 when it was purchased by the Municipality. In 1963, it became part of the Public Utilities Board, and in 1995, it was corporatised as PowerGas, a wholly-owned subsidiary of Singapore Power Ltd. Initially, the gasworks used coal carbonizing plants, but switched to catalytic gasification plants in 1958. In the late 1980s, gas was manufactured from naphtha. By 1972 there were 860.9 km of gas mains, 104,900 gas consumers, and a steady increase in gas production and sales. Gas was the major source for Singapore's electrical generation and from 1970 to 1976. electrical generation grew by 7.5 per cent. Today, PowerGas operates over 1,800 km of gas mains throughout the island.

'Gazetted' Magazine

Time Magazine, 1986. *Time* magazine was gazetted for publishing an article entitled 'Silencing the Dissenters: Prime Minister Lee Restricts the Opposition's Maneuvering Room' in the Asia edition of *Time* on 8 September 1986. The Prime Minister's Press Office wrote a letter in response which was not printed in full in the following week's edition of *Time*. The magazine was deemed to be engaging in domestic politics and the circulation of the magazine was cut by 50% to 9,000 copies. In October 1986, Time magazine printed the full text of the letter. The circulation was not fully restored for 9 months. The magazine was gazetted under amendments made to the Newspaper and Printing Presses Act in May 1986.

General Election

See **Elections**.

'Golden Girl'

Patricia Chan, 1965-1973. Swimming legend Patricia Chan was dubbed the 'Golden Girl' for her performances in the pool during the 1960s and 1970s. Between 1965 and 1973, she amassed an amazing 39 gold medals in the Southeast Asian Peninsula (SEAP) Games series. Up till 2005, she was the most be-medaled athlete in Singapore's sporting history. Her record was only broken in 2005 by Joscelin Yeo who won her 40th SEA Games gold medal at those Games. Chan made her debut at the age of 11 at the 3rd SEAP Games in Kuala Lumpur in 1965 and won 8 gold medals. She went on to win 10 gold medals each at the 4th and 5th SEAP games (1967 and 1969), and 5 gold medals in the 1971 Games. At the 1970 Asian Games, she won a medal for all the events she competed in (3 silvers and 4 bronzes) and her national record for the 200m backstroke set in 1970 remained unbroken for 23 years. Chan was Singapore's Sportswoman of the Year for five consecutive years (1967-1971), a record unlikely ever to be equaled. She retired after the 1973 SEAP Games in Singapore where she bagged 6 gold medals. The 'Golden Girl' epithet was subsequently used on other women swimmers who ruled the waves, like Junie Sng and Joscelin Yeo.

Golf Championship

Singapore Open Championship, 1905. The first Singapore Open Championship was held in 1905. The winner was CV Miles of the Sepoy Lines Golf Club which was located near the present site of the Singapore General Hospital It was opened in 1895 and had 9 holes. The club disbanded in 1905.

Golf Club

Singapore Golf Club, 1891. Singapore's first golf club was the Singapore Golf Club formed in June 1891 with Justice Sir John Tankerville

Goldney as its first President. The entrance fee was $2.00 and the annual subscription was $6.00. Within 6 months, there were 60 members. 'Golf fever' had struck Singapore. The club placed a limit on membership of 150. In 1894, a pavilion was completed at the cost of $3,000. Although women could not become members of the Club, they were allowed to play on Tuesdays. In 1938, King George VI became patron of the Club and it became known as the Royal Singapore Golf Club. The Club's first champion was JB Robertson. It was an all-white club.

The **first multi-racial golf club** was the Race Course Golf Club formed in October 1924. Its first President was ES Manassah. The **first Asian golfer** was reputedly Dr Harold LH Lim, who took up golf while in Edinburgh doing his medical studies. When the club moved to a new location near Pierce reservoir in 1932, it became known as the Island Club. The Island Golf Club's first champion was SIM Ibrahim. In 1952, it was renamed the Royal Island club. It merged with the Singapore Golf Club in 1964 to become the Singapore Island Country Club.

Golf Course

Old Racecourse, Farrer Park, 1891. On the 17 June 1891, four golfers stepped up to play the first hole of the first golf course in Singapore. The course was located on part of the old racecourse in Farrer Park and was officially opened by Governor Sir Cecil Clementi Smith and his wife, Lady Clementi Smith. The band of the 58th Regiment played and there was a fireworks display. Sir John Tankerville Goldney, a judge on the Supreme Court was the first golfer to tee off. Reports stated that he looked resplendent in his bowler hat, knickerbockers, red coat, starched collar and white tie. Judge Goldney had arrived in Singapore in 1887 with his golf clubs, only to discover that there was no golf course. He noticed that there was a 'nice patch of greenery' at the racecourse operated by the Singapore Sporting Club. At the Annual General Meeting of the Sporting Club in 1891, Judge Goldney proposed that club members be allowed to play golf on the racecourse. Sites were then selected for 9 tees and 9 greens and labourers were paid $7 per hour to prepare the course.

Government House

Bukit Larangan, 1823. The first government House was designed and built by George Dromgold Coleman. Coleman arrived in Singapore in 1822 and was immediately commissioned to build Raffles' first residence on Bukit Larangan (Forbidden Hill or now Fort Canning Hill) in January 1823. Raffles wanted to have a modest residence with a Malayan character. The building was constructed of timber with a thatched (attap) roof. The bungalow had a 100-foot frontage and was 50 feet deep with rough plank walls with Venetian windows and was known named Government House. It stood at Fort Canning until it was reconstructed in 1859 when the military authorities took over Government Hill and fortified it. The Governor then moved to a house off Oxley Road, known as The Pavilion, owned by Dr Thomas Oxley, and then to Leonie Hill House in Grange Road. Both these buildings have been demolished.

The second Government House was designed by Major JFA McNair and built on an estate owned by Charles Prinsep. The house was built in a neo-Palladian Anglo-Indian style and the foundation stone was laid by Lady Ord, wife of the Governor, in July 1867. The house took two years to build and was completed in 1869. It was built almost entirely by Indian convict labour brought in from Bencoolen in Sumatra, and cost $185,000. It has a tropical layout like a Malay house, surrounded by verandahs, louvred windows and panelled doors to promote cross ventilation. A high tower, crowned with a mansard roof dominates the building. It is now the Istana, official residence of the President of Singapore.

Governor
See **Colonial Governor**

Governor's Advisory Council
See **Advisory Council**

Grand Jury
1829. The 1826 Charter of Justice provided for citizens of standing to be appointed Justices of the Peace and to act as members of the Grand Jury. The Court of Judicature of Prince of Wales Island (Penang), Singapore and Malacca was established in 1827 and its judges were the Governor, the Resident Councillors and the Recorder. The first Court hearings were held in Singapore on 22 May 1828 with Governor Fullerton and the Resident Council Kenneth Murchison presiding. The Recorder, Sir John Claridge was then in Penang, and the following gentlemen were chosen by ballot to serve on the first Grand Jury: Edward Presgrave (Foreman) Christopher Rideout Read, William Renshaw George, Alexander Malmanno, Richard Wingrove, Charles Scott, Robert Spottiswoode, Charles Thomas, Hugh Syme, James Clark, George Coleman, John Argyle Maxwell, James Fraser and William Shaw. There were 26 indictments at the session. Although the Charter did not specifically grant the Jury the right to make Presentments or recommendations, it became customary for members of the Grand Jury to take an interest in extra-judicial matters such as the state of the jails or the conditions of bridges. The Recorder, the judge in charge of the Grand Jury did not interfere with this practice and generally supported the Presentments. The Presentments developed into a useful check on the administration of the settlement. The first Presentment was made in February 1829. The Grand Jury brought attention to five items including the lack of security following the withdrawal of the Night Watch, the need for a General Hospital and criticism of the licensing of Public Gaming Houses. The Grand Jury existed until 1873.

Grand Prix
Malaysia Grand Prix 1962. The first races in the Thomson Road Circuit (also known as the Sembawang Circuit) took place between 1960 and 1961. In 1962, the race became known as the Malayan Grand Prix and was organized by the then Ministry of Culture. The first winner of the Malayan Grand Prix was Yong Nam Kee in a Jaguar. After Singapore became independent, the race was renamed the Singapore Grand Prix (Formula Asia) and it was given international racing status. The circuit is well-known for its sticky oil trails left by local diesel buses, monsoon drains and the infamous 'Devil's Bend.' The clockwise track was 3.023 miles long and located in the Old Upper Thomson Road. By all accounts, it was a rather treacherous circuit with difficult features with colourful names like 'The Snakes', 'Devil's Bend', 'Range Hairpin' 'Circus Hairpin' (old Sembawang Circus) and 'Thompson Mile'.

Racers typically did 60 laps around this circuit. The first Singapore Grand Prix was held from 9 to 11 April 1966. It was won by Lee Han Seng in a Lotus 22, driving for George Lee Racing. The Singapore Grand Prix lasted from 1966 to 1973. The last Grand Prix was won by Vern Schuppan driving a March-Ford 722. New Zealander Graeme Lawrence, won the Grand Prix an amazing three consecutive times from 1969 to 1971, driving three different makes: McLaren M4A Cosworth (1969); Ferrari 246T (1970); and Brabham-Ford BT29/30 (1971)

Gurkha

1947. The first Gurkha contingent arrived in Singapore in January 1947. The contingent consisted of 100 of these famous Nepalese fighting soldiers from the former Indian Army. They were brought to Singapore to replace the Sikh Contingent that had been disbanded in 1945. The main duty of the Gurkha contingent was to guard security at major installations. However, they were also used for riot control in the Maria Hertogh riots in 1950, the Hock Lee Bus riots in 1955 and the Chinese student riots in 1956. The Singapore Gurkha contingent is housed at Mount Vernon Camp and is now 700 strong. They are a familiar sight at all foreign embassies and at all major government buildings.

H

Handphone

See *Mobile Phone*

Harbour Board

Tanjong Pagar Board, 1905. In 1905, the British Government expropriated the privately-owned Tanjong Pagar Dock Company and transformed it into the first harbour board, known as the Tanjong Pagar Board. In 1913, it changed its name to the Singapore Harbour Board. It was a corporate statutory body and was Singapore's most important public utility. In June 1964, the Port of Singapore Authority (PSA) was formed to replace the Singapore Harbour Board. In 1996, the PSA regulatory function was taken over by the newly-formed Maritime and Port Authority of Singapore (MPA).

Head of State

Sir William Goode, 1959. The first Head of State of Singapore was appointed in 1959 and was referred to as the Yang di-Pertuan Negara. Sir William Allmond Codrington Goode (1907-1986), who had been appointed Governor of Singapore on 9 December 1957, assumed the office Yang di-Pertuan Negara on 2 June 1959 under the new State of Singapore Constitution. Goode joined the Malayan Civil Service in 1931 and studied law in his spare time. He was admitted to the Bar by Gray's Inn in 1936. From 1936 to 1939 he served as District Officer, Raub and was appointed Assistant Commissioner for Civil Defence, Singapore in 1940. During the Japanese Occupation, Goode was taken prisoner and sent to work in Siam on the Burma railway. He remained in Malaya after the war, and in 1948 became Deputy Economic Secretary to the Federation. In 1949 he was posted to Aden (in modern-day Yemen) as Chief Secretary and Acting Governor (1950-1951). Goode returned to Singapore as Chief Secretary in 1953 and became its last British Governor in 1957. From 1960 to 1963 Goode was Governor and Commander-in-Chief in North Borneo. He retired in 1963. On 3 December 1959, the **first locally-born** Head of State, Yusof bin Ishak was appointed Yang di-Pertuan Negara. At independence in 1965, he became Singapore's first President. See also, PRESIDENT.

Health Lectures

Tanglin Club 1898–1899. A series of seven health lectures were given at the Tanglin Club from 1898 to 1899 by leading medical practitioners on alternate Monday evenings from 7 November 1898. The talks were advertised in *The Straits Times* and cost $2.00 for the whole course of lectures, or 50 cents for each lecture. The lectures were often illustrated by magic lantern demonstrations and experiments. All the lectures were well-attended. The lectures were: 'Contagion and its Prevention' by Dr Simon; 'The Roentgen Rays' by Dr Middleton; 'Water' by Dr Ellis; 'Diet and Exercise in the Tropics' by Dr Fowlie; 'Digestion' by Dr Lim Boon Keng; 'The Care of Children in the

Tropics' by Dr Galloway; and 'The Influence of Dress on Health' by Dr Glennie.

Heart Transplant

Singapore General Hospital, 1990. On 6 July 1990, a team of surgeons at Singapore General Hospital performed Singapore's first heart transplant. The recipient was 59 year-old civil servant Wee Soo Hup. His life expectancy without the transplant had been estimated to be less than 6 months. The donor's heart was 'harvested' by a team led by Dr C Sivathasan and Dr Susan Lim. Sivathasan had returned earlier in the year after studying heart transplant surgery overseas while Lim was Head of the Liver Transplant Programme at National University Hospital. The heart transplant team was led by Dr MC Tong, Head of the Singapore General Hospital's (SGH's) Department of Cardiothoracic Surgery. The other members of the team were Drs Sivathasan, Ong Kim Kiat and Lim Yew Cheng. The operation was part of the SGH Heart Transplant pilot programme funded by research grants from the Ministry of Health. Only two other Singaporeans had undergone heart transplants. Seah Chiang Nee and Fong Peng Wah had heart transplant surgery performed by Dr Victor Chang at St. Vincent's Hospital in Sydney, Australia in 1985.

Heritage Society

Singapore Heritage Society, 1987. The first non-government organization (NGO) dedicated to raising awareness of Singapore's heritage and the need to protect it is the Singapore Heritage Society. The Society was founded in April 1987 by a group of concerned citizens and residents, including architect William Lim (who would serve as its first president), Sharon Siddique (who was to be vice-president), Kwa Chong Guan and Geraldene Lowe. Driven by his concern for heritage in a postmodern city, Lim started the Society with one intention in mind: to alert the government to the need to preserve heritage. The rest of the founding members shared Lim's vision. The group's motivation for the setting up of the Society was largely due to a vacuum that existed at that time in public discourse regarding conservation. The rapid pace of urban development in the 1980s had sparked off a debate about whether there would be any historic Singapore left by the end of the period of modernization.

Heritage Trail

Civic District Trail, 1999. Singapore's first heritage trail was the Civic District Trail opened on 29 August 1999. It was introduced to encourage Singaporeans to rediscover the historic places in Civic District, the oldest part of the city. The second heritage trail, the Singapore River Trail opened on 29 January 2005.

High Rise Apartments

Selegie House, 1963. Before the 1940s, most apartments in Singapore were low-rise. Indeed, many lived in two-storey shophouses. When the Singapore Improvement Trust (SIT) was established in 1927 to provide housing for the public, they built 4-storey walk-up apartments like those found in Tiong Bahru. In the late 1940s, the SIT built the first true 'high-rise' apartments were built in the Middle Road, Selegie Road, Rochor Road and Bencoolen Street area. The Prinsep Street Estate (1949) was designed by Lincoln Page and rose 9 stories up. The tallest flat ever built by the SIT was the 14-storey Forfar House in Queenstown (now demolished). After the Housing and Development Board (HDB) was established in 1960, its first public housing 'skyscraper' complexwas Selegie House, completed in June 1963. It cost $3.8 million and provided accommodations for 4,000 people. The complex was built at the corner of Selegie Road and Albert Street and consisted of one block of 20-storey flats and two more blocks of 10-storey flats. The blocks were linked by four rows of two-storey blocks. Selegie House also included 38 shops. One restaurant and 466 flats. There were 24 2-room flats, 409 3-room flats and 33 4-room flats. All the flats came equipped with modern sanitary services, water, electricity and gas. In addition, provisions were made for telephones and radio. The rent for a 2-room flat was $60 per month, 3-room flat was $90 per month and 4-room flats were $120 per month. In the years to come the HDB built even higher apartments: Marine Parade (1974) – 25 storeys; Bishan Heights (1996) – 30 storeys; and Toa Payoh Lorong 2 (2005) – 40 storeys. In 2010, the highest-ever public apartments, the 50-storey Pinnacle at Duxton will be completed. The first **high-rise private apartments** were those found in Cathay Building, built in 1939 (See HIGH RISE BUILDING). The International Plaza, built in 1976 remains the tallest apartment block at 50 storeys today. It will be eclipsed in 2009 by the 70-storey The Sail at Marina.

High Rise Building

Cathay Building, 1939. The Cathay Building, built in 1939 was the first high-rise building in Singapore. It was designed by Frank Brewer and was 79.5 metres high and contained 80 apartments, a squash court and the 1,300 seat Cathay Cinema. It was also the first 'mixed development' in Singapore. The first movie shown at the Cathay Cinema was *The Four Feathers*, starring Aubrey Smith. Cathay was also the first cinema to reopen after World War II. On Sunday 23 September 1945, it screened the movie *Desert Victory*.

Hijacking

Laju Ferry, 1974. In January 1974, the Shell Oil Refinery on Pulau Bukom Besar was attacked by four terrorists armed with machine guns and explosives. Two of them were Japanese from the Japanese Red Army and the other two members of the Popular Front for the Liberation of Palestine. Their objective was to disrupt oil supplies from Singapore to South Vietnam. The attack did not go smoothly as their boat ran aground on a coral reef and they had to get a boat to tow them to the island. The raid was abortive but in their attempt to escape, the four men hijacked a passenger ferry, *Laju*, takng 5 crew members hostage. At the Eastern Anchorage, they were intercepted and surrounded by Marine Police boats and three Singapore Maritime Command gunboats. Two of the hostages managed to escape but the other three remained hostage. After several days of negotiations, the terrorists agreed to release the remaining hostages in exchange for a party of guarantors. The guarantors included four Singapore Armed Forces Commandos and 8 other government officials, led by SR Nathan, then Director of Security and Intelligence for the Ministry of Defence. On 7 February 1974, the terrorists were transferred by boat and taken to the airport. At the airport, they surrendered all their arms to the police and released the three hostages. On 8 February, the four terrorists left Singapore for Kuwait.

Hindu Temple

Kling Temple 1822. The site of the Kling Temple is marked on the first town plan of 1822 . It is said that an even earlier temple located on what is now Stamford Road but thee is no documentary evidence of its location or existence. Singapore's oldest Hindu temple is the Sri Mariamman Temple built in Temple St. in 1827. The first structure was a simple wood and attap structure built by Narayana Pillay, an Indian contractor who arrived in Singapore with Raffles in 1819. In 1844, a brick building replaced the earlier temple. Much of the present building was not completed until 1863 but using the 1844 plan. The attap walkway was destroyed by fire in 1910 and was replaced by a new walkway designed and built by Swan and MacLaren in 1915. The *gopuram* or entrance tower is most spectacular. It was built in 1925 and replaced a much simpler tower built in 1903. The entrance gate is a massive double-leafed door flanked by square pillars. The top of the boundary wall is ornamented with statues of cows, sacred to Hindus. The temple played an important role in the life of the immigrant Indian community. They often stayed at the temple till they found accommodations.

Hockey

1892. The modern field hockey game emerged at Eton College in England in the 1860s when the first rules were written down. In 1875, the first Hockey Association was formed and the rules were further refined. In 1890, the English, Irish and Welsh hockey associations formed the International Rules Board and umpires were empowered to make decisions. In Singapore, it was reported the hockey was first played on 28 November 1892 at the Padang. Alas, no other details of this match are available.

Horse Race

See **Race Course.**

Horticulture exhibition/show

See **Flower Show**

Hospice

St Joseph's Home, 1985. In 1985, Singapore's first hospice was opened by the Canossian Sisters. St. Joseph's Home was a small brick coloured building in Gek Poh Road, Jurong. The hospice provides a haven where terminally ill patients can seek temporary relief from the ravages of cancer. The hospice has a chapel and gardens and this provides a peaceful and serene ambience for the patients. The aim of the hospice is to alleviate the physical pain of the patient through drugs, and to help the patient deal with the process of dying and death itself. This is in marked contrast to the 'death-houses' that lined Sago Lane from the early 1900s, leading many to refer to it as 'Death Street'. These death-houses were run by charitable Chinese clan associations to care for destitute coolies, amahs and indentured labourers who were dying away from their families in China. They were situated in Sago Lane where there many coffin-makers. The dying had no medical care, just food and shelter, and horrific stories were told about how they might have to sleep in their coffins before they die. When philanthropists in Singapore first wanted to build an in-patient hospice in 1975, the application was turned down by the Government, as it was trying to rid Singapore of the scandal of the death-houses by razing the whole street, Sago Lane, to the ground. Hospice became a dirty word in official circles, and it was not until 1985 that another attempt was made to provide hospice care for the dying.

Hospital, General

1821. The first General Hospital was opened in 1821. It was a wooden shed situated inside the cantonment for British troops on Bras Basah Road. The surgeon in charge was Sub-Assistant Surgeon Thomas Prendergast. There were separate wards for European soldiers, *sepoys* (Indian soldiers) and native paupers. Government officials and merchants were usually treated at home by army surgeons from the General Hospital. Serious and special cases were sent to Penang for treatment. In 1822, the Hospital was moved to a new site closer to the barracks. In 1827, this Hospital collapsed and a new Hospital was built in 1828. By 1830, this third hospital was already in a state of disrepair. The staff consisted of one Assistant Surgeon, one Assistant Apothecary and a few subordinates. Patients were often used as orderlies and dressers, and patients complained about the noise made by the clanking chains of the convicts. When the new Assistant Surgeon, Thomas Oxley arrived in 1831, he promised that a more substantial hospital would be built. The Chamber of Commerce raised $2,700 but plans were stalled. It was not till 1843 that approval was finally given for the new hospital to be built. The foundation stone of the new hospital at Pearl's Hill was laid in May 1844. In 1845, it was ready for patients. The most common problems were fevers, respiratory problems, gastro-enteritis, rheumatism and venereal disease.

After the Indian Mutiny in 1858, both the Tan Tock Seng Hospital and the Seamen's Hospital were taken over by the Government for military purposes and both hospitals were relocated. The Seamen's Hospital was transferred to a house in Stamford Road, near the site of the present YMCA Building, and a new Seamen's and Police Hospital was built in Kandang Kerbau. In 1860, the hospital began treating female patients. A cholera outbreak in the area forced the abandonment of the hospital and a new General Hospital was built in Sepoy Lines, the site of the present Singapore General Hospital. It proved to be a good location as it was high and dry, with good drainage, sea breezes and a plentiful water supply.

The Tan Tock Seng Hospital, built in 1849, was the **first hospital to treat all races**. It was originally built on the slopes of Pearl's Hill and moved in 1909 to Balestier Road. It replaced a series of poorhouses. The first poorhouse (See **Hospital, Pauper**) was an attap hut built in 1830 in Bras Basah Road.

Hospital, Infectious Diseases

Smallpox Hospital, 1872. In 1872, the Smallpox Hospital for infectious diseases was set up on Balestier Plain. The Smallpox Hospital became the Infectious Diseases Hospital in 1904 and was extensively rebuilt. It was named Middleton Hospital after Dr WRC Middleton who became Health Officer of the Singapore Municipality in 1894. DM Craik, the Architectural Assistant to the Municipal Council of Singapore said the design was unpretentious and sensible. The hospital consisted of a series of single storey ward blocks in a park like setting. Each ward was open on all sides with large shutters and verandahs. The Middleton Hospital was the only institute especially reserved for infectious diseases and treated smallpox, chickenpox, polio, typhoid, measles and mumps. The hospital was run by the Municipality with an annual grant by the government. In 1960, it was formally taken over by the Government Hospitals Administration. The Middleton Hospital was absorbed into Tan Tock Seng Hospital in 1985 and was renamed the Communicable Diseases Centre. The hospital has been the AIDS treatment centre since the mid-1980s and handled the SARS epidemic in 2003.

Hospital, Maternity

Maternity Hospital, 1888. The Maternity Hospital opened in Victoria Street in 1888. It employed a trained midwife, Mrs Woldstin. The hospital provided limited midwife training by 1898. In 1895, a Mrs Ganno entered the hospital as a 'pupil sick nurse' and midwife. She was recorded as passing an accreditation examination before a Board of Medical Officers at the end of 1897.The first regular course for Asian midwives was commenced in 1910 as a joint venture between the Government and the Municipal Council. In September 1914, a new free Maternity Hospital with 12 beds was opened in Victoria Street. The old Maternity Hospital was used as the Outpatient Maternity Department of the General Hospital. In October 1924, the Victoria Street Maternity Hospital was demolished and maternity patients were moved to the new hospital at Kandang Kerbau. The old Victoria Street Maternity Hospital was used by Raffles Girls' School.

Singapore's **first government maternity hospital** was the Kandang Kerbau Maternity Hospital. When it opened on 1 October 1924, the hospital had 30 beds and 12 children's cots. It was a free maternity hospital and was headed by Professor JS English, Singapore's **first Professor of Obstetrics and Gynaecology**. On the day of its opening, five babies – three Malays, one Chinese and one Japanese – were born in its premises. In 1966, an incredible 39,835 babies were born in the hospital, making it the busiest maternity hospital in the world. Kandang Kerbau Maternity Hospital held this record till 1976.

Hospital, Pauper

1830. In May 1833, an agreement was made for George Coleman to build a Chinese pauper hospital or poor house. The first poorhouse was an attap hut built in 1830 in Bras Basah Road. It was maintained by the introduction of a pork tax. In 1844, Tan Tock Seng donated $7,000 to build a hospital for diseased paupers. Cham Chan Seng bequeathed $2,000 to the hospital and public subscriptions soon raised sufficient funds to build the hospital. The foundation stone of this hospital was laid at Pearl's Hill in May 1844. The foundation stone for the European Seamen's Hospital was laid at the same time, also at Pearl's Hill. The old Pauper Hospital served as a convict Hospital until 1873, when the convict station was broken up and the convicts returned to India. In 1849, the Tan Tock Seng Hospital opened its door 'for the sick of all nations'. The hospital was administered by a committee of Management that included Whampoa Hoo Ah Kay as Treasurer, and Seah Eu Chin.

The Government only provided medicines and medical attendance. In 1854, two wings were added to increase the available accommodation. Tan Kim Ching, son of Tan Tock Seng, provided money for the extensions. During the Indian Mutiny (1857), both the Tan Tock Seng Hospital and the Seamen's Hospital were taken over by the Government for military purposes. The Government built a new hospital on Joseph Balestier's former estate facing Serangoon Road. The Chinese, Arab and European communities continued to give generously to support the hospital, and in 1858, Lee Teo Neo, Tan Tock Seng's widow, provided funds for a female ward. In 1857, Syed Ali Mohammed Aljunied presented the hospital with 5 acres of land at the corner of Victoria Street, Queen Street and Arab Street. The rents from this land contributed to the upkeep of the hospital. In 1879, Tan Beng Swee covered the cost of building three new wards for the hospital. He was appointed life member of the Committee of Management. In 1892, Gan Eng Seng donated a freehold property at Rochore to the hospital. Many visitors also contributed to the hospital.

The hospital moved to its present site in Moulmein Road at the cost of $500,000 in 1909. The Government bore the cost of land and the buildings, aided by two generous personal donations. The first was a $50,000 donation by Loke Yew and the second, a bequest by Wee Boon Teck of $4,000. The old buildings in Serangoon Road were granted to the Trustees of the Kwong Wai Shiu Free Hospital for 99 years at an annual quit rent of $1.00.

Hospital, Military

Pulau Blakang Mati, 1909. The first military hospital was built on Pulau Blakang Mati (now Sentosa) in 1909. In 1912, a new military hospital was built at the Tanglin Barracks and the Blakang Mati hospital was closed. The building was then used as an educational centre. It is now used to house the Pioneers of Singapore Museum and the Surrender Chamber. In 1938, the military hospital at Tanglin Barracks was not big enough to cope with the extra British personnel based in Singapore. Building was begun on a hospital inside the Alexandra cantonment on a 32-acre plot next to the new railway track. The new Alexandra Military Hospital was opened in 1940 and operated by the 32nd Company of the Royal Army Medical Corps. A contingent of 30 Queen Alexandra Nursing Sisters arrived late in 1940. Staff quarters for Medical and Nursing staff was later built at Alexandra Park.

Hospital, Private

Medical Mission for Women and Children, 1913. Dr Ferguson-Davie, wife of the Singapore Bishop, started a Medical Mission for Women and Children in 1913. About 8,000 patients attended each year. The mission carried out excellent work amongst the poorest women and children of all nationalities. The Mission was later re-named St Andrew's Mission. It was located in Cross Street in the vacant buildings of the Government School. It also operated a shophouse in New Bridge Road which accommodated blind children, and a shophouse in Bencoolen Street where outpatients could be treated. The sum of $100,000 was raised and the foundation stone for the Hospital was laid in August 1922 by Mrs Lee Choon Guan. St Andrew's Mission Hospital was opened in 1923 by Lady Guillemard. The hospital was governed by a Board of Management, the Chairman being the Anglican Bishop of Singapore. Mr and Mrs Lee Choon Guan donated $5,000 towards the hospital. St Andrew's Mission Hospital established the first organized nursing training for local girls in Singapore in 1916. In 1937, the hospital appointed Singapore's first Asian Nursing Sister to her post.

Hospital, Orthopaedic

St Andrew's Orthopaedic Hospital, 1939. The St Andrew's Mission Hospital was built by the Anglican Church in 1939 in the Tanjong Pagar area. That same year, the St. Andrew's Mission started the St. Andrew's Orthopaedic Hospital in Siglap for the treatment of children suffering from diseases of the bone including tuberculosis, and those recovering from poliomyelitis. It was re-opened in Siglap after the Japanese Occupation under joint management with the government. In 1947, the hospital, together with St. Hilda's School, provided a school in the hospital compound. With the wide availability of extensive specialist services in government hospitals, the Orthopaedic Hospital was under utilised and closed in 1970s.

Hospital, Seamen's

Seamen's Hospital, 1832. In May 1832, Dr M Martin established a private hospital for seamen. The hospital charges were initially exorbitant and most seamen went to General Hospital for treatment. In 1833, the Grand Jury made a Presentment on 'the want of an Hospital for sick European seamen'. In 1834, Dr Charles Wilson visited Singapore and saw an opportunity for a surgery where ship's crew could be given medical treatment. He advertised that 'ship's crew promptly attended and comfortable accommodation provided on shore during their sickness, for moderate remuneration.' He set up in Gemmill's new building. Business was good and after 8 months, Wilson expanded his practice. In 1837, the Chamber of Commerce began a campaign for a hospital for European and American seamen and printed and circulated a pamphlet. The Chamber managed to collect $2,700 to build the hospital for seamen. The foundation stone for the European Seamen's Hospital was laid in June 1844. The building was completed in 1845 at the cost of $5,490. The Government paid half, and the community raised the remainder. The subscription list for the hospital included most of the major European trading houses and merchants. The staff consisted of: 1 Assistant Surgeon, 1 Apothecary and Steward, 1 Apprentice, 1 Native doctor, 1 cook, sweeper, watchman and 2 coolies.

Hotel

London Hotel 1839. In May 1839, Gaston Dutronquoy opened the London Hotel in Coleman St. Although the official name was the London Hotel, it was usually referred to locally as Dutronquoy's Hotel. The hotel was on the site of the present Adelphi Complex. The hotel faced the Esplanade and looked out over the sea and was a popular destination for travellers. In Edward Cree's account of his visit to Singapore in 1840, he commented favourably on the dinner served at the hotel. It consisted of curried fowl, pork chops, roast duck, ham, cheese and potatoes. It cost $1 and was served with beer, Madeira and claret. He described Dutronquoy as a 'civil amusing fellow who sings French songs'. The baths were contained in another building away from the hotel and one traveller, Charles Walter Kinloch complained of the inconvenience of this arrangement. However, Kinloch thought that the charges were quite reasonable at $1.50 per day although he thought that charging 50 cents for a bath was exorbitant. Joseph Conrad stayed at the hotel and found much of the material for his Eastern novels there. In 1844, Dutronquoy converted part of the hotel into a small theatre, the Theatre Royal. Later that year, there was a performance of *Charles the Second or The Merry Monarch* and *The Spectre Bridegroom* in the Theatre Royal. In 1845, Dutronquoy moved the hotel to the corner of the Esplanade and High St. George Francis

Train, who visited in 1855 was not impressed with the new site of the hotel and called it a 'pile of ugly buildings covering a good sized farm'. Dutronquoy disappeared in mysterious circumstances and it was rumoured that he was murdered while prospecting for gold near Muar. After he left Singapore, the hotel became the Hotel de l'Esperance. In 1865, it was converted into the Hotel de L'Europe and became one of Singapore's premier establishments. Dutronquoy was also Singapore's **first professional photographer**. (see **Photographer**).

Housing, Condominium

See **Condominium**

Housing, Public

Tiong Bahru, 1936. Singapore's first public housing was built by the Singapore Improvement Trust (SIT) which was created in 1927 and operated until 1959. In 1907, WJR Simpson presented the findings of a study on sanitary conditions in Singapore entitled *First Survey of the Sanitary Conditions of Singapore*. There had been concern for some time about the high death rate from dysentery and cholera. Simpson had been a health officer in Fremantle and in Calcutta and was considered to be the 'first living expert on Imperial health'. Among his key recommendations was that a Trust be set up to oversee town and housing improvement. In its 32 years of life, the SIT had a remarkable record considering that the Trust had initially only limited powers to tackle housing and spent much of its early years building back lane facilities for the sewage system. In 1932, its remit was extended to carry out low rental schemes. By 1960, it had completed 24,000 housing units and more than 700 shops, and more than 150,000 people (10% of the population) were living in Trust accommodation and paying subsidised rents. This achievement in public housing was without parallel in Asia at this time. The introduction of satellite towns and the neighbourhood concept in housing provided the blueprint for the Housing Development Board. The SIT planned and built the first public housing satellite town of Tiong Bahru between 1936 and 1941. It accommodated 6,000 people (see first satellite town). The trust also planned and developed the Queenstown area.

Housing, Public by Private Tender

Tampines Neighbourhood 4, 1994. In 1994, the Tampines Neighbourhood 4 building project became the first housing project given to private sector architects by the Housing Development Board (HDB). Previously, the HDB had been the sole agency involved in public housing. The firm of P & T Consultants Pte. Ltd were chosen from a list of ten teams invited to submit proposals. It was a ground breaking innovation in Singapore and led to to other public housing projects being put out to private tender under the Design-and-Build plan.

Hydrofoil

1978. The first hydrofoil built in Singapore was unveiled on 24 May 1978. The vessel was built in collaboration with the British firm of Vosper Pte Ltd. It could seat 70 passengers and cost $2.5 million to build.

I

Ice-cream parlour

Magnolia Milk Bar & Magnolia Snack Bar, 1969. In the 1960s, Cold Storage opened a number of 'Magnolia Snack Bars' in Malaysia and Singapore to promote their Magnolia brand of dairy products. The outlets were found in Taiping, Kuala Lumpur, Malacca, Penang, Kuantan and Singapore. In Singapore, the first outlets opened in 1969. They were at Capitol Theatre at the junction of Stamford Road and North Bridge Road (Magnolia Milk Bar), and the other next to the Cold Storage Supermarket along Orchard Road (Magnolia Snack Bar). These ice-cream parlours were extremely popular with families, serving up ice-cream with exotic names like 'Knickerbocker Casablanca' and 'Merry Widow'. The parlour at Orchard Road was demolished in the 1970s to make way to the development of Centrepoint Shopping Centre while the Capitol outlet shut down in the 1980s. An attempt was made to recreate the nostalgia of these parlours was the short-lived Magnolia Milk Bar at Centrepoint inside the confines of Times Book Store in 2002. The outlet, which was operated by F&N did not last long and shut down after about a year of operations.

Ice House

Whampoa's Ice House, 1854. The first ice-house was built by Whampoa Hoo Ah Kay and Gilbert Angus in 1854. It was built on the banks of the Singapore River near the corner of River Valley Road and Hill Street. It stocked ice from the United States but the consumption was only between 400 and 500 lbs a day and it soon became unprofitable to sustain the business. The building, called Whampoa's Ice House remained a landmark for many years and was only pulled down in 1981 for the widening of River Valley Road. It was later rebuilt on a new site near to its original location at Clarke Quay. (For more on Whampoa, see **Chinese Consul**).

Ice Machine

1861. The first ice machine was introduced into Singapore on the 1 August 1861. Supplies of ice from overseas had always proved to be unreliable and in 1861, the Ice House had completely run out of ice. Dr Scott imported an ice machine that was installed in the new Singapore Ice Works at the foot of Prinsep's Hill below Captain Wilkinson's house. At the end of July 1861, a block of ice from the new ice machine was sent to the Exchange and was viewed by traders and merchants. This ice block was only a sample. The block measured about a foot square and was 6 inches thick. By the 1 August, the machine was in full operation. The ice was sold at 3 cents per pound and purchasers could buy books of ice tickets which considerably reduced the price. The terms were strictly cash. Demand was brisk and a second machine was ordered. The Engineer and Manager of the Singapore Ice Works was George Usher.

Incinerator, Refuse

Jalan Besar, 1889. The first refuse incinerators built to dispose of refuse collected in the Singapore area were built at Jalan Besar in 1889. Additional ones were later built at Tanjong Pagar and Alexandra Road.

In-Vitro Birth

1983. Singapore's first test-tube baby was born on 19 May 1983 at the Kandang Kerbau Hospital. It was also **Asia's first in-vitro fertisation** (IVF) or test-tube baby to be delivered. The baby boy, Samuel, weighed 2.5 kg and his parents were Mr & Mrs Lee Chye Huat. A team of doctors led by Professor SS Ratnam, Head of the Gyneacology Department at the National University of Singapore, delivered the baby. The team included: Drs Mary Rauff, Ng Soon Chye, Koh Tong Sam, Wong Peng Cheang, C Anandakumar, Victor Goh, Law Hai Yang, and Yeoh Swee Choo, as well as Mrs Helen Leong and Ms Chia Choy May. Ratnam was responsible for starting the In-Vitro Fertilisation and Embryo Replacement Programme in 1982. The IVF project was funded by Tan Sri Runme Shaw, the Lee Foundation, the Shaw Foundation and the Singapore Turf Club. The **first private IVF clinics** were opened in 1987. That year, the Ministry of Health issued guidelines for private hospitals intending to provide fertility clinics. Three private hospitals had earlier asked for permission to offer such treatment but were refused. Applications went to the Advisory Committee on Human Reproduction and Embryology, before the Ministry granted approval. In December 1987, it was announced that Mount Elizabeth Hospital and Thomson Medical Centre had been granted permission to operate in-vitro fertility clinics. It was at the Thomson Medical Centre that the **first IVF triplets** were born. The **first IVF twins**, Daphne and Diana, were born in November 1986 to Mrs Evelyn Loo at the National University Hospital.

Industrial Estate

Jurong Industrial Estate, 1961. The first industrial estate built in Singapore was the Jurong Industrial Estate. Nearly 4000 acres of swamp and wasteland was allocated for the estate and work began in 1961. The first phase of the development was completed in 1968 and by 1973, the second phase was completed. It consisted of a deep water harbour, standard factory buildings, communications, houses and related social amenities. The estate was operated by the Jurong Town Corporation which spearheaded Singapore's industrialisation programme. The programme aimed at creating 80,000 jobs within 10 years. In 1965, a 9-mile (5.5 km) railway was built between Bukit Timah Railway Station and the site of the proposed Mobil refinery in Jurong. By 1967, there were 94 factories in operation within the estate, employing 8,800 employees. The first factory to commence production was the National Iron and Steel Mill which started operations in August 1963. (See IRON MILL).

Inspector of Schools

Allan Maclean Skinner, 1872. In 1872, Allan Maclean Skinner was appointed the first Inspector of Schools. It was a new position and he was appointed following the recommendations of the Woolley Committee Report presented to the Straits Settlements Legislative Council in 1870. The report described the state of education in the colony as being in a 'backward state' and recommended the appointment of an Inspector or Director of Education to re-organise secular education, extend Malay and Chinese vernacular instruction and improve girls' education in the colony. The government ignored all the other proposals of the report but did appoint Skinner as the Inspector of Schools. He held the post for 30 years and made extensive changes. Skinner was appointed to the Straits Settlements Civil Service in 1868 (see under CADETS, CIVIL SERVICE) and was the second cadet to be appointed. He took part in the bombardment of Selangor in 1871. That same year, he was Acting Magistrate in Province Wellesley and suggested making changes to Malay vernacular education to re-establish Malay vernacular schools in the area. He proposed that as many village schools as possible be started, using the local Khatib or teacher at the Mosque to supplement the system already in use for teaching the Koran in Arabic. The Malay and Koran studies were separated with Malay classes in the morning and Koran classes in the afternoon. Under this method, the members of the conservative Malay community were encouraged to send their sons to school. This was one of his major achievements as Inspector of Schools. The number of pupils attending the 'supplementary' Malay schools rapidly increased. In 1872, there were 16 schools with 596 pupils. By 1892, there 7,218 pupils in 189 schools. He also acted as Colonial Treasurer from 1881-1887 and as Acting Colonial Secretary at various times from 1884-1887. He wrote 'Memoir of Captain Francis Light, who founded Penang' which was published in the August 1895 edition of *The Journal of the Malay Branch of the Royal Asiatic Society*. In 1883, he presented a fine specimen of a rare leathery turtle to the Raffles Museum. Skinner retired in 1887 on account of his ill health. He was engaged in writing a history of the Straits Settlements when he died in 1901.

International drink

Singapore Sling, 1915. The first Singapore drink with an international reputation is the *Singapore Sling*. It was created in 1915 by barman Ngiam Tong Boon at the Long Bar of the Raffles Hotel. It consists of one-half gin, one-quarter cherry brandy, one-quarter mixed fruit juices (orange, lime or lemon and pineapple) a few drops of Angostura bitters and topped with a cherry and a slice of pineapple. Most visitors to Raffles' Hotel try the Singapore Sling as it is inextricably linked to the hotel. The other cocktail associated with Raffles' Hotel is the *Million Dollar Cocktail* mentioned in Somerset Maughan's short story, *The Letter*. It consists of gin, sweet vermouth, egg white, pineapple juice and Angostura bitters and is decorated with pineapple.

Internet Service

BITNET, 1987. At the instigation of Professor Bernard Tan, Dean of Science at the National University of Singapore (NUS), the NUS became the first institution in Asia to develop links with international academic institutions through BITNET which was maintained by the EDUCOM consortium of universities. On 13 January 1987, the **first email** was sent from the City University of New York (CUNYVM) to the National University of Singapore (NUSVM) through BITNET. The BIT in BITNET stands for 'Because It's There'. Work on the connection began in 1985 and went full-steam ahead in 1986. The NUS team led by Dr Thio Hoe Thong (Director of NUS's Computer Centre) and Dr Loh Wai Lung (Assistant Director, NUS Computer Centre), worked closely with their counterparts in the City University of New York (CUNY) to establish a network. Sporadic contact was made in late 1986. By mid-Febraury 1987, a 4800 bps leased line had been installed at NUS, and this was subsequently upgraded to 9600 bps in January 1988. This was not only **Singapore's first bitnet node**, but the first such node in the whole of Asia outside Japan and Israel.

The NUS then entered into discussions with the National Science and Technology Board (NSTB), SingTel (Singapore Telecoms) and the Ministry of Trade and Industry to see how the benefits of the internet could be extended to the rest of the research and development (R&D) community outside academia. As a result, **the first national R&D network** in Singapore, Technet, was launched in 1992. Technet allowed R&D workers in academia, government and industry to collaborate more effectively with each other. That year, NUS established the first Gopher server in the region, and the **joint-first World-Wide Web server** in the region (www.nus.sg), pioneered by Dr Tan Tin Wee at the NUS Computer Centre. The other joint-first Singapore website was established by Singapore internet pioneer Dr Jek Kian Jin.

In 1994, SingTel established *Singnet*, Singapore's **first commercial internet access service provider** (ISP) with the help of Technet. In 1995, Technet was sold to a consortium comprising Sembawang Media, ST computer Systems and Singapore International Media and was transformed into Pacific Internet or PacNet, Singapore's second ISP.

Iron Mill

National Iron & Steel Mill, 1963. In August 1963, Singapore's first iron mill, the National Iron and Steel Mill, commenced production. The mill cost $12 million and was financed by two local merchant houses with the Economic Development Board (EDB) as a minority shareholder. It was estimated that the mill would provide employment for 400 workers. The factory was opened by Finance Minister Dr Goh Keng Swee, and six months later, the factory went into full production, with the opening of a new steel re-rolling plant and ship-breaking yard. The re-rolling plant had a capacity of 30,000 tons per year. Two hundred workers were employed at the ship-breaking yard. In January 1965, the mills placed an order for two electric arc furnaces as part of its $10 million expansion plan. In 1967, the Steel Mill was producing 100,000 tons of iron and steel each year.

J

Japanese, Migrant

Otokichi Yamamoto, 1818. Otokichi arrived in Singapore 1862, three decades after he left his native Onoura. Otokichi was only 14 years old when he set sail as a novice sailor on board the cargo ship *Honjumaru*. In December 1832, the ship was caught in a fierce storm and the ship was swept far out into the Pacific Ocean and Otokichi and the crew became castaways. After drifting for 14 months, three of the crew, including Otokichi were still alive when their ship beached on the north-west coast of the United States. From there, Otokichi and his companions were moved to Macau where they were cared for by German missionary Karl Gutzlaff. Later, Otokichi worked for the British trading house of Dent and Company in Shanghai (1843) and he married a Singapore-born woman of German-Malay parentage. She bore him three daughters and in 1862, Otokichi moved his whole family to Singapore. He ran a transportation business, became a British subject and called himself John Matthew Ottoson. He died of tuberculosis in January 1867 at the age of 49.

Judge

Sir Thomas Claridge, 1827. The early judges of Singapore were known as Recorders because Singapore was considered a very small settlement and the rank of the judge assigned to Singapore was equated to that of a Recorder in a County in England. The **first Recorder** to arrive in Singapore following the issue of the Second Charter of Justice was Sir John Thomas Claridge (1792–1868) who arrived in 1827. Claridge was educated at Oxford and called to the bar at the Middle Temple. He was apparently an intelligent but difficult man and he quarreled with his colleagues in the Straits almost immediately upon his arrival. He refused to leave Penang on circuit arguing about the type of ship he was to travel in and he launched virulent attacks on his colleagues who refused to attend court. He was finally recalled in 1829 to face charges of insubordination. Claridge served three jurisdictions in the Straits Settlements – Penang (then Prince of Wales' Island), Malacca and Singapore.

In 1855, the post of **Recorder of Singapore** was created. The first holder of the office was Sir Richard McCausland of the Irish Bar, who arrived in 1856 to become Recorder of Singapore. He sat on the Bench for ten years till 1866, retiring on a pension, living for many years afterwards in Ireland. The **first Asian** to be appointed to the High Court in Singapore was Justice Tan Ah Tah (1906–1976). Tan was born in Kuala Lumpur in 1906. In 1925, he won the Queen's Scholarship to study law at Cambridge. He was called to the Bar in 1930 and spent the next 10 years working in a law firm in Penang. In 1946, he became the first Asian to be appointed Commissioner of Estate, Duties and Stamps. In 1947, Tan was one of the first two Chinese to be promoted to the then Colonial Legal Service and in 1948, he was made a judge of the Singapore District Court. In 1955, he was appointed Judge of the High Court in Singapore and in 1958, acted as Chief Justice of Singapore. In 1971, Tan retired from the bench on reaching the age of 65. The Constitution was amended to allow his service to be extended, and Tan retired for the second time in 1975. He died on 12 August 1976. The **first woman High Court Judge** was Lai Siu Chiu. She was sworn in on 30 April 1994 after serving three years as a Judicial Commissioner.

The **first Chief Justice of the Straits Settlements** was Sir Peter Benson Maxwell (1816–1893). Maxwell was born on 31 January 1816 and received his early education in France and then later at Trinity College in Dublin. He was called to the Bar at the Inner Temple and practiced as a barrister in London. Maxwell was sworn in as Recorder of Penang on 20 March 1856. In 1866, he succeeded McCausland as Recorder of Singapore and a year later, when the territories of Penang, Malacca and Singapore were reorganized into the Straits Settlements and the Court of Judicature replaced by the Supreme Court of the Straits Settlements in 1866, Maxwell became the first Chief Justice of the Straits Settlements. On 26 July 1871, Maxwell retired and in 1883, he went to Egypt to organise the Courts after the British occupation. In August 1885, he resigned his appointment and retired to London where he spent his later years. Maxwell spent much time traveling to Europe. He was keen in archaeology and linguistics, and spoke fluent French, German and Italian. Music was his special hobby and he played the cello with considerable skill. On 14 January 1893, after a brief bout of pneumonia Maxwell died. He was laid to rest in the French cemetery at Grasse.

The **first Chief Justice of Singapore** was Charles Murray Murray-Aynsley. He was born on 28 November 1893 and educated at Marlborough, St Paul's School, and St John's College, Cambridge where he graduated with a BA, LLB in law. From 1915 to 1919, he was in military service, and in 1920, he was called to the Bar at the Inner Temple. After practising in the North Eastern Circuit, he was appointed District Commissioner of British Hondurus in 1927. Murray-Aynsley was appointed Chief Justice of Tonga in 1930 and Chief Justice of Grenada in 1935. He came to Malaya in 1938 as Judge at Ipoh, a post he held till the Japanese occupation. He returned to England on leave after being released from Changi in 1945. On his return to Singapore in 1946, he was appointed the Colony of Singapore's first Chief Justice. McElwaine was knighted in June 1950 and he retired in August 1955 to become Chief Justice of Tanganyika.

Independent Singapore's first Chief Justice was Wee Chong Jin (1917–2005). Wee was born on 28 September 1917 in Penang. He was educated at the Penang Free School and then later at St John's College, Cambridge (1935-1938) and called to the Bar at the Middle Temple in London. He practiced as an advocate and solicitor in both Penang and Singapore from 1939 to 1957 before being appointed to the High Court in August 1957 at the age of 40. In 1963, at the age of just 46, he became Chief Justice of Singapore. Two years later, he became independent Singapore's first Chief Justice. In 1966, he chaired the only Constitutional Commission ever convened in post-independence Singapore. In 1988, with the establishment of the Singapore Academy of Law, Wee became its first President. He retired as Chief Justice in 1990 after 27 years at the helm of Singapore's judiciary. From 1973 to 1991, he was also Chairman of the Presidential Council for Minority Rights. He is Singapore's longest serving Chief Justice. In 1987, Wee was conferred and honorary Doctor of Civil Law

(DCL) by Oxford University. He died on 5 June 2005.

Judicial Commissioner

Chan Sek Keong, 1986-1988. On 1 July 1986, Chan Sek Keong became Singapore's first Judicial Commissioner. He was born in Ipoh, Perak in 1937 and received his early education at Anderson School, Ipoh. He read law at the University of Malaya in Singapore and graduated among the top three in his class; the inaugural group of graduands from the Law Faculty in 1961. He was admitted to the Singapore Bar on 31 January 1962 and commenced practice at the firm of Braddell Brothers. In 1969 joined the firm of Shook Lin & Bok, rising quickly to become the firm's managing partner. In 1988, Chan was elevated as Judge of the Supreme Court. On the bench, Chan was well known for his erudite and carefully-crafted judgments. On 1 May 1992, Chan was appointed Attorney-General of Singapore, a post he held till 2006 when he was appointed Chief Justice.

Junior College

National Junior College, 1969. Singapore's first junior college was National Junior College (NJC) at Linden Drive. Opened on 20 January 1969, the junior college was the first to provide strictly pre-university Higher School Certificate courses, culminating in the GCE 'A' level examinations for its students. The **first junior college principal** was Lim Kim Woon and the NJC had an initial intake of 600 students. It operated a six-day week on a single session basis. The college was built at a cost of $1.6 million and was equipped with an audio-visual demonstration room, 10 science laboratories, 30 classrooms, 9 tutorial rooms, an assembly hall and a canteen. Students were selected on scholastic achievement with a special emphasis on second language proficiency, extra curricular activites and sporting ability. Government-sponsored ASEAN students were admitted into the National Junior College. The selective nature of the college was demonstrated by its pioneer batch of students who won a number of Colombo Plan awards and scholarships to Oxford and Cambridge.

Junk from China

1821. The first junk from Amoy, China, arrived on the 13 February 1821. The Captain, Ti Chio, immediately went to see Tan Che Sang, one of Singapore's early Chinese pioneers. Tan took him to the Master Attendant's office to meet the Harbour Master, William Flint. However, Tan failed to get Ti Chio to visit Sultan Hussein. After delaying for 4 days, he was told by Tan to visit the Sultan to pay his respects. The Sultan and his followers were annoyed by the fact that Ti Chio had delayed his visit and refused to pay the customary port dues to the Sultan. He was detained for 4 hours before Tan arranged for him to be released. The incident disturbed the mercantile community and they were worried that it might stop other junks from coming to Singapore. They called a PUBLIC MEETING in protest.

Jury Trials

1826. The Second Charter of Justice – which brought English law into Singapore and which also established the Court of Judicature of the Prince of Wales' Island, Malacca and Singapore – provided for grand and petit juries. The Charter provided that the Grand Jury would comprise no less than 13 and no more than

23 persons. Its duty was to receive complaints and accusations in criminal cases, hear the evidence adduced on the part of the State and find bills of indictment in cases where they are satisfied a trial ought to be had. It was called the Grand Jury only because it had more jurors than an ordinary or petit jury which consists of 12 men empanelled to try and determine any question of fact according to the law and the evidence in court. Because of the paucity of records of early trials in Singapore, it is difficult to ascertain exactly when the jury was first used. However, the few reported cases indicate that jury trials were indeed practiced between 1827 and 1855. In 1873, the Grand Jury was abolished and special and common juries were instituted. The jury system was abolished in Singapore in 1969.

K

Kidney Transplant

1970. The first kidney transplant in Singapore was carried out in 8 July 1970 in the Bowyer Block at Singapore General Hospital. The patient was Mrs Doreen Tan. The surgeon was KT Chan. Mrs Tan was seriously ill with kidney failure when she received the kidney belonging to a young national serviceman, Yee Kwok Tong aged 20. Twenty years later, the Singapore General hospital had a reunion of 40 kidney transplant including Mrs Tan and the surgeon responsible. In 1983, the National Kidney Foundation created history when, with the help of Singapore Airlines, it flew in an American kidney to be transplanted to Mdm Choo Tong Lian. It was also the first time a **kidney kept in cold storage** for 48 hours was transplanted here.

Knighthood

Sir Song Ong Siang, 1936. Song Ong Siang, a distinguished lawyer who had devoted his life to municipal work and to volunteer soldiering in Singapore, was the first Singapore Chinese to receive a knighthood from King George V. He was also the **first local-born law graduate**. Song was born in June 1871 and was the eldest surviving son of Song Hoot Kiam (of Hoot Kiam Road fame). He was educated at St Joseph's Institution and later at Raffles Institution where he won the Queen's Scholarship to study law (1888). Song studied at Cambridge and in 1893, he was called to the Bar. When he returned to Singapore, he established the firm of Aitken & Ong Siang with his old Raffles Institution schoolmate, James Aitken. Song was active in the Straits Chinese community and became an Unofficial Member of the Legislative Council. He replaced Dr Lim Boon Keng in the Legislative Council in November 1919 and again in 1921. He worked hard to improve the status of the Straits Chinese community and, together with Dr Lim Boon Keng, he helped start such important institutions as the Singapore Chinese Girls' School and the Straits Chinese British Association.

The **first and only Eurasian** to be knighted was Sir George Oehlers, **first Speaker** of the Legislative Assembly. Oehlers was born in 1908 and studied law in England. He was called to the Bar in 1931 and returned to Singapore and practised law as a senior partner in the firm of Oehlers and Choa. He was appointed Municipal Commissioner in 1936 and he held the post till 1941. In 1947, Oehlers was once again nominated to the Municipal Commission. Oehlers left Singapore in 1954 to study parliamentary procedure in London and when he returned in 1955, he became the first Speaker of the newly-formed Singapore Legislative Assembly. Oehlers died in 1968.

L

Land Lease

North Beach, 1819. In June 1819, Raffles authorized the provision of 12 building land lots along North Beach. Raffles reserved 6 lots and 6 more were sold to Europeans on application. Raffles gave one lot to Carnegy & Company, one for F Ferrars, one for T Macquaid, one for Captain Flint and kept two. In April 1826, 51 leases were granted. The leading Chinese businessman Tan Che Sang acquired 22 of these leases.

Land Reclamation Project

South Boat Quay, 1822. The first reclamation project took place in 1822. Raffles insisted that the small hill on the South side of the Singapore be levelled and the earth used to fill up the swampy south bank of the Singapore River. This area became known as South Boat Quay. The project made the reclaimed site suitable for building. The land was divided into plots and allotted to merchants. By 1860, 75% of all business in Singapore was transacted from godowns and offices along Boat Quay. The hill was on what is now Raffles Place (originally 'Commercial Square'). Boat Quay was renovated in July 1989 and the area is now a popular restaurant and caf precinct. The second reclamation project was 18 acres of land at Telok Ayer in 1887.

Law Agent

William Napier, 1833. William Napier, nicknamed Royal Billy, was appointed Singapore's first law agent in 1833. He was Lieutenant-Governor of Labuan and presided at the investiture of James Brooke in 1848. Napier was also a good friend of Admiral Keppel and returned from England in 1848 on board Keppel's ship, the *HMS Napier*. Napier was a larger-than-life figure and together with Edward Boustead and George Coleman, he founded the *Singapore Free Press* in 1835 which he edited until 1846. In 1844, Napier married Coleman's widow. Napier played a leading role in the public affairs of the settlement. He became a trustee of the Singapore Institution (later Raffles Institution) in 1836 and acted as legal advisor to the Temenggong of Johore. He was also the first Chairman of the Straits Settelements Associaiton which was founded in January 1868. In 1845, Napier became the first Freemason to be initiated in Singapore. Napier Road, which is named after him, led to his house at the junction of Tanglin Road and Napier Road, which he built in 1854. The **first Chinese law agent** was Wuing Boon Whatt.

Law Society President

Tan Chye Cheng (CC Tan), 1963. The Advocates and Solicitors Society was established in 1963 to represent the interests of lawyers in Singapore. The Society became known as the Law Society in 1970. All registered advocates and solicitors are automatically members of the Society. Fifteen members of the Society are elected to the Council of the Society every year and the members of the Council elect a President and Vice-President. The Law Society seeks to maintain and improve the standards of the legal profession in Singapore and represents, protects and assists members of the profession. The first President was Tan Chye Cheng (more popularly known as CC Tan) who served in 1963, 1964 and 1967. Tan was born in 1911 and educated at St Joseph's Institution. He was called to the English Bar in 1928 and to the Singapore Bar in 1929. In 1947, he formed the firm of Tan, Rajah and Cheah with AP Rajah and Cheah Heng Sin. Tan was a founder member and **first President of the Singapore Progressive Party**. He was a member of the Singapore Advisory Council in 1946 and was elected to the Singapore Legislative Council in 1948 and 1951. He was also President of the Singapore National Olympic Council and President of the Singapore Island Country Club. He died in 1991.

Lawyer

John Simons Atchison, 1859. The first qualified lawyer was John Simons Atchison, who was admitted to the Singapore Bar in 1859. Atchison was a brilliant but eccentric character. As he was related to H Simons of Messrs Paterson and Simons and Company, his office was at the latter's warehouse. He had been admitted as an attorney at Westminster in 1855 and came to Singapore in 1859. He always dressed in patent leather shoes, cotton drill trousers, a fancy cotton waistcoat and dark blue frock. He also wore a black silk hat. One of his eccentricities was that he drank enormous quantities of soda water. He drove everywhere in a small carriage driven by a pony. Atchison lived in *Blanche House* near the Teutonia Club (now Goodwood Park Hotel). Atchison spent a lot of time agitating against the Government, especially the Executive Council. He was the first Honorary Secretary of the Singapore branch of the Straits Settlements Association that was established in March 1868 to safeguard the interest of the commercial sector in Singapore. He died in Bangkok in 1875 where he had gone on a retainer in a big case.

Lawyer, Local-Born

Song Ong Siang, 1893. Song Ong Siang was born in June 1871, the eldest surviving son of Song Hoot Kiam. He studied at St Joseph's Institution and then at Raffles Institution where he won the Guthrie Scholarship for five years as 'Dux' of the Chinese class. In 1888, he won the prestigious Queen's Scholarship to study law at Cambridge. He was called to Bar in 1893 and when he returned to Singapore, he and his old friend from Raffles Institution, James Aitken established the law firm of Aitken & Ong Siang. Song was very active in the Straits Chinese community and became an Unofficial member of the Legislative Council. He replaced Dr Lim Boon Keng on the Council in November 1919, and again in 1921. In 1924, he was nominated to the Legislative Council and he retained his seat until 1927. From 1894 to 1899, he was the Assistant Editor of the *Straits Settlements Law Reports*. Together with Dr Lim Boon Keng, Song worked hard to improve the status of the Straits Chinese community. They started important institutions like the Singapore Chinese Girls' School and the Straits Chinese British Association. Song was a trustee of the Anglo-Chinese School, a member of the Raffles College Council (1934) and Vice-President of the Oxford and Cambridge Society of Malaya. Song and Lim also produced the *Straits Chinese Magazine* which ran for 11 years from 1897. Today, he is best remembered for his book, *One Hundred Years' History of the*

Chinese in Singapore. Song was also founder-member of the Singapore Volunteer Infantry Chinese Company formed in 1901, and the first Chinese to rise to the rank of Captain (1915). In 1907, Song married Helen Yeo Nee Neo at the Prinsep Street Presbyterian Church where he became an elder. He was President of the Chinese Christian Association from 1893 till his death in 1941. Song was also a keen rifleman and represented Singapore in matches against Ceylon and Calcutta. In 1899, he won the Governor's Cup for shooting. In 1927, he was awarded the Commander of the British Empire, and in 1936, he was knighted for his services to Singapore. He died in September 1941, aged 70.

See also **Knighthood**.

Lee Kuan Yew Distinguished Visitor

Sydney Brenner, 1985. The first Lee Kuan Yew Distinguished Visitor was Professor Sydney Brenner in January 1985. The eminent molecular biologist, who won the 2002 Nobel Prize for Medicine, gave four lectures based on the theme of 'Revolution in Biology' at the National University of Singapore. The Distinguished Visitor Programme was set up in 1983 to bring eminent scientists and scholars to Singapore to interact with staff at the university, the public and relevant industries.

Lee Kuan Yew Scholarship

See **Scholars**.

Legislative Assembly, Singapore

1955. Elections for the first Legislative Assembly were held under the Rendel Constitution in 1955. The new constitution provided for 25 elected members and 7 nominated members. For the first time, 6 local Ministers would control Education, Health, Housing, Trade and Industry. The British retained the 3 key ministries of Finance, Law, External Affairs, External Defence and Internal Security. The Governor retained the right of veto over laws passed by the Legislative Assembly. The Labour Front won 10 seats, the Progressive Party 4 seats, the Alliance (United Malays National Organisation-Malayan Chinese Association-Singapore Malay Union) 3 seats, the PAP 3 seats, the Democratic Party 2 seats and there were 3 Independents. The Labour Front was invited to form a government. They formed a coalition with the Alliance party and David Marshall became the first Chief Minister. (See also CABINET).

Legislative Council, Singapore

1948. The first Singapore Legislative Council was formed in 1948. The Council for the first time had more non-officials than officials. This gave the Council a non-official majority. There were 9 officials nominated by the Governor. The non-officials included four nominated by the Governor (the pre-war method of selecting non-officials) three elected by Chambers of Commerce, European, Chinese and Indian, and for the first time there were 6 non-officials elected by the people. The successful candidates were Sardon bin Haji Zubir (Independent) won the seat of Rural East; SC Goho (Independent) won the seat of Rural West; Mohammed Javad bin Namazie (Independent) and John Laycock (Progressive Party) won the two seats for Municipal North East; and CC Tan (Progressive Party) and Nazir bin Ahmad Mallal (Progressive Party) won the two seats for Municipal South West.

The first fully-elected democratic election for the Singapore Legislative Assembly was held in 1959. There were 51 seats under contention and the PAP won 43 seats to take power. The Singapore People's Alliance won 3 seats, the UMNO-MCA Alliance won 3 seats and there was 1 Independent. Lee Kuan Yew became Prime Minister. The Governor was replaced by the Yang di-Pertuan Negara or Head of State. The last British Governor, Sir William Goode became the **first Head of State** as an interim measure. Yusof Ishak took over as Head of State 6 months later.

Legislative Council, Straits Settlements

1867. The first Straits Settlements Legislative Council was formed in April 1867. The Colonial Office appointed a Governor who ruled with the help of the Executive and Legislative Councils. The Executive Council consisted of the Governor, the General Officer commanding the Troops based in the Straits Settlements, the Colonial Secretary, the two Resident Councillors of Penang and Malacca, the Attorney-General, the Colonial Engineer and the Treasurer. Under the Presidency of the Governor, the Executive Council served as a Cabinet and met in private at the Governor's request. The advice of the Executive Council was not binding on the Governor. The Legislative Council consisted of the Executive Council plus the Chief Justice and 4 nominated non-officials. The Council met in public and debates were reported in the press. The Governor initiated most legislation and had the power of assent or veto over the bills. The official members were obliged to support the Governor but non-officials were free to speak and vote as they pleased. The first Nominated Unofficials were: William Henry Read, FS Brown (from Penang), Thomas Scott and Dr. Robert Little. The first Clerk of Councils was HF Plow.

Lemon Grass Factory

Perseverance Estate, late 1800s. The Perseverance Estate in Geylang was the first factory that turned lemon grass or *serai* into citronella oil. The land was owned by Syed Abdul Rahman Alsagoff who came to Singapore and established Alsagoff & Co in 1848. Family members were not only merchants but were also involved in civic and public affairs. Originally the land was used as coconut plantations and the area was known as Geylang Kelapa. In the latter half of the 19th century, the Alsagoff family hired an English manager, J Fisher to develop the Perseverance Estate for the cultivation of lemon grass or *serai*. Since then, the area has been known as Geylang Serai. The factory was situated on Changi Road and contained 16 stills, 8 for citronella and 8 for patchouli oil. The factory was capable of producing 144 bottles per day. Pint bottles were used for local consumption and quart bottles for export. Citronella is considered a useful cure for rheumatism and is also know to have antiseptic properties. It is effective against mosquitoes. The estate won many medals for its products. The Citronella Press Factory ceased to function and the site became the tramway terminus at Geylang in 1910.

Letter to the Editor

Straits Times, 1845. The first letter written to the editor was published in *The Straits Times* on 29 July 1845. The letter argued that some of the fees received by St Andrew's Church should go towards paying for an organist.

Library, Public

Singapore Library 1845. Between 1823 and 1844, the library created at the Singapore Institution (later Raffles Institution) was available to anyone for a small fee of 25 cents per month. However, it was distinctly a school library. In 1843, it was proposed to start a public library by subscriptions. A prospectus was printed and circulated. In August 1844, a public meeting was held to establish a library. JC Smith was the first Secretary and Librarian while William Henry Read was its Treasurer. There were 34 shareholders who paid $30 each and a month subscription of $2.50 per month. Smith Elder and Company was appointed as London agents for the Library and £200.00 per month was given to them for the purchase of books. On 22 January 1845, the Library was opened. Opening hours were 6.00 am to 9.00 pm every day except Sunday. In 1849, the proprietors of the Library proposed setting up a museum, and at its Annual Meeting, it was agreed that a Singapore Library Museum would be established. In 1862, the Library moved to the old Town Hall where it occupied two rooms on the ground floor. The available space soon proved to be insufficient and in 1876, the library moved back to Raffles Institution and was housed on the first and second floors of the new wing. In 1874, the Government decided to establish a Museum and Library. The old Singapore Library was renamed the Raffles Library and became the Raffles Library and Museum. A new building was planned at the junction of Stamford Road and Orchard Road, and it was opened by Governor Frederick Weld on 12 October 1887.

The Library housed a valuable collection of literature dealing with the Malay Archipelago, including two important collections: the Logan Collection and the Rost Collection. The Logal Collection belong to James R Logan, editor of the *Journal of Indian Archipelago* and was acquired in 1880. The Rost Collection was purchased in 1897 from the executors of the Rost estate. Dr Reinhold Rost was Librarian at the India Office in London. In 1907, there were 320 subscribers to the Library. There was a spacious reading room and the walls were adorned with portraits of former Governors, principal residents of the Colony and a large photograph of Raffles. When the main block became too small, a further block was added at the rear and this was opened on 13 February 1907. The building was extended again in 1916 and 1926. In 1960, a new Library was built on the site of the former British Council Hall. In 2005, the National Library at Stamford Road was demolished and the collection moved to a brand new building on Victoria Street.

The **first regional library** was Tampines Regional Library which opened on 3 December 1994. The National University of Singapore Library became the **first academic library in the region to offer on-line access** to overseas databases through the library On-Line Search Service. In 1995, it became the first academic library in the region to launch Library InfoGate, an electronic document management and retrieval system which offers desktop access to selected library collections all over the world.

Light Rail Service

Bukit Panjang Light Rail System, 1999. In 1999 the Bukit Panjang Light rail system opened. it was built at the cost of S$283 million and is 8 kms long.

Lighthouse

Horsburgh Lighthouse, 1851. The first lighthouse was designed by John Turnbull Thomson in 1844. Construction began in 1847 and it was completed and operational on 27 September 1851. The structure was erected on Pedra Branca at the Eastern approaches to the Singapore Strait and was named the Horsburgh Lighthouse after James Horsburgh, Hydrographer of the East India Company. According to the official notice to mariners, the light was exhibited between the hours of sunset and sunrise from the 15 October, 1851. The light could be observed as a revolving bright light which gradually attains its brightest period once every minute. It then declines until it totally disappears to the distant observer. The lantern which is open all round is elevated 95 feet (29 metres) above the level of the sea at High Water Spring Tide and can be seen from the deck of a ship at a distance of 15 nautical miles. The lighthouse was a pillar of dressed granite and the lantern was covered by a spherical dome which is painted white. The Raffles Lighthouse was erected in 1854 and became operational on 1 December 1855. In 1988, both lighthouses were automated.

Literary Society

Chinese Philomatic Society, 1896. Singapore's first literary society was the Chinese Philomathic Society founded in 1896 by Dr Lim Boon Keng. The society brought together a number of Straits Chinese for the regular study of English literature, Western music and the Chinese language. Lim was President and Song Ong Siang was Vice-President. Other members included Chan Kim Boon, Tan Boo Liat, Tan Jiak Kim, Lee Keng Kiat and Seah Liang Seah. The society was to provide three future presidents of the Straits Chinese British Association: Dr Lim Boon Keng, Tan Jiak Kim and Song Ong Siang.

Literary Prize

See **Book and Literature Prizes.**

Liver Transplant

National University Hospital, 1990. The first liver transplant was carried out on a 25-year-old production worker, Ms Surinder Kaur on 29 September 1990, by a team of doctors from the National University Hospital. The team was led by Dr Susan Lim, the second woman doctor in the world to perform a liver transplant. The operation lasted five hours. Lim was assisted by 4 surgeons and 2 anaesthetists. Kaur had been diagnosed with auto-immune liver disease and had been given only 6 months to live before the operation. The donor was Goh Boon Chai, a construction worker who fell four storeys to his death on 28 September 1990.

Local Battalion

See **Battalion**.

Lottery, State

Konan Saiken, 1942. Singapore's first state lottery was held in July 1942 during the Japanese Occupation. A Government Lottery called *Konan Saiken* was held by the Japanese Administration to help increase revenue and to prevent inflation. The tickets cost $1 each and the top prize was $100,000 While the 2nd prize was $50,000. There were ten 3rd Prizes of $10,000 each and fifty 4th Prizes of $1,000 each. Lottery mania swept Singapore and Malaya and the motto was 'Poor Today, Rich Tomorrow'.

Tickets were available at the offices of Dr Lim Boon Keng in Club Street; SC Goho in Meyer Chambers; and Ibrahim bin Haji Yaacob at 146 Cecil Street. The draw was open to the general public and was held on 10 September 1942 at Syonan Ko-Kai-Do. The 1st Prize ticket (No 607940) was held by Letchuman Chettiar, who bought 223 tickets in the hope of winning a prize. He announced that he would give part of his prize to charity and part to the Nippon War Fund for wounded soldiers. The lotteries continued until August 1945.

Loyalty Pledge

1966. The Singapore Pledge was written in 1966 by S Rajaratnam, then Minister of Culture. Rajaratnam, a former journalist, revealed that he dreamt of building a Singapore that its people could be proud of and felt that language, race and religion were divisive forces. He sent the draft of the text to then Prime Minister Lee Kuan Yew, who polished it before submitting it to Cabinet for approval. It was introduced in its present form to all schools in the third term (July) of 1966. The Pledge read:s

We the citizens of Singapore
Pledge ourselves as one united people
Regardless of race, language or religion
To build a democratic society
Based on justice and democracy
So as to achieve happiness, prosperity and progress for our nation.

Lung Transplant

2000. On 19 November 2000, surgeons at the National Heart Centre at the Singapore General Hospital performed Singapore's first lung transplant. The 54 year-old recipient was Thanvanthri Nadesen Veerappan who had been suffereing from pulmonary fibrosis and doctors had estimated that he had only weeks to live without a transplant. The 9-hour operation was carried out by Drs S Sivathasan, and Tong Ming Chuan with Dr T Agasthian in attendance. The lungs were removed from Madam Yap Chee Kian, a 39 year old woman who died of a brain haemorrhage at the National Neuroscience Institute. Thanvanthri made a good recovery and went home one month after the operation.

M

Malay Graduate of Nanyang University

Jaafar Kassim, 1971. The first and only Malay graduate of Nanyang University was Jaafar Kassim. Born the eldest of 13 children on Pulau Tekong Besar, Jaafar was sent to the only school on the island, a Chinese school when he was 6 years old. After his Primary School Leaving Examinations, Jaafar chose to continue his secondary and pre-university education in the Chinese stream at Whampoa Government Secondary School. He graduated from Nanyang University with a Bachelor of Arts in Chinese Language, Literature and Philosophy in 1971.

Malay Orchestra

Orkestra Melayu Singapura, 1991. The first Malay Orchestra was formed in September 1991. the Orkestra Melayu Singapura was led by Mohammed Mokhtar Abdullah, a composer and musician. It was supported by the People's Association and consisted of mainly Western brass and woodwind instruments but also included a gong and a Malay drum. The orchestra was launched in January 1992 by Mohammed Maidin, Parliamentary Secretary to the Ministry of Information and the Arts. It gave its debut performance on 11 April 1992.

Malaya Cup

See **Malaysia Cup**

Malaysia Cup

1921. What is now the Malaysia Cup started out in 1921 as the *HMS Malaya Cup*, after the battleship that visited Singapore and Kuala Lumpur in 1921. The first finals was between Singapore and Selangor on 1 October 1921 in Kuala Lumpur. Singapore won the inaugural cup 2-1. Both teams featured large numbers of European players. In 1925, the Malaya Cup was played for the **first time in Singapore** and once again, Singapore beat Selangor 2-1 at the Anson Road Stadium. In 1933, Singapore won the Malaya Cup with the largest margin ever when it beat Selangor 8-2 in the finals at Anson Road. In 1967, the cup was renamed the Malaysia Cup to reflect the changed political circumstances of both Malaysia and Singapore. The first winner of the Malaysia Cup was Perak who beat Singapore 2-1 in the finals. Singapore's **first win in the Malaysia Cup** was in 1977 when she beat Penang 3-2 in the finals after extra time. The team, coached by the legendary Choo Seng Quee, was considered one of the finest ever assembled in recent memory. In 1994, Singapore pulled out of the Malaysia Cup competition following a dispute with the Football Association of Malaysia over gate receipts. It has not been involved in the tournament since. In all, Singapore won the Malaya Cup or Malaysia Cup a total of 24 times.

Marathon

1982. The first Singapore Marathon was held in 1982. It was won by Raymond Crabb from England in a time of 2:24:19. The fastest woman competitor was Winnie Lai-chu Ng from Hong Kong in a time of 2:55:11. From 1982 until 1998, the marathon was held in even-numbered years. Since 1999, it has been held annually.

Market

Market Street, 1822. Singapore's first market of record was the fish market near the north end of Market Street. It was situated on the river bank in the middle of a bazaar of shops including shops retailing market produce. Its location was ideal as the sheltered river bank provided a safe landing place for fishing boats. However, when Raffles visited Singapore for the last time in October 1922, he objected to the position of the market as he had designated it as part of the new commercial area. Since the Chinese were to be located further south in Telok Ayer, Raffles decided it would be convenient to locate the market there. The town committee recommended that the market be relocated to the eastern extremity of Telok Ayer Bay. They argued that it was a central location and could be built over the sea. Farquhar disagreed saying that the site frequently had a heavy surf beating on that part of the shore. Another location further to the west near the Thian Hock Keng temple was inspected. A prominent Chinese merchant, Tan Che Sang visited the site and offered to build the new Market at his own cost but on the condition that he could collect the rents. This offer was refused.

A site was finally selected at the south end of Market Street midway between the two sites under discussion. In February 1824, the new market was ready. It was a simple timber structure partially built over the water on timber piles. However, many of the vendors refused to leave the old market and business carried on in the old market for some time after the new market was completed. Francis Bernard, the former Master Attendant, then in charge of the police force, tried to encourage the vendors to move by sounding the Town Gong as a signal for the smooth transfer to the new market. However when the Gong was sounded there was panic and pandemonium and the whole fracas threatened to develop into a riot. Less than a year after its completion, the market was found to be inadequate.

In 1834, George Dromgold Coleman submitted his design for an octagonal building to be built in brick. It was twice the size of the market that it replaced and was formed by 2 concentric rings of brick piers arranged in an octagonal. This market was completed in 1834 and was continually used until it was replaced in 1894. The site was affected by the reclamation project in Telok Ayer that started in 1879. In 1894, the market was re-sited on reclaimed land at the edge of the shoreline. A new building was designed by James McRitchie, the Municipal Engineer. Its cast iron structure was manufactured in Glasgow by P&W McClellan and was erected by Riley Hargreaves and Co. (later known as United Engineers Pte Ltd). This is the building we now know as *Lau Pa Sat* or the Old Market. In the 1960s, rapid urbanisation in the city area made it seem inevitable that the market building would be torn down. However, it was gazetted as a national monument in 1973 and later extensively renovated. Today it is a popular cooked food centre.

Masonic Lodge

Masonic Hall, 1856. In 1844, the practicality of opening a Masonic lodge in Singapore was discussed and a number of Singapore-based merchants applied to the United Grand Lodge of England for a warrant of constitution. This was obtained and in December 1845, JC Smith, Charles A Dyce and Thomas O Crane were appointed the first Master and Wardens of the new Zetland Lodge. William Napier was the first brother to be initiated in Singapore. The meetings were held in a house in Armenian Street. In 1856, a Masonic Hall was opened on the Esplanade. The present Masonic Hall on Coleman Street was opened in 1879.

Master Attendant

Francis James Bernard, 1819–1820. The first Master Attendant in Singapore was Francis James Bernard. He was Master Attendant from February 1819 to April 1820. The post of Master Attendant was similar to that of Harbour Master but it was combined with other duties such as Post Master and Marine Storekeeper. Raffles appointed Bernard to the post on a salary of $300 per month. However, his appointment was provisional as Raffles was keeping the post for his brother-in-law, Captain William Lawrence Flint who was still in Europe. Bernard was born in 1796 and joined the Bengal Pilot Service as a volunteer in 1810 at the age of 14. By the time he was 19, Bernard was a second mate.

In 1815, he then went to Calcutta, and in June 1818, he married Esther Farquhar at St John's Cathedral in Calcutta. The couple joined Esther's father, Major William Farquhar in Malacca. The family sailed from Malacca to Penang on the brig the *Ganges* which Bernard owned and commandered. They joined Raffles on his trip south to Singapore in 1819. The brig was commandeered by Raffles for use by the East India Company to provide storage until provision could be made for stores to be built ashore.

Captain Flint arrived in Singapore on 23 April 1820 and took over the post of Master Attendant the next day. Bernard stayed on in the role of assistant in charge of the police force at the salary of $150. He and Esther had 5 children. Bernard left Singapore in March 1827 on the British brig *Meridian*. He did not return to Singapore and made his way to the Celebes. He died at Batavia on 19 December 1843.

In May 1971, Captain Goh Choo Keng became the **first local Port Master of Singapore**. It was his second 'first' as he was also the first Singaporean to head the Marine Department in 1970. He held both posts concurrently. Captain Goh joined the Marine Department in 1965 after obtaining his Master's Foreign-going Certificate. He was sent to Britain for an Examiner's Course and returned in 1967.

Master Plan

1954. The first Master Plan for land use in Singapore was written between July and December 1954 and published in December 1955. The Master Plan was proposed by the Singapore Improvement Trust (SIT) and was written by a Diagnostic Survey team under the leadership of Sir George Pepler, Town Planning Advisor to the Colony of Singapore and Manager of the SIT. The Master Plan contained a written statement of the main proposals, a Colony map at a scale of 2.5 inches to a mile, a Town map at the scale of 8 chains to the inch, a Central Area map at the scale of 4 chains to the inch and Programme maps showing the stages by which the the proposed development should take place. The Master Plan divided Singapore into 3 areas; Central Planning Area, Urban Planning Area and the Rural and Islands Planning Area. The objective of the Plan was to 'secure that the right land shall be available at the right time to meet the variety of needs of people in Singapore for homes, workplaces and recreation'. The Plan noted that more than half of the population lived in the Central Planning Area and recommended that there be a redistribution with the construction of new suburbs, new towns and expanded villages. The Plan felt that the encouragement of secondary industry was vital and recommended ample provision for industrial land in certain zones. As much of the land was in private hands, the Plan proposed the formation of a development corporation to be set up to acquire and develop land for industrial purposes. Redvelopment was most needed in the Central Planning Area. The Plan recommended a careful selected programme of demolition of those blocks which most needed it. They counselled againt the advancement of wholesale demolition to be replaced by grandiose schemes. The Plan pointed out the serious need for a rapid housing programme and estimated that Singapore would need 185,000 permanent homes and 47,700 temporary homes to be built over 18 years to conquer the housing problem. The Plan also urged the need for planning for open space and adequate roads and public utilities.

Maternal and Child Health Clinics

Maternal and Child Health Clinics, 1923. In 1910, Mrs Blundell, a Municipal nurse, was appointed to investigate the conditions of early life of infants and to advise mothers on child care. As a result of her investigations, the first regular course for Asian midwives was commenced in 1910 as a joint venture between the Government and the Municipal Council. In 1912, a European sister was employed to visit and advise mothers. The Maternal and Child Health Service continued to grow. In 1923, the first two Municipal Maternal and Child Health Clinics were opened at Kreta Ayer and at Prinsep Street. The first clinics were held in rural areas in 1927. Nurses conducted clinics beside the road, in people's homes and in garages. The first permanent rural clinic was established in Bukit Timah in 1929. The benefits of these clinics can be demonstrated by the drop in the infant mortality rate, which nearly haved from 1920 to 1940. See also NURSE TRAINING.

Mayor

Ong Eng Guan, 1957. The first Mayor of the City of Singapore was Ong Eng Guan who was elected Mayor of the Singapore City Council in December 1957. He was re-elected as Mayor in December 1958 and resigned in April 1959 to stand for election to the new Legislative Council. Ong Eng Guan was born in Malacca in 1925. He was educated in both Chinese and English and went to the University of Melbourne to study accountancy. He gained a Batchelor of Commerce degree and a Diploma in Public Administration. He was active in student politics while at the university, and became President of the Australian Overseas Club. He was also the founder President of the Asian Students Federation. The Federation united Asian students in the fight against Western imperialism. He returned to Singapore to work as an accountant.

He became the Treasurer of the People's Action Party at its formation in November 1954 and was also Secretary of the Editorial Board for *Petir*, the party magazine. He was also Chairman of the PAP Funds Committee and served on the PAP Local Government Committee. In 1957, he stood as a PAP candidate for Hong Lim for the first fully elected

City Council elections. The PAP won 13 seats out of 32 contested. Ong Eng Guan was elected Mayor. The inaugural meeting of the City Council was a memorable day. There were riots outside the Town Hall, Ong was arrested and the council had to postpone its inaugural meeting until the following day. The council soon became known as the most controversial municipal council in the World. Meetings were described as bedlam and pandemonium. By early 1959, the city council was no longer functioning properly and the Minister for Local Government stripped the Council of its powers.

Ong Eng Guan resigned in April 1959 to stand for election in the Hong Lim electorate in 1959 Legislative Council elections. Following the elections, he became Minister for National Development and also had a seat on the Internal Security Council. He was later forced to resign from the party for 'arbitrary and unprincipled acts without consultation or discussion with colleagues'. In April 1961, he contested the Hong Lim by-election or the 'Ong-Lim' by-election as it was jokingly called, and defeated the PAP candidate Jek Yeun Thong. He then set up the United People's Party. In July 1965, he resigned his seat in parliament and left politics.

Medical, Syndrome

See **Disease, Named After Singaporean.**

Medical school

Straits and Federated Malay States Government Medical School, 1905. The first medical college in Singapore was the Straits and Federated Malay States Government Medical School founded in 1905 in a building formerly used as a Female Lunatic Asylum. In all, there were 23 students in the first batch: 9 Chinese, 6 Eurasians, 5 Tamils, 1 Malay, 1 Ceylonese and 1 European. The first Principal of the College was Dr CD Freer, an ex-colonial Surgeon Resident of Penang and was appointed as a house surgeon to the General Hospital in 1890. Teaching was done by government doctors, 2 army surgeons and 5 private practitioners: Drs Lim Boon Keng, Murray-Robertson, David Galloway, Fowlie and Black. The first batch of 7 students graduated in 1910. They were: Chen Su Lan, EW De Cruz, WF Cargey, J Granapragasam, SR Krishnan, JS Lee and MW Chill. The first woman to graduate was Miss E Nune in March 1911. That year, a new building was provided with funds donated by Tan Chay Yan. It was named in his father's memory and became the Tan Teck Guan Building in the grounds of the Singapore General Hospital. In February 1926, a new three-storey building was opened. After the College received a large donation in 1912 from the King Edward VII Memorial Fund, it changed its name to the King Edward VII Medical School (1913). In 1923 it became the King Edward College of Medicine and in 1949, it merged with Raffles College the University of Malaya.

Meteorological Observations

1820–1825. The earliest meteorological observations were recorded at Fort Canning between 1820 and 1825 by Lieutenant-Colonel William Farquhar. The first instance of an earthquake felt in Singapore was at 9.00 pm on 24 November 1833.

Metric Weights & Measures, Introduction

1971. Metric weights and measures were officially introduced and adopted all across Singapore in February 1971. The Metrication Act was passed by Parliament that year and a Metrication Board was establish to help coordinate efforts to get Singaporeans to think and work in the metric system.

Military base

See **Army Camp**.

Miss Universe Pageant

1987. The first Miss Universe pageant to be held in Singapore took place in May 1987. The event was staged at the World Trade Centre and televised to a world-wide audience. The winner was Miss Chile, Cecilia Borocco, who won a tiara and US$250,000 worth of prizes. She turned 19 just a few days before the finals. The runner-up was Miss Italy, Roberta Capua. Miss Singapore, Nicole Teo bowed out in the semifinals. There were 11 judges including Isobel Sanford, star of the TV sitcom, *The Jeffersons*. The show was presented by Bob Barker and Mary Frann.

Mobile Phone

1988. The first mobile phone service was launched on 16 August 1988 with 3,000 handphones were issued in the first month. The price of each phone was between $2,900 and $3,400 each. The registration fee was $10 and the subscription was $150 fir the first quarter and and then $50 per month. The licence fee was $50 yearly and local calls cost 20 cents per minute and overseas calls were international call rates plus 20 cents per minute. The new handphones weighed between 600 and 700g. About 2,500 people ordered their handphones in June when the introduction of handphones was first announced. The popularity of the handphones placed pressure on the Telecoms to improve reception. Another $18 million was invested in the following year to improve reception in Upper Serangoon and Yio Chu Kang. The number of base stations rose from 37 to 57.

Mobilisation, National Servicemen

Operation Mobilisation, 1985. On 8 July 1985, the Ministry of Defence conducted Operation Mobilisation, its first open recall exercise. About 10,000 reservist troops were involved. This was the first time the Singapore Armed Forces recalled reservists through the mass media. The **first silent mobilization** took place on 22 March 1993. This exercise involved 2,700 reservists who had to report to their centres within 8 hours of activation through pagers and telephones. It was reported that 97% of the reservists mobilized were able to report within the 8 hour target.

Monument, National

Dalhousie's Obelisk, 1850. The Preservation of Monuments Act was passed in 1971 to 'establish and incorporate the Preservation of Monuments Board to preserve for the benefit of the nation, monuments of historic, traditional, archaeological, architectural or artistic interest.' The first monument to gazetted under the Act was Dalhousie's Obelisk. The obelisk was built in 1850 to commemorate the landing in Singapore of the Marquis James Dalhousie, Governor-General of India.

Dalhousie had been advised to take a sea cruise for the sake of his health and as an exponent of free trade, his visit caused some excitement amongst Singapore's mercantile community. He came on the Man O'War ship *Feroze*, and stepped ashore to a 19-gun salute. The Marquis and his wife seemed impressed by Singapore and it was hoped that would lead to increased interest in Singapore. The mercantile community contributed $2,000 to build the obelisk to commemorate the visit. It was designed by Government Surveyor John Turnbull Thomson and was inscribed with the hope that Dalhousie had 'recognised the wisdom of liberating commerce from all restraints under which enlightened policy this Settlement has rapidly attained its present rank among British possessions.' As it turned out, Dalhousie gave little recognition to Singapore and this first memorial was perhaps undeserved.

Memorial, Military or War

See **War Memorial**

Monopoly Set, Singapore Edition

Parker Brothers, 1993. The first Singapore edition of the famous board-game, *Monopoly*, was put out by Parker Brothers in 1993. It features such familiar street names as Tanglin Road, Shenton Way and Emerald Hill. The railway stations are Ang Mo Kio, City Hall, Jurong East and Bedok stations. The jail is Changi prison.

Motorcycle Track

1930s. The first motorcycle track in Singapore was located in the Alkaff Gardens (now Sennett Estate in MacPherson), home of the Alkaff family. The Alkaffs held motorcycle races and even brought in professional riders from Hong Kong and Japan to compete. Their private gardens were located in MacPherson, in what is now Sennett Estate. The Gardens were landscaped in Japanese style and had a miniature Mount Fuji, a pagoda, a lake and two bridges. There was no entrance fee for use of the gardens and the family mixed freely with the public on the premises.

Mosque

Masjid Omar Kampong Melaka, 1820. The Masjid Omar Kampong Melaka at Keng Cheow Street was build in 1820, just a year after Raffles landed. It is also known as the Omar Kampong Malacca Mosque. Since its establishment, the mosque has been rebuilt twice, once in 1855 and then again in 1981-1982. The oldest mosque in the city area is the Masjid Jamae in South Bridge Road which was built in 1826. In 1839, the brick mosque was replaced by a graceful structure with two towers with horizontal mouldings and topped by two domes. The architecture is a mix of Anglo-India, Malay and Chinese style. It is now gazetted as a National Monument.

Mount Everest, Ascent

1998. The first successful ascent of Mount Everest took place in 1998. The expedition team consisted of Edwin Siew, Khoo Swee Chiow, David Lim, Justin Lean, Leong Chee Mun, Robert Goh, Mok and Rozani. On 25 May 1990, Edwin Siew and Khoo Swee Chiow became the first members of the Singapore team to reach the summit.

Mountains, Singapore-named

Temasek Peak, Singapura I Peak & Ong Teng Cheong Peak, 2005. The first mountains named in honour of Singapore are: Temasek Peak (4,374 metres); Singapura I Peak (4,589m); and Ong Teng Cheong Peak (4,743m). A team of four Singaporeans set out on 20 July 2005 to climb three virgin peaks in Kazakhstan's Tien Shan range. They celebrated their success by naming the peaks in celebration of Singapore's 40th birthday. The team comprised David Lim (team leader), Mohamad Rozani Maarof, Shani Tan, and Wilfred Tok. They were dropped onto the Siemienova Glacier by helicopter and mounted their assault on the first peak on 24 July. 'Temasek' was their choice for the first peak (ascended 24 July) as it was Singapore's original name. 'Singapura I' (ascended 26 July) represented the kind of challenges the nation overcame; and the last peak was named after the late President Ong Teng Cheong who did much to promote mountaineering in Singapore (ascended 28 July).

Movie

See **Film**

MRI machine

National University Hospital, 1991. The first Magnetic Resonance Imaging (MRI) machine was installed by National University Hospital in 1991.

MRT Line

North-South Line, 1987. Following a Comprehensive Traffic Survey in 1981 that showed that a rail system was crucial, the Singapore Government authorised the building of a Mass Rapid Transit system. The $5 billion project comprised 67 km of rail with 42 stations. Twenty-seven of these stations were above ground and 15 under ground. The North-South line was implemented first as it was used to carry people across town to the Central business District. In 1988, the Mass Rapid Transit Corporation was established. The **first section** to be completed was the section from Yio Chu Kang to Toa Payoh in November 1987, The project was opened in stages. Prime Minister Lee Kuan Yew launched the network on 12 March 1988. The final section was completed in July 1990, 2 years ahead of schedule.

Municipal Commissioner, Chinese

Tan Seng Poh, 1870. The first Chinese to be appointed to the Municipal Commission was Tan Seng Poh. He was appointed in 1870 and served three consecutive terms of 3 years each. Tan was born in Perak in 1830 and accompanied his sister to Singapore when he was 9 years old. His sister married Seah Eu Chin, the Teochew tycoon and Tan was educated in Singapore. Later, he headed a Teochew syndicate that gained control of the Singapore Opium Farm. When Seah retired in 1864, Tan carried on the Seah family business together with Seah's two sons, Liang Seah and Peck Seah. This gave him control over vast gambier and pepper estates. Historian Carl Trocki estimated that these estates provided employment for 100,000 people. Between 1870 and 1879, Tan Seng Poh, together with Cheang Hong Lim and Tan Hiok Nee formed the Great Syndicate that controlled the Singapore, Johor, Malacca and Riau opium and spirit farms. He was made Justice of the Peace in 1871, and died in 1879.

Museum

Singapore Library Museum 1849. In August 1844, a meeting was held to establish a

Singapore Library. At a meeting of the Library in January 1849, it was decided to form a museum with a view to collecting objects of historical and archaeological value. This first museum was called the Singapore Library Museum and was situated together with the Library inside Raffles Institution. The Temenggong of Johor presented the museum with two gold coins. In 1862, both the library and museum were moved to the newly-built Town Hall (now Victoria Concert Hall). In 1874, the museum and library were taken over by the Government and renamed the Raffles Library and Museum. The collection was moved to the first purpose-built Museum at the junction of Stamford Road and Orchard Road on 12 October 1887. At that time, the museum collections had a strong interest in natural history and its collections included zoology, botany, geology, and ethnology specimens predominantly from the Malay region. The zoological specimens included a whale skeleton, a Malayan Sun Bear, a huge Seladang (buffalo), a giant crocodile (shot by GP Owen) and a Siberian tiger. The archaeological specimens included artifacts and primitive tools. The centerpiece of the ethnological collection was a painting of Sir Frank Swettenham by John Singer Sargent.

The Raffles Museum became a key research institution. During the Japanese Occupation, the collection was supervised by Professor Hidezo Tanakadate who maintained good relations with British scientists who had been working at the Museum before the Occupation. It was renamed Syonan Hakabutsu Kan. William Birthwhistle managed to protect many of the important exhibits, including Raffles' letters. In 1965, the Museum took on a new identity and role. It was renamed the National Museum in 1969 and the shift in focus and exhibits caused the zoological specimens to be removed and redistributed to a variety of institutions include the Singapore Science Centre, the Muzium Negara in Kuala Lumpur and the Zoology Department of the National University of Singapore. The last collection is now known as the Raffles Museum of Biodiversity.

In 1993, the Museum came under the control of the National Heritage Board and was renamed the Singapore History Museum. In 2006, the Museum, which was temporarily housed at River Point, returned to its Stamford Road premises and was renamed the National Museum of Singapore (namos)

The **first private museum** was opened by lawyer Woon Wee Teng in January 2005. Located at 235 Cantonment Road, the 47-year old lawyer houses his collection of Buddhist relics. His thousands of Buddha figurines, statues, paintings and other Buddhist relics are housed in the three-storey house. Singapore's **first toy museum** is the MINT Museum of Toys opened by toy collector, Chang Yang Fa. Located in a five-storey shophouse at 26 Seah Street, MINT stands for 'Moment of Imagination and Nostalgia with Toys'. Chang, who collected the 50,000 toys over the past 25 years, values the collection at over S$5 million.

Music Conservatory

Singapore Conservatory of Music, 2001. The signing of an agreement between the National University of Singapore (NUS) and the Peabody Institute of the Johns Hopkins University on 26 November 2001 led to the establishment of Singapore's first conservatory of music at NUS, the Singapore Conservatory of Music. In August 2003, the Conservatory was renamed Yong Siew Toh Conservatory of Music in honour of Yong Siew Toh, a music teacher whose family donated S$25 million through the Yong Loo Lin Trust to the Conservatory. The Yong family believed that this gift is a fitting contribution to honour her life and her dedication to music. The Yong Siew Toh Conservatory of Music offers a 4-year undergraduate music degree programme in collaboration with the Peabody Institute, one of the world's leading music schools. The Conservatory provides aspiring professional musicians with the musical skills and perceptions necessary to sustain careers in music, whether as solo or ensemble performers, composers, teachers, recording engineers, critics or scholars.

Music Performance, Public

1831. The first public entertainment was given in 1831 by Signor Masoni, a violinist. Unfortunately no records exist of this recital.

Musical, Local Flavoured

The Samseng and the Chettiar's Daughter, 1982. The first musical with a local flavour was *The Samseng and the Chettiars' Daughter* directed by Australian director John Tasker and based on Kurt Weill's *The Threepenny Opera*. The production brought together many well-known names in Singapore theatre. The **first locally-produced musical to become an international hit** was Chang & Eng. Based on the true story of the 'original' Siamese twins, Chang and Eng Bunker, it was produced and directed by Ekechai Uekrongtham and debuted at the 1997 Festival of Asian Performing Arts.

Musical recital
See **Concert**.

Musical Society

Amateur Musical Society, 1865. The first local musical society formed among the English community in 1865 was the Amateur Musical Society. The leader was the organist of St. Andrew's Cathedral, Mr Fenton. Their first concert was held on 28 December 1865 in the Upper room of the Town Hall (now Victoria Concert Hall). Music was provided by an orchestra made up of members of the society. Admission was $2 and tickets were available from John Little & Co. The members of the society had problems finding a piano of concert quality but were eventually lent a good piano. Proceeds from the first concert went towards buying a first rate piano from England. The concert consisted of a wide variety of choral and instrumental pieces including the *Overture to the Caliph of Baghdad*, Haydn's 1st Quintet and Locke's *Music for Macbeth*. Thomas Crane (see first Auctioneer) and his son Charles sang a duet 'Larboard Watch' and lawyer Charles Burton Buckley sang 'The Village Blacksmith'. *The Straits Times* wrote that the concert was a success from start to finish.

N

National Anthem

Majullah Singapura, 1959. The National Anthem 'Majulah Singapura' was sung for the first time on 3rd December 1959. On 30 November 1959, the Singapore State Arms, Flag and National Anthem Ordinance was passed. The Singapore National Arms, Flag and Anthem were presented to the nation on 3 December 1959 as part of Loyalty Week when the new Head of State, Yusof bin Ishak was installed during a ceremony on the steps of City Hall. The anthem 'Majulah Singapura' means Onward Singapore. It was written by Encik Zubir Said. It was originally written to commemorate the City Council and was first performed by the Singapore Chamber Ensemble during the opening ceremony of the newly renovated Victoria Theatre on 6 September 1958.

The words *Majulah Singapura* were displayed on a banner in the renovated Victoria Theatre and the song was based on that. The song proved to be popular and with some revisions, it was accepted as the National Anthem. In May 2000, the Anthem was re-arranged by Phoon Yew Tien. He transposed it into the key of F, used a slower tempo and scored it for more instruments. The new version was played and recorded for the first time by the Singapore Symphony Orchestra conducted by Lim Yau on the 20 November 2000. Zubir Said was born in Minangkabau in Central Sumatra in 1907, and had a prolific career writing film music as well as festive and patriotic songs. He was 51 when he composed 'Majulah Singapura'. He was conferred with the *Sijil Kemuliann* or Certificate of Honour by the Singapore Government in 1963. He died in Singapore on 16 November 1987 at the age of 80.

National Day Parade

9 August 1966. The first National Day Parade was held on the Padang on 9 August 1966 to commemorate the first anniversary of Independent Singapore. At 9.00 am on 9 August 1966, President Yusoff bin Ishak arrived at the steps of City Hall to mark the beginning of the first National Day Parade. The President was met by Defence Minister and Colonel of the Artillery, Dr Goh Keng Swee. Prime Minister Lee Kuan Yew and many of his Cabinet colleagues were present. The President reviewed the parade as a 21-gun salute sounded from the grounds of nearby Raffles Institution. On the Padang was the honour guard of the Infantry Regiment, Local Defence units, police units, cadets and a number of cultural troupes. The marchpast took 90 minutes and consisted of 23,000 men and women and children. Many of the Cabinet members and Members of Parliament wore military uniforms and joined in the parade. Ong Pang Boon (Minister for Education) and Jek Yeun Thong (Minister for Culture) wore officer cadet uniforms of the People's Defence Force. The members of the parade marched behind the men of the newly formed Singapore Armed Forces Training Institute and the Gurkha Police. Also in the parade were the Girls' Life Brigade Band and the drill team of Raffles Institution. There was a huge lion dance on the Padang with 60 lions and dragons. The parade marched on to Tanjong Pagar through Chinatown. It was the first military parade ever held in Chinatown and huge crowds lined the route and the streets and houses were decorated with flags. The parade was televised to enable many more people to watch.

National Day Rally, Live Broadcast

National Theatre, 1971. The first National Day Rally to be broadcast live on television was the Rally on 15 August 1971. Prime Minister Lee Kuan Yew addressed an audience of 3,500 at the National Theatre at the National Day Concert and Rally.

National Flag

See **Flag**

National Monument

See **Monument**

National Reserve, Wetlands

Sungei Buloh Nature Park, 2001. On 10 November 2001, Minister of National Development Mah Bow Tan announced the designation of Sungei Buloh Nature Park as a nature reserve under the National Parks Act. Officially opened on 6 December 1993, this 87-hectare of mangrove, fresh water ponds and secondary forest was designated a forest reserve from as early as 17 April 1890. The fresh water and secondary forest habitats may have been subsequently introduced by early settlers in the Sungei Buloh (meaning 'Bamboo River' in the Malay language) area since the Straits Settlement Government Gazette Reports of the Botanic Gardens described the area to consist entirely of mangrove swamp in 1890. To mark its new status as Singapore's first wetland nature reserve, Sungei Buloh Nature Park was re-named Sungei Buloh Wetland Reserve.

National Service (Part-time)

1954. In 1952, the Colonial Government enacted a National Service Bill to introduce limited part time service in the Singapore Military Forces for British citizens and citizens of the Federation of Malaya. The government defended the Bill by stating that 'self defence is one of the major tasks and responsibilities of self-government'. There was little trouble with registration and about 98% of the eligible students registered. Registration began on 5 April 1954 at the Singapore Volunteer Corps (SVC) Headquarters in Beach Road. On 1 July 1954, the first batch of recruits reported to the SVC Headquarters to be kitted out. Recruits were to attend training classes two evenings per week to be trained in the use of the rifle, the Bren gun and other military subjects. However, continuing boycotts at the Chinese High School and Chung Cheng High School forced the government to end this first attempt at National Service and it was not re-introduced until 1967.

National Service (Full-time)

1967. The National Service (Amendment) Bill was passed on 14 March 1967. The Bill introduced compulsory National Service for males born between 1 January 1949 and 30 June 1949. Registration began on 28 March 1967 at the Central Manpower Base at the Old Kallang Airport. About 9000 youths were called up. Due to limited facilities and trainers, only 10% of those called up were admitted to 2 years fulltime service, followed by ten years of reserve service. The remaining 90% would serve part time in the People's Defence Force, the Special Constabulary or the Vigilante Corps. There was an active response to the introduction of the Bill, and anti-NS marches took place at New Bridge Road, Rochore Canal Road and Kim Keat Road. Tear gas shells were used to disperse the crowd and 13 people arrested. This did not deter the government, and the **first two National Service battalions** were formed on 1 April 1967 at Taman Jurong Camp. They were the Third and Fourth Battalion of the Singapore Infantry Regiment 3. The batch reported for duty on 17 August 1967 and formal training began on 11 September. The first National Service enlistees were given a National Service Medallion at a special dinner, and they were presented with medallions by the Chinese Chamber of Commerce.

Natural History Society

Singapore Natural History Society, 1921. On 30 May 1921, a meeting was called at the Board Room of the Straits Trading Company, of all residents interested in forming a Naturalists' Society. Under the chairmanship of Dr Gilbert Brooke, those present agreed to form the Singapore Natural History Society with FN Chasen from the Raffles Museum as Honorary Secretary. Its first President was Major JC Moutlon, also from the Raffles Museum. Brooke, the Straits Settlements Chief Health Officer was its Vice-President. The Patron of the Society was Governor Sir Laurence Guillemard. The two main objectives of the Society were to develop a friendly intercourse between local naturalists and to increase and disseminate knowledge concerning natural history by means of papers, discussions, field excursions, formation of collections and publication of transactions. The inaugural meeting of the Society was held on 8 August 1921 at Raffles Museum. Ian Burkill, Director of the Botanic Gardens presented a paper entitled 'The Present State of Our Knowledge of the Vegetation of Malaya'. The society's first excursion was to Bukit Timah on 31 August 1921. The highlight of the day was the live capture of a Black Cobra at Watten Estate. The snake was afterwards sent to the London Zoo; it arrived safely. The **first copy of the journal** of the Society, *The Singapore Naturalist*, was published in July 1922 by the Methodist Publishing House. The journal contained a range of papers and the publication of transactions as well as the reports of all meetings of the society. At the first Annual General Meeting held in February 1922, it was announced that membership was close to 80. The **first paper presented by a woman** was 'Some Native Superstitions' presented by Mrs EF Howell and read to the Society in August 1923.

Naturalised Chinese

Seah Eu Chin, 1853. In 1853, Seah Eu Chin became the first Chinese to be granted a certificate of naturalisation under the Indian Act XXX of 1852. Governor Blundell sent a message concerning 'the satisfaction it has afforded him to enrol the name of so talented and so respectable a Chinese resident'. Seah was born in 1805 in Swatow, China. He came to Singapore in 1823 and worked his passage to Singapore by acting as a clerk on board a Chinese junk. On his arrival in Singapore, he became a commission agent, first in Kling Street (now Chulia Street) and later in Circular Road, supplying junks trading between Singapore and the regional ports. His business was successful and he invested widely in property. He was the first to start pepper and gambier planting on a large scale and he was also a trader in cotton goods and tea. In 1840, Seah became a member of the Singapore Chamber of Commerce and wrote a series of articles in the *Journal of the Indian Archipelago* on 'The Chinese in Singapore' He was one of the first Chinese to be made a Justice of the Peace and was often asked to sit on the Grand Jury. He retired from business in 1864 at the age of 60 and spent the rest of his life cultivating his interest in Chinese literature. He died in 1883, leaving four sons and three daughters.

Naval Reserve

Straits Settlements Royal Naval Volunteer Reserve, 1934. In 1934, the first Naval Volunteer Force was set up in Singapore. It was called the Straits Settlements Royal Naval Volunteer Reserve (SSRNVR). In 1963, the Volunteer force was handed over to Malaysia and became the Singapore Division of the Malaysian Royal Navy Volunteer reserve. After independence in 1965, the force became the Singapore Naval Volunteer force. It was often referred to as 'Dad's little navy'. This formed the basis for what was to become the Republic of Singapore Navy.

Navy, Republic of Singapore

Sea Defence Command, 1967. When Singapore became independent in 1965, the Naval Reserve took over the existing ships and this formed the basis for Singapore's navy. The Naval Reserve consisted of volunteers and three small ships, the *Republic of Singapore Ship (RSS) Laburnum*, later renamed *Singapura*, the *RSS Panglima* and the *RSS Bedok*. They were berthed at the Telok Ayer basin. The *RSS Panglima* and *Bedok* continued to patrol Singapore waters guarding the waves of the new nation. The navy was officially inaugurated in May 1967 and became the Sea Defence Command. The base was moved from Telok Ayer Basin to some old British Army buildings on Blakang Mati. There were no berths for the ships and they had to anchor offshore or tie-up on moorings. In 1968, the Sea Defence Command became the Maritime Command. In 1974 the base was shifted to a 220 acre site on Pulau Brani in Keppel Harbour. In November 1969, the School of Maritime Training opened and the first batch of 'regulars' passed out of the base at Blakang Mati. In January 1969 the first batch of four naval cadets were sent to Auckland Naval Base for midshipman training. They were Fernando Allen, Lim Khoon Bock, Lim Eng Lian and John Ng Teck Song. In June 1968, the first 6 patrol boats were ordered by the Sea Defence Command. They were 33 metres long and were 150 tons each and powered by two 2,750 hp engines capable of 31 knots continuous speed. They were built by the Vosper Thorneycroft Group. Two were built in the United Kingdom and 4 were built in Singapore. Their 40mm Bofors and 20mm Oerlikon guns were a considerable increase in firepower. The first patrol boat to be completed was the *RSS Independence*. On 1 April 1975, Maritime Command became the Republic of Singapore Navy.

NETS

1986. NETS, the nation-wide cashless shopping and payment project was launched on 18 January 1986. The project is run by Network for Electronic Transfers (NETS) Pte Ltd.

News Broadcast

The first **radio news** was broadcast on 1 March 1937 following the inauguration of the radio station by the Governor Sir Shenton Thomas. The **first news broadcast on television** was made at the inauguration of a pilot monochrome television service on 15 February 1964. The 'News in English' was accompanied by a 5-minute newsreel.

Newspapers

Singapore Chronicle, 1824. The *Singapore Chronicle* (later *Singapore Chronicle and Commercial Register*) was the first newspaper published in Singapore. Established in 1824, by the former Master Attendant, Frederick James Bernard, it closed down in 1837. The first issue of The Singapore Chronicle was published on 1 January 1824. The first issue of the second newspaper, the *Singapore Free Press*, founded by William Napier, appeared in October 1835. Singapore's **first Chinese monthly magazine** was *Tung Hsi Yang K'ao* (literally, Inquiry of the Eastern and Western Oceans) published by Karl Guzlaff for the society for the Diffusion of Useful Knowledge in 1837. The magazine was filled with news and illustrations as well as literary compositions such as 'An Ode to London'. The monthly ceased publication on the eve of the Anglo-Chinese War (1840). The closure of this magazine signalled the end of the first phase of the history of Chinese periodicals in Singapore. The early periodicals such as this were printed by European missionaries. The emphasis was on preaching Christianity rather than news reporting. When China was thrown open to foreigners after 1842, the missionaries and their presses returned to China.

The **first Chinese daily newspaper**, *Lat Pau*, was published on 9 February 1881. The name was taken from the Hokkien and Cantonese names for Singapore. It was started by See Ewe Lay who came from a well-established Straits Chinese family in Malacca. His grandfather came to Singapore from Malacca in 1828, and See himself was a comprador of the Hongkong and Shanghai Bank when he started the newspaper. He engaged Yeh Chi-yun, a reporter based in Hongkong as his first writer. Yeh wrote the leading articles and selected and edited the news for the paper. The first issues are no longer available and the oldest copy available is dated 19 August 1887, serial number 1724. The paper consisted of a single sheet printed on both sides and was folded and cut to form 8 pages. The paper went into liquidation in 1923 amidst the Great Depression. *Jawi Peranakan* was the **first Malay weekly newspaper** published in Singapore, in 1876, with an initial circulation of 250 copies. Its first editor was Munshi Mohd Said bin Dada Mohyddin who died in 1888. The first issue of a second Malay newspaper, *Sekola Melayu*, was published on 1 August 1888. Singapore's **first free commuter newspaper** was *Streats*, which hit the newsstands on 3 September 2000.

Night Club

See **Cabaret.**

Nominated MPs

Unofficial Members of the Legislative Council, 1867. During the colonial period, the Governor would nominate members of the public as Unofficial members of the Straits Settlements Legislative Council. In 1867, provision was made for three Unofficial Members. The first nominated European Unofficial was William Henry Read. He had come to

Singapore in 1841 to take over his father's place in the firm of AL Johnston & Company. Read had a long history of public service and was a member of a number of clubs. He was a Senior Lieutenant in the Singapore Volunteer Corps in 1959 and later became Commandant. Among other things, Read was also: Treasurer of the Singapore Library and original shareholder; commodore of the Singapore Yacht Club (1867); and Patron of the Singapore Recreation club. He wrote many letters to the newspapers under the pen-name of Delta, on a variety of issues. He was the first Chairman of the Singapore Branch of the Straits Settlements Association. In 1887, Read left Singapore and wrote a memoir entitled *Play and Politics: Recollections of Malaya by an Old Resident*. He claimed that when he died, others would find 'Singapore' engraved on his heart. A tablet in St Andrew's Cathedral in Singapore commemorates his life and work.

The first Chinese Unofficial nominated to the Legislative Council was Whampoa Hoo Ah Kay. He was appointed in 1869. For more on Whampoa's life, see EXECUTIVE COUNCIL. The **first woman** nominated was Mrs Elizabeth Choy (b. 1915) in 1951. She was born in North Borneo and came to Singapore to study for her Cambridge School Certificate at the Convent of the Holy Infant Jesus. She became a teacher and taught at St Margaret's School and at St Andrew's School. In 1956, she became the first principal of the School for the Blind and remained there till 1960 when she returned to St Andrew's School to teach. She retired in 1974. She married Choy Khun Keng in August 1941 and when the Japanese bombed Singapore, she joined the Medical Auxiliary Services as a volunteer nurse. In October 1943, the Japanese arrested the Choys for smuggling radio parts to the camp in Changi. They were taken to the Kempetai headquarters at the YMCA and tortured. Elizabeth Choy was detained for 193 days while her husband remained a prisoner for 2 years. In 1950, she stood as an independent candidate for Cairnhill constituency in the City Council elections. The British were impressed by her sincerity and fluency in English and nominated her to the Legislative Council in 1951. She stood as a Progressive Party candidate in the 1955 general elections but lost to Lee Choon Eng of the Labour Front.

In 1990, the Singapore government introduced a Nominated Member of Parliament scheme that allowed for six people to be nominated to Parliament. The first NMPs were businessman Leong Chee Whye and cardiologist, Associate Professor Maurice Choo Hock Heng. Their term of office commenced on 22 November 1990.

NTUC FairPrice Supermarket

NTUC Welcome, Toa Payoh, 1973. NTUC FairPrice was born on 1 May 1983. Before that, there were two labour organisation-operated supermarkets: NTUC Welcome and Silo. In July 1973, NTUC Welcome opened its first outlet at Lorong 4 Toa Payoh. When the supermarket opened, Singapore was facing double-digit inflation and food shortage. To prevent profiteering, the Government gave $250,000 to former Welcome chairman Dr Baey Lian Peck to set up a cooperative to beat the profiteers and bring down inflation. In 2005, it had over 70 outlets and is Singapore's biggest supermarket chain.

Nurses

Mrs Ward, 1867. In 1867 the first nurse, Mrs Ward was employed by the Lunatic Asylum.

She was the first female employee of the Medical department. She worked both at the Asylum and at the adjoining General Hospital. The only other attendants at the Asylum were 2 male convicts. In 1885, nuns from the French Convent commenced duty as nurses in the General Hospital. A Hospital Report in 1889 commented on the care shown by the Sisters of Mercy working at the hospital even though they were not trained. The **first trained midwife** was Mrs Woldstein who was employed in 1888, by the Maternity Hospital in Victoria Street. By 1898, there was written evidence that 8 or 10 midwives with 'trustworthy credentials' were working at the Maternity Hospital. Other midwives had been granted certificates of proficiency after some training at the Maternity Hospital.

The Colonial Nursing Association was formed in England in July 1896 to provide for the nursing needs of the colonies. This provided an impetus for discussions on nursing training in Singapore. In 1899, a committee was established to raise money to bring nurses out from England. This committee eventually became the Singapore Nursing Association responsible for bringing out trained nurses from England. The moneys raised were invested and the interest used to pay for nurses to be sent out from England by the Colonial Nursing Association. In 1900, these nurses replaced the nuns from the Convent. In November 1900, it was recorded that the nursing staff at the General Hospital consisted of 1 head nurse, 7 sisters, and 5 probationary nurses.

Nursing Training

1922. The Medical Report for 1883 provided the first debate on nursing training. It stated that 'the absence of proper nursing is a great evil'. In August 1885, nuns from the French Convent commenced duty as nurses at the General Hospital. A report of the Hospital in 1889 commented on the care shown by the Sisters of Mercy working at the hospital even though they were not trained. Dr Hoad, the Resident Surgeon mentions in 1893, the need for nurses to have a Certificate of Hospital Training from a French or English hospital. The first probationer Nurse was recruited by the General Hospital in 1889 but no details of her training are available.

In the case of midwives, some sort of limited training was available at the Maternity Hospital by 1898. Midwife training advanced more quickly and midwives had been granted certificates of proficiency after some training at the Maternity Hospital. In 1895, there is mention of a Mrs Ganno, who entered the Maternity Hospital as a 'pupil sick nurse' and midwife. She was recorded as passing a creditable examination before a Board of Medical Officers at the end of 1897. At first, only married women were taken for midwifery training. The first mention of single women undergoing training was in 1902. Registration of midwives began in 1896. In 1910, Mrs Blundell, a Municipal nurse was appointed to investigate conditions for mothers and infants in Singapore. As a result of her investigation, a joint venture between the Government and the Municipal Council was established for the **first regular training for Asian midwives** in 1910. Mrs Lee Choon Guan donated money for scholarships for the training of local midwives. A Midwives Ordinance was passed in 1915 and four levels of midwifery were recognised. Regular training began at the Maternity Hospital.

In 1899, a committee was set up to raise money to bring nurses from England. The first six trained nurses were sent out from England by the Colonial Nursing Association in 1900. these sisters were able to organise an on-the-job training course for nurses. In November 1900, it was recorded that the nursing staff at the General Hospital included one 3rd year, one 2nd year, and three 1st year probabtionary nurses. By 1921, there were 36 nursing probationers. In 1922, a four-year training course was introduced. The **first local health nurse** was Mrs ME Pereira. In 1916, nursing training for local Asian girls commenced at the St Andrew's Mission Hospital under the guidance of Mrs Ferguson-Davie, wife of the Anglican Bishop of Singapore. It was for two years and was similar to the course at the General Hospital. In 1949, the St Andrew's Mission Hospital introduced training for a 3-year Certificate for the Nursing of Sick Children.

1. Tomb of George Dromgold Coleman, Singapore's first architect. **2.** The renovated Raffles Hotel, one of the winners of the first URA Architectural Heritage Awards (1994).

3. Go Boon Kwan, founder of Ho Ho Biscuit Company (1898), Singapore's first biscuit factory. **4.** The gate to Fort Canning Cemetery, designed by GD Coleman, today. **5.** Fort Canning Cemetery, Singapore's first burial ground, circa 1907.

6. Cavanagh Bridge, Singapore's first steel suspended bridge (built in 1869).

7. Alexander Laurie Johnston, first President of the Singapore Chamber of Commerce (1837).

8. Benjamin Henry Sheares Bridge, Singapore's first viaduct and first bridge to be named after a former President of the Republic.

9. The Singapore-Johor Causeway, Singapore's first land bridge. It was built in 1924.
10. Stamford Canal where the first Indian temple was reputedly built.

11. & 12. The Esplanade-Theatres on the Bay, Singapore's first purpose-built concert hall and performance complex. The Concert Hall was inaugurated in 2002. Singaporeans affectionately refer to the spiked domes as 'The Durians'.

17. Convent of the Holy Infant Jesus, Singapore's first convent school, founded in 1852. It is now CHIJMES, a lifestyle and dining hub.

13. Armenian Church, Singapore's first Armenian Church was completed in 1835 and is Singapore's oldest surviving church.

14. Old Portuguese Church of St Joseph's in Victoria Street. The original church was completed in 1825 but completely rebuilt in 1906 and then again in 1912.

15. Cathedral of the Good Shepherd, consecrated in 1846. Its predecessor church, the first Roman Catholic church in Singapore was in 1833 just opposite its current location.

16. St Andrew's Cathedral. The present building was completed in 1861. Its predecessor, St Andrew's Church was Singapore's first Protestant church. It was built in 1837 but was torn down in 1852 after being struck by lightning.

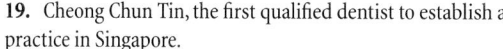

18. Dr Robert Little, Singapore's first coroner and one of the the first Nominated Unofficials.

19. Cheong Chun Tin, the first qualified dentist to establish a practice in Singapore.

20. Dr WRD Middleton, Singapore's first Municipal Health Officer. He gave the first demonstration of an X-Ray machine in 1898.

21. Dr Lee Choo Neo, Singapore's first woman doctor. She graduated from the King Edward VII Medical College in 1919.

22. & 23. The King Edward VII Medical College, Singapore's first medical school. Today the building is known as the College of Medicine Building and is a National Monument. Pictures taken in the 1930s.

24. & 25. Tiong Bahru, Singapore's first public housing estate and 'satellite town' built by the Singapore Improvement Trust in 1936. It is now a conserved area.

26. Thong Chai Medical Institute, the first free clinic in Singapore. It was founded in 1867.

27. Tan Kim Seng Fountain, the first public fountain.

28. Tan Kim Seng, philanthropist and organiser of Singapore's first Chinese Ball in 1852.

29

30

29. The Pavilion at the Singapore Cricket Club. It was recorded that cricket was first played on the Padang in 1837. The Cricket Club was established in 1852 and its first pavilion was a small wooden one. It was demolished and rebuilt several times. This picture depicts the second pavilion to be built.

30. The Old Race Course at what is now Farrer Park. This racecourse was the site of several firsts. It became Singapore's first horse-racing ground in 1886 and remained there till it moved to the Bukit Race Course in 1933. In 1891, it was also the site of the first golf course.

31. Caricature of Justice Sir John Tankerville Goldney, first President of the Singapore Golf Club, Singapore's first. The Club was established in June 1891.

32. The Old Golf House at Buffalo Road. This was the Club House of Singapore's first multiracial golf club, the Race Course Golf Club, formed in October 1924.

33. Singapore's first commercial digital radio service, SMART Radio, was launched on 19 November 1999. This made Singapore the first country in Southeast Asia to provide commercial digital radio services.

34. Tombstone of Stephen Hallpike. In 1831, he and his wife started Singapore's first boarding house in High Street.

35. Members of Singapore's first literary society, the Chinese Philomathic Society. It was founded in 1896 by Dr Lim Boon Keng.

36. The Botanic Gardens' first Director, Henry Nicholas Ridley, who arrived in Singapore in 1888 to take charge of the Botanic Gardens. His strong advocacy and promotion of rubber cultivation led some to call him 'Mad Ridley'.

37. Dr Nathaniel Wallich of the Royal Gardens in Calcutta. Wallich was a good friend of Raffles and the allter was greatly influenced by him to establish a botanic garden in Singapore. The very first botanic garden was a 19-hectare site bordered by Hill Street and Canning Rise. Raffles donated $1,000 towards the upkeep of the gardens

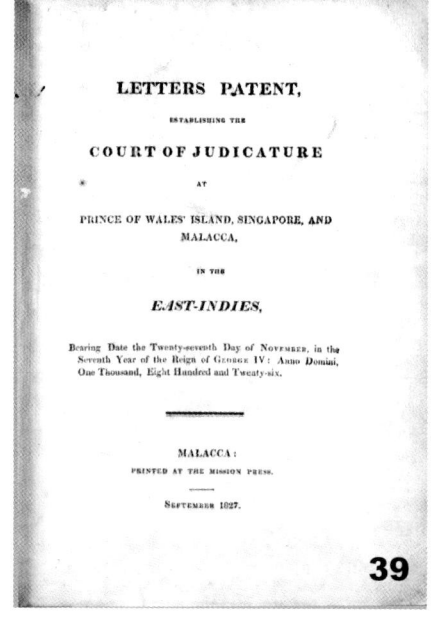

38. Sir Peter Benson Maxwell, first Chief Justice of the Straits Settlements.

39. First page of the Second Charter of Justice establishing Singapore's first court, the Court of Judicature of Prince of Wales' Island, Singapore and Malacca.

40. Sir Song Ong Siang, Singapore's first local-born lawyer.

41. Sir Thomas Braddell, Singapore's first Attorney-General.

42. The Masonic Lodge on Coleman Street. The original Masonic Hall was established in 1856 at the Esplanade. This hall was completed in 1879.

43. The Old Parliament House was Singapore's first court house.

44. William Henry Read, Singapore's first nominated European Unofficial (1867).

45. A view of one of Singapore's first markets, the Telok Ayer Market (highlighted). The original wooden building (1824) was replaced in 1834 by this octagonal building of brick designed by GD Coleman.

46. The present-day Telok Ayer Market designed by James MacRitchie, and completed in 1894. It replaced Coleman's market which had to be torn down due to land reclamation works.

47. The interior of today's Telok Ayer Market.

48. Ellenborough Market (on stilts), possibly Singapore's second market.

49. Whampoa's Ice House at Clarke Quay. This is a reconstruction of the 1854 original which was pulled down in the 1960s.

50. Whampoa Hoo Ah Kay, Singapore's first Chinese Unofficial member of the Legislative Council.

51. Dalhousie's Obelisk, Singapore's first gazetted National Monument. The obelisk was built in 1850 to commemorate the landing in Singapore of the Marquis James Dalhousie, Governor-General of India. It was gazetted in 1971.

52. The Raffles Library and Museum on Stamford Road. This was Singapore's first purpose-built museum and it was completed in October 1887. The first museum was established January 1849 and was part of the Singapore Library (established in 1844). The collections were originally housed at the old Raffles Institution in Bras Basah Road.

53. Sungei Buloh Wetland Reserve, Singapore's first wetland park. It was opened in 2001.

52

53

54. St James Power Station, Singapore's first municipal power station. It was built in 1927.
55. St James Power Station, view of the engine room.

56. Capitol Building, formerly known as the Namazie Building, was built in 1922. In 1969, the first ice-cream parlour, the Magnolia Milk Bar opened on its ground floor.

57. Flint Building, formerly occupied by Emmerson's Tiffin Room, established by Charles Emmerson, Singapore's first veterinary surgeon.

58. Criminal Investigation Department (CID) Headquarters in Robinson Road. In 1884, the first detective branch of the Singapore Police Force was established. This eventually became the CID.

59. Singapore's first group of Queen's Scholars 1886-1887.

60. Thomas Dunman, Singapore's first Commissioner for Police.

61. Early picture of the Singapore Chinese Girls' School, Singapore's first English-medium school for girls (1899).

62. The Fu Tak Chi Temple on Telok Ayer Street, reputedly Singapore's first Chinese temple. It was established in 1820 and its original wooden building was replaced by this building in 1824.

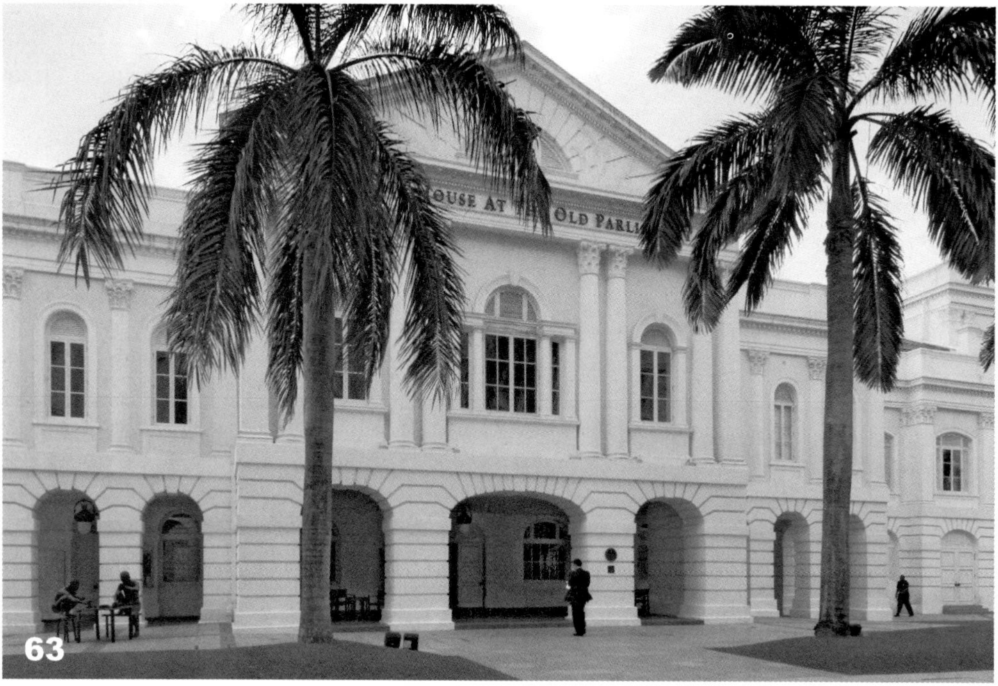

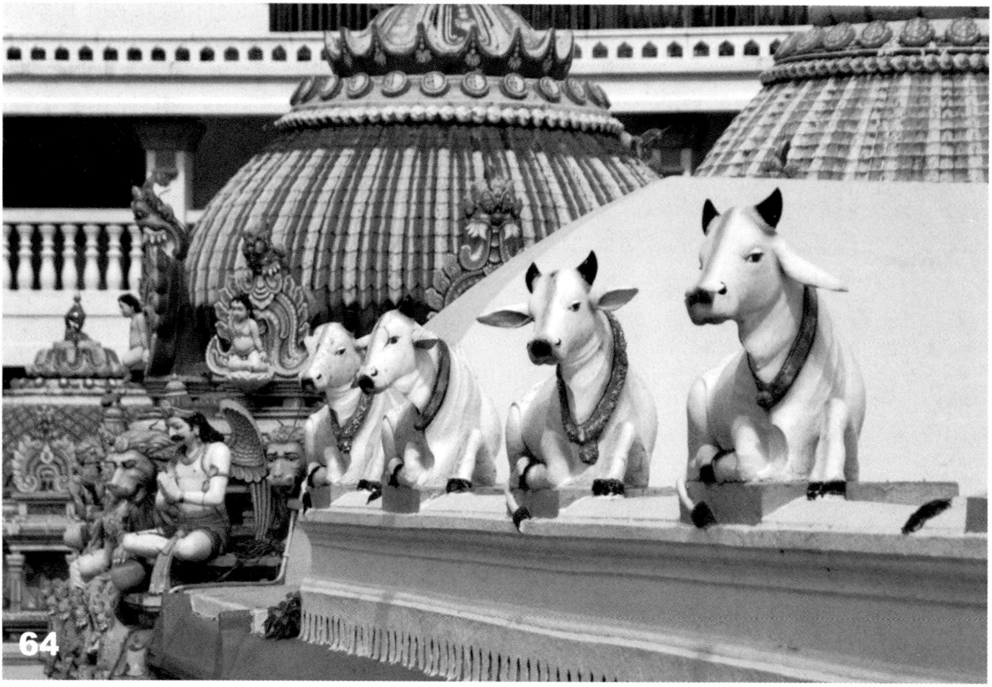

63. The Old Parliament House, now the Arts House was Singapore's first Legislative Assembly building.

64. & 65. The Sri Mariamamam Temple, Singapore's first.

66. The first rickshaws were introduced in Singapore in 1880.

67. The first 'auto-car' was imported into Singapore in 1896 and belonged to well-known local lawyer, Charles Burton Buckley who referred to the car as his 'coffee machine'

68. Singapore's first car repair facility, established by two Australian brothers, CFF and TJB Wearne in 1906 in Orchard Road.

69. Singapore's first auto club, the Singapore Automobile Club met for the first time in 1907 outside the Singapore Club in Fullerton Square. Members of the club are seen here on an outing at Tyersall, the estate belonging to the Sultan of Johore.

The Singapore Traction Co., Ltd.

The first Company to operate passenger vehicles in Singapore began business in 1886.

Trolley-Bus.

In 1905 Singapore Tramways laid down Tramways, the motive power of which was electrical energy.

In 1926 The Singapore Traction Company began dismantling the old Tramway plant and in 1928 had replaced it with a fleet of Trolley Buses.

Singapore has now the largest *Single Unit* Electric Trolley Bus Passenger Service in the World, covering approximately 25 miles of route and owning A FLEET OF 108 TROLLEY BUSES.

These serve a population of nearly half a million with modern, safe and comfortable services. This service carries nearly 40 million passengers a year at relatively low fares.

The Company has planned its Scheme of operation not only to meet immediate needs but has left scope for development for which it has ample financial resources.

In addition to the Trolley Bus Service, the Company operates an efficient Service of Omnibuses which travel as far afield as the Naval Base on the North Side of the Island.

Omnibus.

70. Advertisement of the Singapore's first bus company, the Singapore Traction Company (1925) depicting a trolley bus and an omnibus. The first trolley buses were introduced in 1927.

71

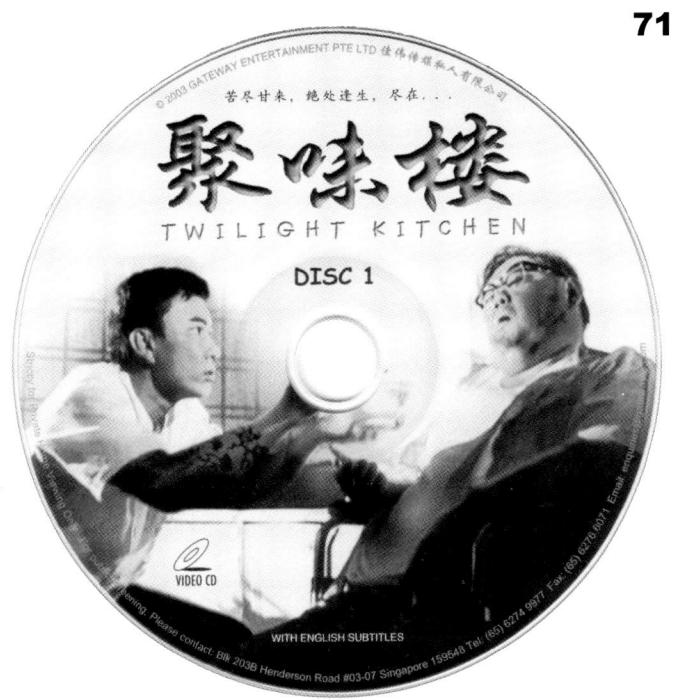

71. *Twilight Kitchen* was Singapore's first community film (2003). It starred Moses Lim and Zhang Wenxiang

72. Dr Lim Boon Keng, also known as the 'Sage of Singapore' was the first person in Singapore to cultivate rubber.

73. Early rubber plantation in Singapore.

72

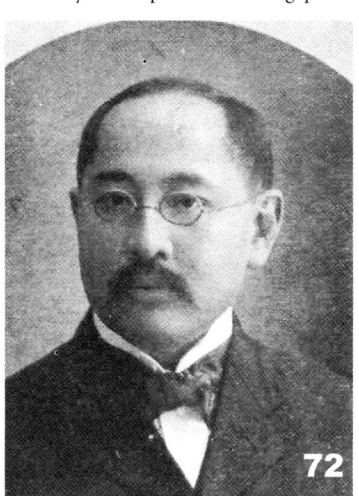

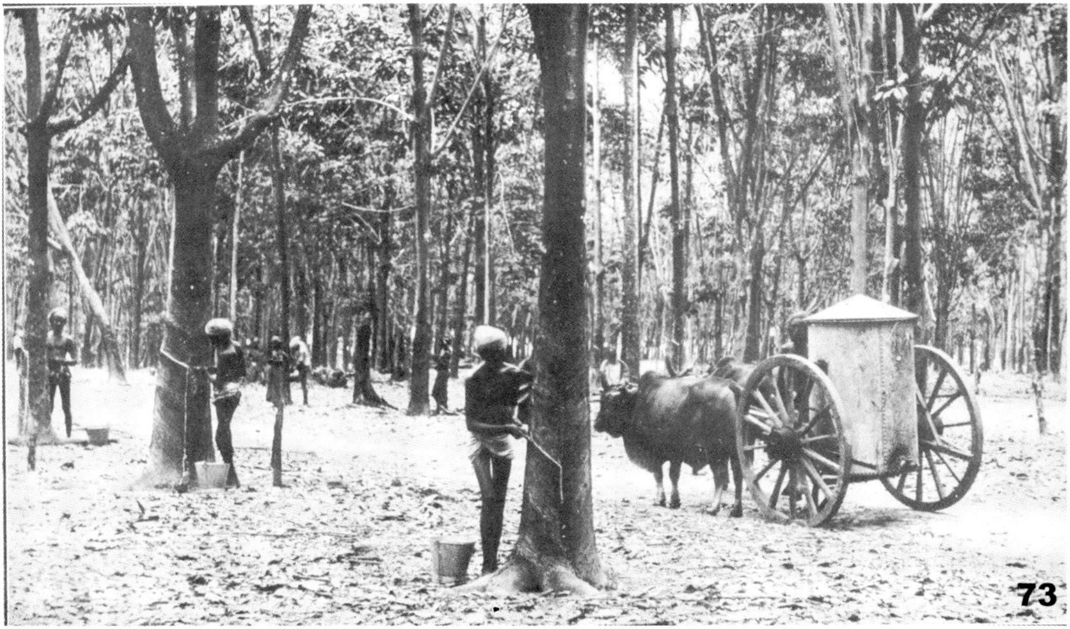

73

74. The Prinsep Street Presbyterian Church, originally known as the Malay Chapel was Singapore's first Presbyterian church. It was founded in 1842. In 1930, Singapore's first Boys' Brigade Company was established here.

75. Early scouts of Singapore's first official Scout Troop, the First Sands Troop (circa 1913).

76. The Cenotaph, Singapore's first war memorial. It was built in March 1922 and dedicated to the memory of those who died in World War I.

O

Observatory

Kallang, 1840. On 12 September 1840, Second Lieutenant Charles Morgan Elliot of the Madras Engineers came to Singapore to establish a 'magnetic observatory'. He selected a site at the bend of the Kallang River just to the left of the Kallang Bridge and built an observatory of wood with an attap roof. The floor and pedestals were made of granite. In January 1841, he took over the task of tide reading and established a tide gauge. He also took regular observations of rainfall and temperature. He stayed in Singapore for over 4 years and then left to build a magnetic observatory for Rajah Brooke in Sarawak. He travelled extensively in the Indonesian Archipelago and wrote a technical paper for the *Philosophical Transactions of the Royal Society* and was made a Fellow of the Royal Society. He returned to the East to make further studies in the Archipelago and died there in 1852. The observatory was later moved to Fort Fullerton at the mouth of the Singapore River.

Official Dinner

Crawfurd's Dinner, 1824. Singapore's first official dinner was given by Resident John Crawfurd, to celebrate the 5th Anniversary of the raising of the British flag on the island by Raffles in 1819. We have an account of the dinner from the diary of Walter Duncan, a young mercantile assistant working at the firm of AL Johnston and Co. Duncan wrote that there were about 75 Europeans living and working in Singapore in 1824, and that 50 of them were invited to the dinner. According to his diary, the speeches were long and dull and that the wine ran out. Dinner was served at a very 'late' hour of 7.30 pm. This was a time when dinner was usually served at 4.30 pm and then people went for a walk or a drive after dinner. The major event of the evening was the toast to Raffles, described in the speech as a 'distinguished individual'. The dinner guests then drank a toast to 'The Prosperity of Singapore'. The guests left at 10.00 pm.

Oil Crisis

1973. The international oil shock in 1973 and the recession that it brought about Singapore's the first oil crisis. From 1965 to 1973, Singapore experienced high rates of economic growth. The oil crisis slowed this double-digit growth considerably. In 1974, GDP growth was 6.3% and in 1974 it fell again to 4.1%. However, while growth plummeted, the average growth rate of GDP remained at about 5% per year, high by the standards of other countries.

Oil Mills

Singapore Oil Mills, 1882. The first coconut oil mill was the Singapore Oil Mills. It was built in 1882 at the corner of Havelock and McKenzie Roads. In 1889, Herman Mulinghaus of the Straits Trading Company (see TIN SMELTER) also saw the possibilities in the rising coconut industry and started the Bintang Oil Mills. In 1899, he bought out the Singapore Oil Mills. The combined works sat on a 10-acre plot overlooking the Singapore River. The works produced between 30 and 40 tons of oil a day. The residue of the copra after the oil was removed was sold as oil cakes used for cattle feed. Tallow for candles was also produced at the works.

Oil Refinery

Shell Refinery, Pulau Bukom, 1961. Singapore's first oil refinery was built by Shell in 1961 on Pulau Bukum. For this, Shell was awarded Pioneer Certificate Number 1 by the Singapore Government. On its centenary in 1991, Shell was awarded Singapore's first Distinguished Partner in Progress award in recognition for its contribution to Singapore. In 2005, the Bukom refinery produced 50,000 barrels per day and is the largest Shell refinery in the world in terms of crude distillation capacity, making Singapore a key regional supply and trading centre for oil in the East. Ninety percent of the products from the Bukom refinery are exported to countries in the region and beyond. Together with refineries operated by Esso, Mobil, Caltex, Maruzen and SPC, Singapore's total refining capacity is about 1 million barrels per day making it the third largest refining centre after Houston and Rotterdam. The strategic location of Singapore and its deep-water harbour have contributed to Singapore's success as a refining centre.

Oil tanks

Pulau Bukom, 1891. The first three oil tanks were built on Pulau Bukom in 1891 for the bulk storage of kerosene for cooking and lighting. The *SS Murex* brought 3,000 tons of kerosene in to the tanks. After 1896, the arrival of the motor car meant that large quantities of fuel were needed in Singapore. The introduction of airplanes further increased the demand for fuel.

Olympian

Chua Boon Lay, 1936. The first Singaporean to make an appearance at an Olympic Games was footballer Chua Boon Lay (1902–1976) who was a veteran of the All-China football team at the Berlin Games in 1936. Chua became player-manager of the Malayan Chinese team in the All-China National Games in Shanghai in 1935. After the final match against Hong Kong, three Singaporeans were selected for trials for the 1936 Berlin Games. They were: Chua Boon Lay, Chia Keng Hock and Lim Chwee Chua. Only Chua was able to make the journey and he was selected. The **first Singapore athlete to represent Singapore** at the Olympic Games was Lloyd Valberg (1922-1984) who took part in the High Jump event. Valberg jumped 6 feet 3 inches and was placed eighth. He was accompanied by the Manager, the late Jocelyn de Souza who was the **first Olympic Chef de Mission**. The **first Singapore woman** to participate in the Olympics was Tang Pui Wah who ran took part in the 100m sprint and the 80m hurdles at the Helsinki Games in 1952.

Olympic Medal

Tan Howe Liang, 1960. The first Olympian from Singapore to win a medal in the Olympics was Tan Howe Liang in 1960 at the Olympics in Rome. He won a silver medal in the Lightwieght Weightlifting competition. He lifted 380 kg to beat 33 rivals. In 9 Sep 1960, at the Palazetto Dello Sport Hall in Rome, Tan Howe Liang, then aged 27, put Singapore on the world map when he lifted a total of 380kg in the lightweight (67.5kg) category to beat 33 rivals (except Russia's Viktor Busheuv who took the gold) for the lightweight Silver medal. Prior to his Olympic performance, Howe Liang established a world record in the Jerk (lightweight division) with a lift of 347 pounds at the 6th British Empire & Commonwealth Games in Cardiff in 1958. That year, he also took home a gold at the 3rd Asian Games in Tokyo. He easily lifted a gold performance at the inaugural SEAP Games in Bangkok in 1959. Tan won his second Commonwealth Games gold medal in 1962 in the middleweight division. Tan Howe Liang is the only Singaporean who had won a medal at all the major international games – the Olympics, Commonwealth, Asian and SEAP (all gold except for the Olympics). He became the first weightlifter in the world to be awarded the International Weightlifting Federation (national honour) Gold Award in 1984. After retiring from competition, Tan coached many younger weightlifters, including Chua Koon Siong who was another champion, Tung Chye Hong and Teo Yong Joo.

Open-Heart Surgery

Singapore General Hospital, 1965. The first open-heart surgery using an artificial heart-lung machine was conducted at Singapore General Hospital on 28 January 1965. The patient was Miss Chua Ah Moi who had been diagnosed with a 'hole in the heart' in 1962 by a mobile X-Ray unit of the Singapore Anti-Tuberculosis Association. Her condition deteriorated and she needed an operation. The 4-hour operation was conducted by a Malayan medical team under the supervision of Dr McGoon of the Mayo Clinic in the United States. Chua was later discharged after a complete recovery.

Opium Farmer

Tay Han Long, 1820. The first opium farmer was Tay Han Long in 1820. Throughout the 19th century, opium was shipped to Singapore from India. Singapore took about 20% of the opium exported from India. About one-third of the opium that landed in Singapore was shipped on to China, one third was shipped to markets in the surrounding region, and the remainder was sold here. Opium was a major commodity in Singapore and the state of the economy in Singapore depended on the price of opium. Opium contributed to nearly half the revenue of Singapore through a system known as farming. As Singapore was a free port, the government could not generate revenue through port fees or excise charges. Instead, revenue was derived from excise farms. The farmers held the monopoly for collection of taxes on certain particular commodities. There were farms for the collection of taxes on opium, liquor, *biti* (betel nut), pawnbroking and the markets. However, the most lucrative farm was opium. An opium farm gave the farmer the monopoly on retail sale of prepared opium and the collection of taxes on it. The farmer was usually not a single person but represented a syndicate of investors. In 1819 and 1820, opium was sold through 4 opium shops licensed by Colonel William Farquhar at a monthly rent of $395 per month. However, this did not generate enough revenue, and opium farming was introduced in 1820. The system evolved by trial and error. The tender for the farm was for a period of between 1 and 3 years and was usually decided by public auction, although occasionally it was decided by sealed tenders. Little is known of the early opium farmers and there are few records. The first opium farmer was Tay Han Leng, the father of Tay Ho Swee who later became part of an important syndicate. There was fierce rivalry between the Hokkiens and Teochews over control of this important commodity and many of the riots in the early 19th century are due to struggles over the wealth generated by opium. Until 1849, Hokkiens dominated the opium industry. Tay Han Leng paid an annual rent of 7,345 Spanish dollars, which was 46.1% of total revenue. The **first important syndicate** to emerge was run by Kiong Kong Tuan, Tay Eng Long and Cheang Sam Teo in 1846-1847. From 1870 to 1879, the opium and spirit farms in Singapore, Johore, Malacca and Riau were controlled by 'The Great Syndicate' of Cheang Hong Lim, Tan Seng Poh and Tan Hiok Nee (sometimes spelt Tan Yeok Nee).

formerly a performing unit of the People's Association Cultural Troupe. The Patron was then Deputy Prime Minister Lee Hsien Loong and the Music Director was Hu Bing Xu. The objective was to develop a Chinese orchestra of international standing. In 2002, the orchestra performed *Marco Polo and Princess Blue* as part of the Opening Festival of the Esplanade-Theatres on the Bay. In 2002, Tsung Yeh was appointed Music Director. In 2005, the orchestra went on its first European tour to London, Newcastle and Budapest.

Orchestra, Amateur

1860. The first amateur orchestra was formed in 1860 for the purpose of providing music for the Amateur Dramatic Society. Two of the musicians were members of the musical D'Almeida family. In 1865, the orchestra of the Amateur Musical Society gave a concert. The leader was the organist of St. Andrew's Cathedral, Mr. Fenton. It was held on 28 December 1865 in the upper room of the Town Hall (now Victoria Concert Hall). The concert consisted of a wide variety of choral and instrumental pieces including the Overture to the Caliph of Baghdad, Haydn's *1st Quintet* and Locke's Music for Macbeth. *The Straits Times* wrote that the concert was a success from start to finish. The **first Malay orchestra** was set up on January 19th 1992 by the People's Association. See MALAY ORCHESTRA.

Orchestra, Chinese Professional

Singapore Chinese Orchestra, 1996. In May 1996, the Singapore Chinese Orchestra became Singapore's first professional Chinese orchestra with its official home at the newly-refurbished Singapore Conference Hall. The orchestra was

Orchestra, Professional

Singapore Symphony Orchestra, 1977. The Singapore Symphony Orchestra gave its inaugural concert on 24 January 1979. In 1977, the semi-professional Singapore Philharmonic Orchestra under Conductor Yoshinao Osawa played Tchaikovsky's *1812 Overture* at the opening night of the Arts Festival. The performance stimulated a huge amount of interest in the concept of setting up a professional symphony orchestra in Singapore. In October 1977, Defence Minister Dr Goh Keng Swee met with Tan Boon Teik and Associate Professor Bernard Tan of the Singapore Youth Orchestra to intitiate a national orchestra.

Tan Boon Teik became its **first Chairman** and Dr Goh became the **first Patron**. Choo Hoey (b. 1934), who was then conducting the Athens State Orchestra, was invited to be the conductor. Dr Goh proposed that the orchestra should begin with a small group of full-time professional musicians. Recruitment of musicians would be from abroad but a programme of local talent development should be put in place. The first 8 musicians were selected; 4 violin players, a viola player, a bass player, a cellist and a French horn player. Musicians were hired from prestigious international music schools. For example the entire woodwind section came from Eastman Music School in the United States. The first Leader of the orchestra was Pavel Prantl. The first concert was held on 24 January 1979 at the Conference Hall. The concert opened with Rossini's *Barber of Seville*. They also played Schubert's *Unfinished Symphony* and Beethoven's *Emperor Concerto* (featuring Singaporean pianist Ong Lip Tat), Ives' *Unanswered Question* and *Dance of the Yao People*.

The first Anniversary concert featured Singapore pianist Seow Yit Kin playing Grieg's *Piano Concerto*. The fifth Anniversary featured Daniel Hiefetz playing Mendelssohn's *Violin Concerto* in E Minor. The orchestra gradually expanded in size and by 1993, there were 86 full time members and 12 freelance musicians. In 1980 the Singapore Symphony Chorus was formed under the leadership of Lim Yau. In 1980 the orchestra went on tour for the first time to Penang and Kuala Lumpur. After 1980, the orchestra made its home in the Victoria Concert Hall. It is now based in the Esplanade-Theatres on the Bay. The **first general manager of the SSO** was Tan Siew Loon (1921-2002). Tan, who spent most of his life as an administrator in the then-Radio Television Singapore was seconded to the National University of Singapore to set up the Centre for the Arts. In 1980, he helped set up the SSO but left six months afterwards to return to radio.

Orchid Show

1931. The Orchid Society of South-east Asia was founded in 1928 as the Malayan Orchid Society. It held its first orchid show in Singapore in 1931. Its first post-war orchid show was held in 1957. The **first International Orchid Show** was held on 26 to 29 August 1993 at the World Trade Centre.

P

Pager

1973. Singapore's first tone pagers were introduced in 1973, and international paging service introduced in 1991.

Park, Public

People's Park, 1889. The first public park was a space at the foot of Pearl's Hill called 'People's Park'. It was handed over to the Municipality in 1889 for use as a public park and recreation ground. Today, People's Park Complex occupies this site.

Parliament, Sitting

8 December 1965. The first sitting of the Parliament of independent Singapore took place on 8 December 1965. The Yang di-Pertuan Negara Yusof bin Ishak gave a moving speech. At the conclusion of the speech, the House was adjourned under Standing Orders. The date was significant as it was 24 years to the day after the Japanese started bombing of Singapore. At the first business sitting on 13 December 1965. the Singapore Independence Bill was presented to Parliament. Together with the Singapore Constitution (Amendment) Bill, it completed the constitutional change from Singapore as a state in a Federal monarchy into the independent Republic of Singapore. As an independent republic, the government took new responsibilities for Defence and Foreign Affairs.

Patent Holder, Chinese

Lim Tiang Swee, 1880. The first Chinese to apply for a patent was Lim Tiang Swee of Lim Kong Wan & Son in October 1880. He applied for a patent for a machine for 'cleaning cargo rice, converting same into white rice to be worked by steampower'.

Penicillin

Tan Tock Seng Hospital, 1945. The first penicillin injection was given at Tan Tock Seng Hospital in 1945. Dr Benjamin Chew, a physician at Tan Tock Seng Hospital gave a penicillin injection to his colleague Dr Clarence Smith who had a lung abscess. Drugs were in short supply during the Japanese Occupation and the penicillin was smuggled into the hospital by hospital pathologist, Dr Leo S da Silva. Dr da Silva had heard that the United States Air Force had dropped medicines into the Sime Road Internment Camp and he obtained the penicillin from the camp.

Pharmaceutical Factory

Columbia International Corporation Ltd, 1967. In March 1965, Singapore's first pharmaceutical factory opened in Jurong Industrial Estate. The Columbia International Corporation Ltd was opened by Finance Minister Dr Goh Keng Swee and it was granted pioneer status by the Singapore Government (1963). The factory was a joint-venture between local industrialists and industrialists from Taiwan, Hong Kong and the United States of America.

Philosophical Society

Straits Philosophical Society, 1893. The first philosophical society, the Straits Philosophical Society was founded in March 1893. Its objective was to critically discuss philosophy, history, theology, literature, science and art. The membership was limited to 15 and preference was given to graduates of universities, fellows of British and European learned societies and persons of distinguished merit. The society met monthly and dined together before a paper was read and discussed. The annual subscription was $25 and the entrance fee was $5. The first members were Reverend George M Reith, Sir John Bonser, Sir Walter Napier, Henry Ridley, RW Hullett, Sir Bromheaad Matthews, J McKillop, Dr Galloway, Arthur Knight, Tan Teck Soon, Thomas Shelford, Dr GD Haviland, RN Bland and CW Kinnersley. The first President was Major-General Sir Charles Warren. The society was dominated by the leadership of three men; WR Collyer who was President from 1894-1901 and from 1902-6; Henry Ridley who was President from 1907-12 and Arthur Knight who was Secretary for twenty years. A selection of the essays read before the Society from 1893-1910 was published in 1913 in a volume edited by Henry Ridley and entitled *Noctes Orientales*.

Photograph in Newspaper

Malaya Tribune, 1914. The first photograph to be printed in a Singapore newspaper appeared in the *Malaya Tribune* on the 9 February 1914 on page 7. It was a photograph of the King of Albania, HSH Prince Wilhem of Wied. The *Malaya Tribune*, an English language newspaper started publication on 1 January that year.

Photographer

Gaston Dutronquoy, 1839. Gaston Dutronquoy was the first recorded resident photographer in Singapore. He owned the London Hotel in Coleman Street and operated his studio in the hotel. Dutronquoy was a native of Jersey in the Channel Islands and arrived in Singapore in March 1839. He placed an advertisement in the local newspaper describing himself as a painter of miniatures and portraits. In 1843, he became Singapore's first professional photographer, claiming in an advertisement that he was 'the complete master of the newly invented and late imported daguerreotype.' He further claimed that 'Ladies and Gentlemen could have their likeness taken in astonishing space of two minutes.' It is not known whether Dutronquoy actually established a photographic studio in his hotel as he was often busy either promoting his hotel or his theatre business. The earliest **photographic studio** of note was GR Lambert & Company. The studio was opened in 1875 by GR Lambert who arrived in Singapore from Dresden. He remained in the business until 1885 when he sold it to Alexander Koch who managed it from 1885 to 1905. Lambert was a photographer by special appointment to His Majesty the King of Siam and to his Highness the Sultan of Johore. Lambert was well known for his production of photographs in natural colours by purely chemical and mechanical means. GR Lambert & Co had branches in Deli, Sumatra, Bangkok and Kuala Lumpur. The firm did not appear in any commercial directory after World War I and presumably dissolved before 1914.

Photographic Exhibition or Salon

Japanese Club Exhibition, 1926. In 1926, an exhibition was organized by the Japanese Club at Selegie Road. The works displayed were mainly from overseas Japanese members. Only one Singapore participant, a Dr Chia won a prize. On 24 March 1935, an international Photographic Exhibition was held in Singapore. It included 83 works from Singapore, Hong Kong, and Malaysia and it was held at Prince Edward Road. The first post-War salon of photography was organized in 1950 by Loke Wan Tho and Dr Carl Alexander Gibson-Hill, on behalf of the Singapore Art Society. The **first Malayan Photographic Exhibition** was held in 1953. It was later renamed the Pan-Malaysian Photographic Exhibition, and then Singapore National Photographic Exhibition. In 1978, the ASEAN Salon replaced the Singapore National Photographic Exhibition.

Photographic Society

Strait Photographic Association, 1887. Singapore's first photographic organization was the Strait Photographic Association, established in 1887. The first president was David Chalmers Neave, the founder of Fraser & Neave Company and it was located in Hill Street. In 1894, the members started participating participate in international competitions. They sent their photographic works to Indonesia, Jakarta and won prizes in the competition. The second photographic society was the Singapore Camera Club which was established in 1924. It should not be confused with its post-War incarnation of the same name, which was founded in 1950.

Pier

P&O Pier, 1852. The first commercial pier to be built in Singapore was the Peninsular & Oriental (P&O) Steam Navigation Company coal-bunkering pier at Tebing Tinggi in Keppel Harbour. It was built in 1852. With the increase in steamer traffic coming to Singapore, the storage and supply of coal became urgent. Coal was transferred by lighter to Boat Quay and then transferred back to the next steamer requiring coal. It was time-consuming and inefficient. Bad weather could hold up the operation and heavy seas could swamp the sailing lighters. Many tons of coal were lost this way. In 1845, P&O inaugurated its first scheduled steamship service through Singapore. They needed a pier for their coal bunkering operation. As there was no wharfage available in the Singapore River, P&O took advantage of the deep water in New Harbour, as Keppel Harbour was originally called, and built a coal bunkering pier on a headland west of St James. In 1862, the Messageries Maritimes shipping company opened another coal bunkering pier at Pulau Brani. Keppel Harbour began to expand and within a few years, became the major gateway to the port of Singapore.

Pilot, Air Plane

See **Air Plane**

Pilot, Ship's

Jacob Clunies, 1840s. The first pilot for the Pacific and Oriental (P&O) Steam Navigation Company was Jacob Clunies. Clunies had a shipbuilding business in Singapore in the 1840s and he did much to open up New Harbour (later Keppel Harbour). Clunies died in No 3 Coleman Street, then a boarding house, in June 1866.

Pineapple Canning Factory

JP Bastiani, 1888. The pioneer of pineapple canning was a retired French sailor Joseph Pierre (JP) Bastiani. He was born in 1847, to a family of farmers in Corsica, the youngest of ten siblings. His father died when he was very young, and together with his eldest brother, Bastiani developed a small but thriving business preserving fruits and vegetables, utilizing the newly-invented tin can. In 1863, at the age of 16, Bastiani left Corsica to seek his fortune in France. He worked for several years in several chateaux in Bordeaux, Burgundy and the Loire Valley. His interest and knowledge of viticulture grew rapidly, but he soon found himself attracted to the charms of Paris. It is unclear what happened when Bastiani was in Paris, but by the early 1870s, he left for the Far East. It has been speculated that a failed liaison caused his departure from the French capital. Interestingly, Bastiani travelled in the same ship as the great novelist Joseph Conrad.

On Conrad's advice, Bastiani settled in Singapore. In 1874, he secured a shop in Singapore named J Bastiani. Drawing on his various talents and experiences, he was soon involved in several distinct businesses. The company styled itself as 'Preservers of Pine Apples and Other Fruits Indigenous to Singapore' and also dealt with wines. His ability to communicate in French, English, Italian and Spanish allowed him to deal smoothly with food and wine merchants around the world. Bastiani's business flourished. He imported wine to Singapore and re-exported them to Batavia, Bangkok, Phnom Penh, Hanoi, Hong Kong and Australia. His large wine cellar was legendary throughout the region, and he counted among his clients, many planters and civil servants. Ever the generous host, Bastiani converted the upper floor of his building into an international hall for entertaining. He shared with his chef, his culinary secrets of his Mediterranean specialities and brasserie fare of his years in Paris. He was particularly fond of the wood-burning oven installed at the back of his small rear garden, built to his exact specifications.

Bastiani's second business also made him famous in Europe and America. He experimented with the preservation of tropical fruits and won many silver medals at world fairs throughout the world. His culminating achievement was his extraordinary *Mangoustans au Sirop* which won first prize in the 1889 Exposition Internationale in Paris. He was soon exporting his produce to the best shops in London, Marseille, Naples, Hamburg and New York. In 1890, Bastiani made his first trip to Australia, and fell in love with the country. Thereafter, he visited Australia frequently. In 1905, Bastiani was ready to return to Europe and wound up his business. He purchased a small wine shop in Paris and went into semi-retirement, becoming famous throughout Paris as a wine expert and storyteller. Bastiani eventually closed his business when his health deteriorated, and retired to Corsica. It is not known when he died.

Chinese traders quickly saw the potential of this new industry, and set up a number of rival canneries and the Chinese soon came to dominate the industry: Tan Hwa Hee and his Chop Tek Watt brand; Seah Liang Seah who marketed his pineapples under the Lion brand; Seah Eng Keong's Chin Giap & Co; Lim Nee Soon and Tan Kah Kee. These were just some of the industry's most successful and colourful characters in the industry. The pineapple canning industry became the third largest export industry in Malaya and Singapore. In 1906, it was reported that some 16 factories produced over 700,000 cases of preserved pineapple.

Plantation House

Carnie's Hill, 1840. The first large plantation house was built for Charles Carnie in 1840. The estate was called Carnie's Hill and it originally covered 67 acres and stretched from Orchard Road to Bukit Timah Road. This was the first house to be built in the direction of Claymore and Tanglin. The area is now known as Cairnhill, after Charles Carnie.

Play

The Revenge, **1833.** The earliest record of amateur theatricals in Singapore appeared in the 21 March 1833 issue of *The Singapore Chronicle*. The plays were staged in Cross Street in Telok Ayer. Tickets were sold at $1.00 and $2.00 and could be purchased at Merryweather & Co. The doors were opened at 6.00 pm and the performance started at 7.00 pm. The play performed was Edward Young's tragedy, *The Revenge* (1806). It was followed by a farce, Henry Fielding's *The Mock Doctor or The Dumb Lady Cured*. There was also a recitation and some comic and sentimental songs. The *Chronicle*'s editor was very critical of the performance and claimed that the acting 'afforded some amusement from the burlesque character of the performance.' It would be another 16 months before the second performance. This time, it was Goldsmith's comedy, *She Stoops to Conquer*. The *Chronicle* described the performance as affording 'universal satisfaction'.

Pledge

See **Loyalty Pledge**

Plus size boutique

Woman of Substance, 2003. Singapore's first women's online plus-size store was Woman of Substance. It was established on 12 September 2003 but had closed down by the end of 2005.

Poetry Festival, International

2003. Singapore's first International Poetry Festival took place in January 2003. It was organised by The Literary Centre and featured 27 local and international writers. It was the first independent festival of its kind in the region.

Police Academy

Police Depot, Shenton Way, 1923. The first Police training establishment was the Police Depot founded in 1923 in Shenton Way. It was used to provide basic training for recruits, Constables and Inspectors. In the 1929, the Police Depot was moved to extensive premises in Thomson Road. In 1945, the Police Depot was renamed the Police Training School. In August 1969, it was renamed the Singapore Police Academy. The Academy offered basic 6 month preparatory training courses for regular recruits, a 3-month training course for National Service recruits and longer courses for officer cadets. It also offers a range of specialised courses for professional development.

Police Band

Second Straits Settlements Police Band, 1925. The first Police Band in Singapore was formed in 1925 at Tanglin Barracks. The bandmaster was FE Minns. He advertised for bandsmen as far afield as the Punjabi and Sikh Regiments of the British Indian Army. The band was known as the 2nd Straits Settlements Police Band. After the end of the Japanese Occupation, the band was re-formed into the Singapore Police Band. Between 1963 and 1965, it was known as the Royal Malaysia Police Bank, Singapore. It is now called the Polis Republik Singapura Band. The **first Singaporean band-leader** was Ridzwan Mulok who also became the **first Singapore Police Force Director of Music**. Before 1963, the band wore white tunics with shoulder flaps. During the Malaysia period, the band wore sarong and songkoks. The band now wears blue trousers with yellow lining and white tunics. It plays regularly at National Day Parades and State functions.

Police Force

1819. Singapore's first police force was set up in 1819 and consisted of 11 men: 1 sergeant, 8 constables, 1 jailer and 1 Malay writer. The 'force' was run on a monthly budge of $300. Francis James Bernard, Singapore's first Master Attendant (see **Master Attendant**) was the **first Police Chief**, Magistrate, Chief Jailor, Marine Storekeeper and Assistant to the Resident. Bernard was able to keep law and order among the various communities through the headmen of the each community. A 'sampan' squad of two rowing sampans (small boats) was set up to patrol the harbour. It consisted of a Sub-Inspector, 2 corporals and 12 constables. The Marine Headquarters was at the Cavanagh Bridge Police Station.

Police Station

1823. The first police station was built in 1823. In the early years, the Master Attendant was head of the police force and in charge of the prison. The **first Master Attendant** in Singapore was Francis James Bernard. He was Master Attendant from February 1819 to April 1820. The post of Master Attendant was similar to that of Harbour Master but it was combined with other duties such as Post Master and Marine Storekeeper. Bernard was appointed to the role provisionally by Raffles on a salary of $300 per month. He was only employed provisionally as the post was being kept for Captain William Lawrence Flint who was still in Europe. Bernard lay claim to a piece of land on the South side of the river opposite Ferry Point. His house was one of the first built and was ready within 4 months of the British flag being hoisted (February 1819). The house was a long low building on the seafront. It was used as a public office and the first Police Office was located there. A strong room was built under the Police Office to hold prisoners.

Police Superintendent or Commissioner

Thomas Dunman, 1843. Since 1831, there had been extreme lawlessness in Singapore, with a large number of burglaries and there were demands for an extended police force. In 1843, a public meeting was called and the meeting noted the prevalence of crime and called for better management of the police force. In September that year, the Government appointed Thomas Dunman Deputy Magistrate and the **first Superintendent of Police**. Dunman was born in 1812 and came to Singapore as a young man to work as a clerk in the firm of Martin, Dyce & Company. He remained there for 9 years. At the time of Dunman's appointment, the Resident Councillor was *ex officio* Commissioner of Police. However, in June 1857, the two roles were separate and Dunman became Commissioner of Police. He held the post till his retirement in 1871.

Dunman was well-respected and is credited with providing security to households and for raising and training an efficient and effective police force. His handling of the 1854 riots was much praised, and it earned him a commendation from the Governor-General and was presented with a sword-of-honour. Dunman owned a large coconut plantation called Grove Estate in Tanjong Katong and built a house there and three bungalows along the seashore. After he retired in 1871, he remained on his estate for four years before returning to England. Dunman also owned a piece of land at the corner of Bras Basah Road and Victoria Street which was dubbed 'Dunman's Corner'. He made a gift of this land to the Presbyterian Church in Singapore and the land was held by the Dunman Trust and provided funding for the upkeep of the church. He married Mary Ann Crane, second daughter of Thomas Crane, a well-known auctioneer and merchant, and they had 9 children. Through this marriage, Dunman also became related to the D'Almeida family. Dunman was extremely active in public service, serving as: Municipal Councillor, Committee member of the Masonic Lodge; shareholder of the Singapore Library; and gifted amateur actor. Dunman died in Bournemouth in 1887 at the age of 73.

The **first Singapore-born Commissioner** of Police was John le Cain. He joined the Straits Settlements Police Force in 1939 as a probationary inspector and was posted to the Tanjong Pagar Police Station. The following year, he joined the Special Branch. During World War II, le Cain was interned by the Japanese at Changi Prison and Sime Camp. He returned to Special Branch at the end of the Japanese Occupation. In January 1946, he was one of only 4 Asian officers to be promoted to the rank of Assistant Superintendent of Police. He became Deputy Superintendent in 1953, Superintendent in 1957 and Assistant Commissioner in 1960, and Commissioner on 31 March 1963. He retired in 1967.

Police, Woman Officer

Mary Quintal, 1949. Women police were enrolled for the first time in March 1949. They were taken on as members of the Special Constabulary (Active Unit) and approval was given for one Inspector, one Sergeant, 4 Corporals and 34 Constables. Their instruction was in English. The training was held over 3 months and the women were instructed in General Law, Police Duties, Powers of Arrest and in simple squad drill, marching and saluting. In addition they were given practical training in making arrests, traffic control and giving evidence. They were also taken on instructional tours to Courts, Fire Brigade, Police headquarters, Boys and Girls homes and Child Feeding Centres. Prior to their final posting, they were attached temporarily to Traffic, Radio, CID and Divisional HQ stations to give them all round experience. Their uniforms were dowdy and impractical and they wore calf length skirts of khaki drill, grey shirts, navy blue berets and laced up shoes. In 1969, a more comfortable and appropriate uniform was introduced. This experiment was so successful that arrangements were made to expand the expand the number of women the following year. Today there are over 900 women in the Police Force, almost 14% of the regular force.

One of the first group of police women was Mary Quintal. Within 5 months she was given the rank of Inspector Extra Constabulary. In 1951, she became a substantive Inspector. In 1961, she was appointed as

Assistant Superintendent of Police. By 1969, she has become the Officer Commanding Women Police. She retired in 1974 after 25 years of service. Mandy Goh Peng Neo entered the Police Force in 1952. She had a successful career in the Police Force and was appointed Assistant Superintendent of Police in 1974 and took over from Mary Quintal as Office Commanding Women Police. In 1979, Goh became the **first woman to be appointed to an operational land position** when she became Administrative officer in charge of Toa Payoh Police Station. From 1979 to 1980 she achieved another first by becoming the Officer in Charge of the Arms and Explosives branch. In 1982, she became the **first woman head of the Anti-Vice Enforcement Unit**. She became Acting Deputy Superintendent of Police. The **first female commander of the Traffic Police** was Superintendent Ng Guat Ting who was appointed on 7 January 2005. Superintendent Ng joined the police force at the age of 19 and was 43 years old on the date of her appointment. Before joining the Traffic Police, she was Commander of Clementi Police Division (1999-2001); and Deputy Director of Operations (2001-2004). She succeeded Assistant Commissioner Teo Kian Teck.

Political party

Kuomintang, 1912. The first local legal political party was the Kuomintang (KMT) in 1912. It was banned by the British in 1914. The **first post-war political party** was Malayan Democratic Union formed on 21 December 1945.

Polo

Singapore Polo Club 1899. The first attempt to introduce polo into Singapore was in 1891. However, the lack of a proper ground prevented the formation of a club. In 1899, the Singapore Polo Club was formed largely due to the efforts of Lieutenant-Colonel Pennefather, Captain Duff and WS Symes. Club members were able to play at the Singapore Racecourse at Farrer Park twice a week. The first game was played in February 1899. The Racecourse made an ideal polo ground as it was level and the rain kept the grass green. The King's Own Royal Lancaster Regiment was stationed in Singapore between 1899 and 1900 and did much to encourage and promote the game. The presented a cup to the Club known as the KOR Cup. The Club followed the rules of the Indian Polo Association and most of the horses are Walters. In 1899, the Club had a membership of 78 with 26 active playing members.

Polyclinic

Queenstown, 1963. Polyclinics were formed by combining Out Patient Departments with the Maternal and Child Health Clinics. They were set up to provide patient-centred continuing care and preventive primary healthcare services to the community. The **first polyclinic** was built in Queenstown in 1963. It included medical, dental clinics and a laboratory. It covered the area from Ghim Moh to Dover and Ayer Rajah and included Margaret Drive and Stirling Road. In 1990, Tampines Polyclinic became the first polyclinic to provide X-ray services. It was also the first polyclinic to introduce a health screening package for adults. The screening included diabetes, tuberculosis, cholesterol and blood sugar levels as well as overall medical checks.

Polytechnic Institute

Singapore Polytechnic, 1954. The first polytechnic institute built in Singapore was the Singapore Polytechnic in October 1958. In 1953, the Colonial Government set up the Dobby Committee to consider proposals for the establishment of a polytechnic. The *Dobby Report* recommended that a polytechnic be set up in Singapore and AW Gibson was commissioned to work out the details of the proposal. The Singapore Polytechnic Ordinance was passed in October 1954 to establish a polytechnic. On 27 October 1954, the Singapore Polytechnic was established as an autonomous body. The government provided a 10-acre site in Prince Edward Road and funds were provided by the Singapore Legislative Assembly. DJ Williams was appointed its **first Principal** in January 1956. In 1957, work began at the Prince Edward Road site and classes began in a variety of locations. The nautical classes were held in the Sailor's Institute in Connell House; the town planning and surveying classes in Tanjong Katong Technical School; and shorthand and typing classes at the Belvedere School in Tanglin Road. In September 1958, registration for the first 2,800 full- and part-time places commenced. The Polytechnic had 5 Departments – Electrical and Mechanical Engineering; Architecture and Building; Commercial Studies and Accountancy; Nautical Studies and General Education – offering a variety of 58 courses.

The Prince Edward Road Campus was opened on 24 February 1959 by the Duke of Edinburgh, Prince Philip. Following the publication of the *Chan Chieu Kiat Report*, the polytechnic focused on the training of professional and technician diploma students with a long term view of developing the Polytechnic into a College of Advanced Technology. Professional diploma courses were replaced by degree courses in engineering, accountancy and architecture. In 1968, a decision was taken to transfer the degree courses to the University of Singapore and the polytechnic was restructured to concentrate on technical courses to provide skilled technicians for the rapidly industrialisation taking place in Singapore. The School of Industrial Technology and the School of Nautical Studies offered full and part-time technician diploma and certificate courses. In addition a 2-year full time Industrial Technician certificate was introduced. By 1970, the Polytechnic was bursting at its seams and in 1971, a decision was made to move to a 37-hectare site in Dover Road. The new campus was officially opened by then Prime Minister Lee Kuan Yew on the 7 July 1979. By then, there were 8,000 students at the Singapore Polytechnic, 5,000 of whom were full-time students and 3,000 part-time students.

Population census

See **Census**.

Port Master

See **Master Attendant**.

Post Office

Maxwell's House, 1827. The first post office was started in a room at the front of John Argyle Maxwell's house (now Old Parliament House) in 1827. One half of the room was used for the post office and the other half by the Master Attendant's marine office. By 1843, the space became inadequate and the Post Office was moved to a small building behind the house that had originally been designed as a coach house. The surroundings were noisy but the building was more spacious. The introduction of monthly mail service by paddle steamer in 1845 added to the problems of the Post Office and greatly increased its business. That year, when the Police Office moved to William Napier's house in High Street, the Master Attendant's Office and the Post Office were moved to the old Police Office at Ferry Point. It was a godown built by Captain Methven in 1820 and was made of brick and lime and had an attap roof. **Parcel post** between the Straits Settlements and the United Kingdom was introduced on 1 October 1885.

The **first Chinese Post Office** was in 81 Market Street and it was established in 1876. Up till that date, letters to and from China, including remittances, were handled by a small number of Chinese merchants. The Straits Government felt that it would benefit the Chinese labourers if they had access to a cheaper and safer form of forwarding letters. After communications with the Imperial authorities in China, the Government arranged to open a Chinese Post Office in Market Street. It was hoped that this would break the monopoly of the Chinese letter collectors. However, a serious riot, instigated by the letter collectors, took place on the morning the new post office opened. It was badly damaged and the Superintendent of Police, RW Maxwell was stoned, knocked down and beaten. After the riot was quelled, the letter collectors were taken out and put on board the *Pluto*, 3 miles out in the harbour. A week later, the Post Office reopened. In 1877, it was moved to the General Post Office. The number of Chinese letters rose from 80,000 in 1880 to 280,000 in 1889.

Postage Stamp

East India Company, 1854. The first postage stamp in Singapore was issued by the East India Company in 1854. They were in denominations of half, one, two and four *annas* and featured the side profile of Queen Victoria with the word 'India' on the stamp. The **first issue of Straits Settlements stamps** came out on 1 September 1867. In 1877, the Straits Settlements joined the Universal Postal Union whose mission it was to ensure fair postal rates throughout the world. In 1876, the Chinese clubbed letter collectors started a riot to protest the formation of the British postal agency in Singapore, seeing it as a threat to their livelihoods. Parcel post between the Straits Settlements and the United Kingdom was introduced on 1 October 1885. The charge was 1s 4d per pound and the limit was 50 pounds. The service was rarely used as there was no parcel delivery service in the United Kingdom and parcels were delivered to the P&O Offices in London for collection. After an Inland Parcel Post was established in the United Kingdom in 1883, parcel post became more popular. In the early years of postal traffic, all letters were entered into a book. However, this did not provide any form of compensation in case of loss. **Registration was first introduced** into Singapore in January 1858 and the fee charged was 12 cents. The indemnity was only paid in cases of total loss and capped at $10.00.

Postcard

1879. The first international postcards were introduced into the Straits Settlements in 1879 by the Postal Department. They were blank on one side and on the other side there was space for the destination to be written and an imprinted postage stamp. They were on sale for

1 cent and the postage was 3 cents. They could be sent anywhere in the world. Private postcards cost 8 cents for postage. On 15 December 1884, local postcards for use within the Straits Settlements and the Malay States were introduced by the Postal Department at 1 cent per card. In 1897, the Department allowed privately printed postcards to be sent at the same rate as official postcards. This created a boom in demand for privately printed postcards. However, they had to be of regular size with the words POSTCARD imprinted on the address side. Between 1897 and 1902, the Department issued its own picture postcards but the growing popularity of privately printed postcards soon forced the Department out of the market. The **first privately printed postcards** were produced in 1898 and were usually of coloured paintings of local scenes. Many of the early picture postcards were printed overseas but some early ones are attributed to GR Lambert, the famous local photographer. Postcards provide a valuable archival resource for historians as they portray the community as it evolves.

Postmaster & Postmaster-General

Lieutenant A Dow, 1819. For the first four years of British settlement, the mail was handled by Cantonment Adjutant Lieutenant A Dow. He was succeeded by Lieutenant Henry Ralfe and later by Lieutenant CE Davies. In February 1823, the **first civilian Postmaster**, Charles Ryan was appointed. In December that year, the post of Postmaster was terminated. However, Ryan continued to act as the Postmaster until he resigned in 1824 to become storekeeper in the firm of Napier & Scott, remaining there for 3 years. In March 1827, he left Singapore and sold his nutmeg plantation (Ryan's Hill) to Hugh Syme. The property was later renamed Duxton Hill. Ryan returned to Singapore in 1828 and worked as a clerk to the Assessment Fund. He died in 1840 in Singapore, apparently from alcoholic poisoning.

From 1824 to 1858, the Master Attendant took charge of postal services in Singapore. From 1 May 1824, Captain Flint, the Master Attendant, became Postmaster with an additional allowance of $50 a month for the extra work. In June 1825, Edward Coles was appointed to assist Flint in postal work and was referred to as the Acting Postmaster. Coles was later transferred to another post and Flint resumed his duties as Postmaster and remained in that office till he died in October 1828. In 1858, the positions of Master Attendant and Postmaster were finally separated and the new Post Office department was headed by William Cuppage, formerly Assistant Postmaster. He had the help of two clerks, three sorters and four peons to deliver the mail. Cuppage remained as Postmaster until he retired in 1871, after working nearly 42 years in Government. From 1869, he appointment was designated acting Postmaster-General and his salary raised to $300 per month. In 1871, Henry Trotter, formerly from the postal department in Ceylon, took over from Cuppage and became **Singapore's first Postmaster-General.**

Power Station

Mackenzie Road, 1905. In 1905, the tramway company in Singapore (Singapore Electric Tramways) converted from steam to electric power. The power was provided by a power station built by the tramway company under an Authority given by the Municipality. The power station generated power for the use of the tramways and for the supply of electricity to the Municipality and the Government but to no other party. This provided power for a limited number electric street lights. The power station was located in Mackenzie Road adjacent to the Rochore Canal, from which is obtained an ample supply of water. The station was 190 feet long and 48 feet wide. There were two main traction sets of 500 kilowatts, one steam lighting set, one motor generator lighting set and banks of associated switching gear. The generators were made by Dick Kerr & Co. Inside the boiler-house, there were 8 Lancashire boilers arranged in 2 banks of four. Each boiler was capable of evaporating 6000lbs of water each hour with a working pressure of 175 lbs. per square inch. The main contractors were Yates and Thom (of Blackburn). The cost to public and domestic users was 18 cents per unit. Supplies of power from the company power station to the town were terminated in October 1926 when a new system was introduced. Instead of the tramway power station providing power for electric lights, a municipal power station was built that would provide power for electric lights, and also for the tramway. The **first municipal power station** was St James Power Station built in 1927. See also, STREET LAMPS.

Prefabricated Flats

1964. The first ten blocks of prefabricated Housing Development Board flats were completed in September 1964. They were built at the Macpherson Road–Aljunied Road estate. Building time was halved and costs reduced. Apart from cost considerations, prefabrication eliminated the problem of the acute shortage of skilled carpenters in Singapore. Singapore was the first city in Southeast Asia to use prefabrication for its public housing projects.

President

Yusof bin Ishak, 1965. In August 1965, when Singapore became an independent state, separate from Malaysia, Yusof bin Ishak, hitherto, Singapore's Yang di-Pertuan Negara or Head of State, became its first President. Born on 12 August 1910 at Padang Gajah, Trong in Perak, the eldest son in a family of nine, Yusof was educated at the Malay school at Kurau, Perak and later at the Malay school in Taiping. In 1921, he commenced his English studies at King Edward VII School in Taiping. In 1923, his father, Ishak bin Ahmad, a civil servant, was posted to Singapore and the family moved here. Yusof then enrolled briefly in Victoria Bridge School (1923-1924) before gaining admittance to Raffles Institution, the premier government school. He passed his Cambridge School Certificate with distinction (1927) and spent two further years in the Queen's Scholarship class. He was an active sportsman, playing hockey, cricket, water-polo and boxing and was Singapore's light-weight boxing champion in 1933. Yusof was also the most outstanding cadet in the School Cadet Corps and was the first student ever to be commissioned 2nd Lieutenant in the Corps. Yusof was also a school prefect and co-editor of the school's magazine, *The Rafflesian*.

When he left school in 1929, he and two friends started a fortnightly sports magazine, aptly called *Sportsman*. In 1932, he joined the staff of *Warta Malaya*, then the leading Malay newspaper and within a few years, was made Acting Editor of the paper. In 1938, Yusof and a few friends decided to start their own newspaper. He resigned his job at *Warta Malaya* and established the Utusan Melayu Press Ltd. The first issue of the newspaper, *Utusan Melayu*, was published in May 1939, with Yusof as Managing Director. During the Japanese Occupation (1942-1945), Yusof remained in Malaya and the paper ceased publication. When the Japanese surrendered in 1945, he returned to Singapore and resumed publication of *Utusan Melayu*. In 1957, Yusof decided to move the *Utusan*'s operations to Kuala Lumpur and moved there to supervise the construction of Utusan Building. While in Kuala Lumpur, he was elected President of the Press Club of Malaya.

Outside journalism, Yusof was active in public affairs and in 1959, was appointed Chairman of the Public Service Commission. In December 1959, he was appointed self-governing Singapore's first local head of state or Yang di-Pertuan Negara. On 9 August 1965, when Singapore became an independent republic, Yusof became its first President. In his last years in office, Yusof Ishak was often ill, but that did not deter him performing his duties and from reaching out to the people. He died of heart failure on 23 November 1970 and was buried at Kranji War Memorial, following a state funeral. Yusof was survived by his wife, Noor Aishah and three children. For his contributions, Yusof was conferred the First Class Order of the Darjah Kerabat (The Most Esteemed Royal Family Order of Brunei) by the Sultan of Brunei (1960); the Darjah Kebesaran Sri Maharajah Mangku Negara (S.M.N.) by the Yang di-Pertuan Agong of Malaysia (1963); and Honorary Doctor of Letters, University of Singapore (1969). See also, HEAD OF STATE

President, Elected

Ong Teng Cheong, 1993. In 1991, constitutional amendments were put in place to transform Singapore's presidency into an elected office. Technically, the transitional provisions in the Constitution designated the incumbent President as the first elected President. At the time, the post was held by Dr Wee Kim Wee. The **first presidential elections** were held on 28 August 1993, and Ong Teng Cheong defeated Chua Kim Yeow to become Singapore's first elected president. Born on 22 January 1936, Ong was educated at the Chung Cheng Primary School, and the Chinese High School before proceeding to the University of Adelaide where he graduated with a degree in architecture. He worked briefly in Adelaide before returning to Singapore. In 1965, he was awarded the Colombo Plan Scholarship to pursue his Master's degree. He left for Liverpool University where he obtained his Masters in Civil Design. On his return in 1967, he joined the Ministry of National Development as a Town Planner but he left the civil service in 1971 to start his own architectural firm, Ong & Ong, with his wife Ling Siew May as partner. In the late 1960s, Ong began his involvement in grassroots activities, and he was noticed by the then Member of Parliament for Jalan Kayu, Hwang Soo Jin. It was Hwang who introduced Ong to then Prime Minister Lee Kuan Yew.

Ong entered the political fray when he contested the 1972 general elections under the PAP banner. He was elected Member of Parliament for Kim Keat constituency and remained and MP till 1993 when he resigned to stand for President. In 1975, Ong was appointed Senior Minister of State for Communications, and in 1977, Acting Minister for Culture. In 1978, be became Minister for Communications and in 1981, Minister for Labour. Two years later, Ong was made Minister Without Portfolio and Secretary-General of the National Trades Union Congress (NTUC). In 1985, he was appointed Second Deputy Prime Minister, and in 1990, Deputy Prime Minister.

During his years in Cabinet, Ong is best remembered for his many initiatives, especially in the arts scene. He chaired the Advisory Council on Art and Culture (1989) and was instrumental in forming the National Arts Council and championing the building of the Esplanade Theatres on the Bay. Ong was also concerned about the learning of Chinese in schools and presided over the Chinese Language Review Committee (1992). As Minister for Communications, he realized the vision for a mass rapid transit system, and as a trade union leader, his concern for the working class never wavered. It was Ong who mooted the idea of the Orchid Country Club and the Pasir Ris Resort for union members. Under his watch, union membership grew from 190,000 to 230,000.

As President, Ong acted independently, debunking skeptics who thought that he would be a mere rubber-stamp for the Government's programmes. In 1994, he disagreed with the Government over the interpretation of his powers under Article 22H of the Constitution and referred the issue to a special Constitutional Tribunal. The Tribunal ruled in favour of the Government's interpretation. In 1999, when his six-year term was up, Ong, who had been suffering from lymphoma, declined to seek re-election. He died on 8 February 2002 from lymphoma.

President Scholars

See **Scholars**.

Priest, Singapore-born Catholic

Reverend Lionel Cordeiro, 1925. The first Singapore-born Catholic priest was Reverend Lionel Cordeiro. Born in Singapore in 1898, Cordeiro was ordained a priest in the Cathedral of the Good Shepherd on 27 December 1925. At the time of his death in December 1966, he was parish priest of St Matthew's Church in Tangkak in Johore. Cordiero taught for some time in St Francis Xavier's Seminary in Punggol before transferring to the parish of St Peter and Paul, and later at St Teresa's Church. He later transferred to Batu Gajah in Perak where he became known for his work in educating the poor. After World War II, Cordeiro was assigned to the parish of St Andrew in Muar where he worked for the next 20 years. He continued working in Johor till his death.

Prime Minister

Lee Kuan Yew, 1959. Born on 16 September 1923 at 92 Kampong Java Road, Singapore, Lee was the eldest child of Lee Chin Koon and Chua Jim Neo. His grandfather, Lee Hoon Leong gave him the name 'Harry'. Lee was educated at Telok Kurau Primary School and then at Raffles Institution where he won the Sir John Anderson Scholarship for being the top student in Malaya. He proceeded to read economics at Raffles College but his education was interrupted by the Japanese Occupation. During the Occupation, he operated a successful black market business selling a tapioca-based glue called *Stikfas*. He also worked as a transcriber of Allied wire reports for the Japanese. He was also English-language editor of the Japanese *Hodobu*, an information or propaganda department from 1943 to 1944. After the War, he left for London, originally to read economics, but subsequently changed to law and managed to obtain a place at Fitzwilliam College in Cambridge where he graduated in 1949 with first-class honours in Law with a star for distinction in the final examinations. He was called to the Bar at the Middle Temple in 1950, and thereafter, he returned to Singapore where he pupilled with John Laycock in the firm of Laycock & Ong.

Lee immediately became active in the political scene, becoming legal adviser to many left-wing trade unions and defending students of the University of Malaya during the infamous *Fajar* trial in 1954. On 21 November that year, Lee and a group of fellow English-educated intellectuals founded the socialist People's Action Party (PAP). The Party also included the Chinese-educated left-wing group led by Lim Chin Siong. The PAP's inaugural conference was held at the Victoria Memorial Hall. Lee was elected Secretary-General of the Party and he held on to this post continuously (save for a brief period in 1957) till 1992.

In 1955, Lee was one of only four PAP candidates to contest the general elections. He was elected Member of Parliament for Tanjong Pagar. From 1955 to 1959, Lee worked assiduously to consolidate his position within his Party and his Party within Singapore's political firmament. In 1959, the PAP won a landslide victory and Lee became Singapore's first Prime Minister. Since then, he led his Party to 8 general election victories. Lee stepped down as Prime Minister in November 1990 and handed the reins of power to Goh Chok Tong. He remained in the Cabinet as Senior Minister till August 2004 when he was made Minister Mentor when his elder son, Hsien Loong took office as Singapore's third Prime Minister.

See also **Chief Minister**

Printing Press

Mission Press, 1823. Within four months of Raffles' arrival in Singapore, the London Missionary Society applied for land to set up a mission. The head of the mission in Malacca, William Milne sent Samuel Milton to help form a mission in Singapore. In 1822, Milton was joined by Claudius Henry Thomsen who brought with him a small press. Thomsen became the pioneer of the printing and publishing industry in Singapore. Shortly after his arrival, he applied for a printing permit and in January 1823, the permit was received and he established the Mission Press.

Operations began in the private residence of one of the missionaries where Raffles Hotel now stands. The Press was active in printing and bookbinding and was soon printing all public documents for the Government in English and Malay. The Mission Press was eventually able to print works in English, Malay, Chinese, Thai and Arabic. The press was later bought by the Singapore Institution (later renamed Raffles Institution) and many of the earliest books published in Singapore carry the imprint of the Institution Press as well as that of the Mission Press.

Singapore soon became a publishing centre for Christian literature in Chinese, Bugis and Malay. When the London Missionary Society left Singapore for China, the Society took the large press as well. The Society left a small lithographic press which was used by Benjamin Peach Keasberry who refused to leave Singapore with the other members of the Society. He continued to print books under the Mission Press imprint. The press also published the *Journal of the Indian Archipelago and Eastern Asia* as well as letterheads for merchants, bills of lading, a steady stream of religious publications and two of Singapore's earliest newspapers, *Tifang Jih Pao* (1845) and *Jit Sheng* (1858). When Keasberry died in 1875, the press was bought by John Fraser and DC Neave and the press was renamed Printers Ltd.

It survived until 1942. Their most enduring publication was Charles Burton Buckley's *An Anecdotal History of Old Times in Singapore* (1902). The **first Indian press** was Denothaya Venthira Press run by SK Madadoom Saiboo. It was located at No 1 Mohammed Ali Lane, off South Bridge Road. It published two periodicals and four literary works in Tamil. The press also printed works in English, Malay and Arabic. The **first Japanese press** was the Japanese Commerce Museum in Middle Road. It published translations of laws, surveys and studies prepared by its scholars. Malay presses began to emerged during the 1920s. These included Bintang Press, Geliga Limited, Qalam and the Melayu Raya Press.

Prison

Bras Basah Goal, 1841. Originally, convicts were housed in temporary huts near the Bras Basah Canal. At the convict population grew, this subsequently developed into a long row of attap-sheds stretching from Bras Basah Road to Stamford Road. In 1841, a decision was taken to erect a jail for the Indian convicts along Bras Basah Canal at the foot of Fort Canning Hill. The original huts were gradually replaced by permanent buildings that the convicts built. The boundary wall was first constructed, followed by a brick building within its confines. The building was later used as a convict hospital. This brick building initially housed convicts in irons and local prisoners. The rest of the convicts were housed in temporary structures within the prison walls. Those employed in positions of trust were allowed to erect small huts for themselves in the style of a native village just outside the wall, in which they were allowed to have their wives and families.

In 1847, Singapore's **first purpose-built prison** was constructed at Outram Road from plans prepared by John Turnbull Thomson. The foundation was laid in February 1847. The prison was extended in 1879 from designed by Major JFA McNair, who was Executive Engineer and Superintendent of Convicts. McNair learnt photography and he photographed convicts for identification purposes. Later, it became popular for ladies and gentlemen to visit the prison to have their photographs taken. Outram Prison was rebuilt in 1929 by Captain Edward Lake and it continued in use till 1968 when it was demolished to make way for the Outram Road Housing project which was in turn torn down in 2004 to make way for further development.

Public Meeting

1821. The first public meeting was held by Singapore's merchants and traders in 1821. In February that year, the first junk arrived from Amoy. The Temeggong and the Sultan demanded dues from the junk captain, Ti Chio, as was the traditional practice in the Malay world. He refused to pay as he had heard that the port was duty free. He was thrown into the stocks by the Sultan's followers. The merchants objected strongly as they were anxious to keep the port free of taxes and duties as laid down by Raffles. They called a public meeting and presented a letter Lieutenant-Colonel William Farquhar, the Resident. Although he saw the protest as interference on the part of the merchants, he responded rapidly to their protest. The chiefs were given an allowance in place of the customary dues and the port remained duty free. See **Junk from China**.

Public Service Commission

1951. Singapore's Public Service Commission (PSC) can trace its origins to the British Civil Service Commission (1855). Prior to World War II, the recruitment of top civil servants in Singapore was in the hands of the Secretary of State for the Colonies who relied on the UK Civil Service Commission and the Crown Agent for the colonies to select candidates. In 1947, the Colonial Office established a commission under Sir Harry Trusted to consider the terms and conditions for the public services. The Trusted Report called for the establishment of a Public Services Commission and proposed that the civil service be divided into four divisions (Divisions I to IV). In Singapore, legislative councillor NA Mallal moved a motion calling for the setting up of a PSC and for a Select Committee to consider the constitution and terms of the commission (1948). The idea received a lukewarm reception till 1949 when a Select Committee was established and recommended that a PSC be established. The Committeee, chaired by CWA Sennett (then Commissioner of Lands) recommended that the commission have a statutory and independent character. On 23 December 1949, the Legislative Council passed the Public Services Commission Ordinance (brought into force on 1 January 1951). The three-man PSC's **first chairman** was Frederick Gordon-Smith. The first woman to become Chairman of the PSC was Professor Gloria Lim who was appointed in 1982.

Pugilistic Competition

Gay World Stadium, 1967. A pugilistic competition was held at the Gay World Stadium from 21 May to 27 May 1967. It was the first event of its kind in Singapore and was organized by 32 pugilistic organisations and the People's Association under the Chairmanship of Sim Peng Boon. There were three sections: pugilistic arts, lion dance and dragon dance. The organizers hoped that the event would promote pugilistic virtues of loyalty, chivalry and helpfulness irrespective of sect, denomination or place. The opening night was attended by 10,000 people. The event was opened by the Prime Minister Lee Kuan Yew. In his remarks, Lee said that pugilistic organisations played an important role in helping to build a tough and rugged people for the Republic of Singapore.

Q

Quarantine Station

St John's Island, 1874. In 1873, the Master Attendant, Henry Ellis suggested that a quarantine station be built on St John's Island. The first quarantine station was completed in November 1874. There was provision in the plans for a steam cutter, a hospital and a quarantine burial ground on Peak Island.

Queen's Medal (Sandhurst)

Tan Teck Guan, 1980. The first Singaporean to win the prestigious Queens Medal at Sandhurst Royal Military Academy was 2nd Lieutenant Tan Teck Guan in July 1980. He was the first non-British winner for 12 years.

Queen's Scholar

See **Scholars.**

R

Race Course

Farrer Park Racecourse, 1886. The forerunner of the Singapore Turf Club was the Singapore Sporting Club which was formed in December 1843 by a few amateur racing enthusiasts. In 1886, the Government gave the Club a 999-year lease of Farrer Park at a peppercorn rent on the condition that the ground 'should be always clear of brushwood and be maintained in good order to the satisfaction of Local Government.' The Club's Committee then organized to have a track laid. The first race was held at 11.00 am on 23 February 1886 for the Singapore Cup which carried a prize of $150. The day was reportedly bright and clear and a national holiday had been declared to celebrate the 24th anniversary of Raffles' arrival. The bugle sounded at exactly 11.00 am and the first race began. The pre-race favourite, *Colonel* won by a commanding three lengths. The horse was owned by a Mr Forbes and ridden by William Henry Read, founder of the Club. The first Chinese to own racehorses was Tan Keng Swee. He won the Maharajah of Johore's Cup at the Spring Meeting in 1879. In 1929, the Race Course was acquired by the Singapore Improvement Trust for public housing. The Trust purchased the lease from the club for $1.5 million, enabling the Club to buy 244 acres of rubber estate in Bukit Timah to develop a new racecourse. In 1933, Sir Cecil Clementi opened the Bukit Timah Racecourse which he declared to be 'the finest in the East.' This racecourse remained in use until it moved to Kranji in 1999.

Radio Station

Empress Place, 1936. Singapore's first broadcasting station was set up at Empress Place in 1936 by a private commercial organisation, the British Malaya Broadcasting Corporation. The station then moved Cathay Building in 1937. In 1940, the Straits Government purchased the entire holdings and operated the service as the 'Broadcasting Station, Post and Telegraph Department, Singapore and the Federated Malay States' and moved the station to Caldecott Hill. From February 1942 until August 1945, the radio station was operated by the Japanese Military Administration under the name of *Syonan Hoso Kyoku*. In September 1945, the radio station came under the control of the Publicity and Printing Unit of the British Military Administration. With the return of civil government in 1946, the station became known as 'Radio Malaya'. On 4 January 1959, Radio Singapore was born. It was officially opened by Chief Minister Tun Lim Yew Hock, who delivered a five-minute talk after the 1.30 pm news.

Radio transmission

1936. The first radio broadcast in Malaya was in the year 1921 when AL Birch, an electrical engineer from the Johore Government brought the first radio set into the country. He established the Johore Wireless Association and commenced broadcasting through 300-meter waves. The following year, amateurs began broadcasting from two experimental stations. Singapore went on the air for the first time in 1936 when a private company, the British Malaya Broadcasting Corporation commenced operations. The broadcasting listening station licence in its present form was first issued in May 1947. The first radio transmission commenced on 1 June 1936. It was operated by the British Malaya Broadcasting Corporation and the signal emanated from a government building in Empress Place. The station call sign was ZHL operating on the frequency of 1,333 KHz in the 225-meter band. Normal service began on 1 March 1937 with an inauguration speech by Governor Sir Shenton Thomas. The introduction of shortwave transmissions in July 1938 brought radio to a much greater area.

Railway Station

Tank Road Station, 1903. The first station in Singapore was the Tank Road station. It was the city end of the Singapore-Kranji Railway completed in January 1903. The Tank Road Station was rather grand with a clock tower. It proved to be an unsatisfactory location as it was 2 miles from the main commercial centre. It remained the terminus for passengers but in 1907 an extension was built to take goods to Keppel Harbour.

Railway Track

Singapore-Kranji Line, 1903. In 1903, the Singapore-Kranji Railway opened. The construction of the line was done under the supervision of CE Spooner of the Federated Malay States Railway (FMSR). The line south through Malaya was arrived in Johore Bahru and was completed in 1909. This gave rail access on a one-metre gauge line from Johore Bahru to the Thai border. In 1913, the Singapore-Kranji line was purchased by the FMSR. Railway wagons and passengers were taken across the Straits of Johore on barges and launches. The Causeway was completed in 1923, linking Singapore with Johore Bahru by rail and road.

Rally, Asian Highway Motor

Vientiane to Singapore, 1969. The first Asian Highway Motor Rally was flagged off on 16 April 1969 in Vientiane, Laos. The Rally attracted some 600 participants and the drivers were expected to cover 2,897 km through Thailand and Malaysia before ending the race in Singapore. The Rally was organized to celebrate the opening of the first paved road from Vientiane to Singapore. It was won by Staff Sergeant Joseph Minto of Singapore and his Malaysian-sponsored team. Driving an Opel Commodore, he beat 155 vehicles after a 4-day race.

Ramon Magsaysay Award

Lim Kim San, 1965. Born on 30 November 1916 in Singapore, Lim was educated at Anglo-Chinese School and then at Raffles College where he graduated with a diploma in Arts at the Department of Economics (1939). Shortly after graduation, Lim married Pang Gek Kim, daughter of pawnbroker turned banker, Pang Cheng Yean. It was an arranged marriage and the couple had six children. Lim started out working as a pump attendant at his father's petrol kiosk. During the Japanese Occupation, he suffered a great deal when he was detained and tortured twice by the dreaded *Kempetai*. After the Occupation, he went into business, his keen business sense honed by helping his father run the family business in rubber, commodities, salt, sago and gasoline. He revolutionised the sago business by inventing a machine to produce sago pearl cheaply and efficiently and made his first million in 1950 at the age of 34.

Lim was also successful in banking, taking over the management of his father-in-law's business and became the director of United Chinese Bank and managing director of Batu Pahat Bank (1951). In 1959, Lim was appointed a member, and later deputy chairman, of the Public Service Commission. In 1960, he accepted the honorary position of chairman of the Housing Development Board (HDB). Within the first two years of his chairmanship, the HDB showed promising results. It built 26,168 apartments, about as many as what its predecessor, the Singapore Improvement Trust, did in its 32 years.

Lim entered politics in 1963, and was elected Member of Parliament for Cairnhill constituency under the PAP ticket. He was appointed Minister for National Development. Lim retained his seat in Cairnhill until he retired from politics in 1980. While in Government, Lim was Minister for: Finance (1965-1967), Interior and Defence (1967–1970), Education (1970–1972), Environment (1972–1975, 1979); National Development & Communications (1975–1978); and National Development (1978–1979). He was also chairman of the Public Utilities Board (1971–1978). In 1980, Lim retired from the politics, but continued to serve in other important public appointments: Chairman of the Port of Singapore Authority (1979-1994); Deputy Managing Director of the Monetary Authority of Singapore (1981-1982); Chairman of the Council of Presidential Advisers (1991-2004); and Executive Chairman of Singapore Press Holdings (SPH) (1988-2002). For his public service, Lim was awarded the Order of Temasek (1962); the Ramon Magsaysay Award for community leadership (1965); the NTUC Medal of Honour (1977); and the PAP Distinguished Service Medal (1990). The second Singaporean recipient of the Magasaysay Award was Dr Goh Keng Swee, who was Finance Minister and Deputy Prime Minister. He received the 1972 award for Government service.

Rationing

1942-1945. Food rationing was first introduced during the Japanese Occupation, between 1942 and 1945. The Japanese Military Administration took control of essential food supplies such as rice, sugar, tapioca, salt, flour and milk. After removing the allocation for Japanese military use, the remainder was divided up amongst the rest of the population. **Water rationing** was first introduced in April 1963. Water stocks were down due to the dangerously low levels in the Tebrau Waterworks in Johor, the MacRitchie, Seletar and Pierce reservoirs. The rationing remained for the rest of 1963 and was relaxed in January 1964.

Recall, Open

See **Mobilisation, National Servicemen**

Recorder

See **Judge.**

Red Cross Society

British Red Cross Society, Singapore Branch, 1949. In September 1949, Red Cross work in Singapore began when a Singapore branch was established as part of the British Red Cross Society. The organization took up temporary accommodation in a borrowed office in Empress Place. It later moved to Maxwell Road and then to the Asia Insurance Building.

The branch was officially inaugurated by Lady Gimson, wife of Governor Franklin Gimson. She became the first President of the Singapore branch. In 1959, the foundation stone for Red Cross House in Penang Road was laid by Lady Goode, wife of Governor Sir William Goode and retiring President of the Singapore Red Cross. Red Cross House was opened in 1961, and in 1964, the Singapore branch of the Red Cross ceased to be part of the British Red Cross. In 1965, the Singapore branch of the Red Cross became part of the Malaysian Red Cross. Following Singapore's independence, the Red Cross in Singapore became a national society. In 1968, it became involved in International relief services and opened a night ambulance service. In 1984, the Red Cross Blood Centre opened.

Regatta, New Year's Day

see **Sailing Regatta**

Registration of births and deaths

1872. In 1872, the registration of births was introduced. However, as registration was voluntary, the records were not complete. In 1938, the Registration of Births and Death Ordinance was introduced to make the registration of births and deaths compulsory. In 1948, a National Registration Office opened at Empress Place, and issued paper identity cards to identify individuals born in Singapore. In 1966, the National Registration Act came into force and the National Registration Office and the Registry of Births and Deaths came under the control of the Ministry of Labour. In October 1981, the National Registration Department was established under the Ministry of Home Affairs.

Reporter, Asian Chief

Chia Po Teik. Former Straits Times chief reporter Chia Po Teik was the first Asian to be appointed chief reporter in any British-owned English language newspaper, the *Straits Echo*. He died in 1996 aged 86.

Republic of Singapore Air Force

See **Air Force**

Recorder

See **Judge**

Resident, British

William Farquhar, 1819. The first Resident of Singapore was Colonel William Farquhar, who was appointed to the post by Raffles in 1819. Farquhar joined the Madras Engineers in 1790 at the age of 20 years old. He served in Malacca for 23 years. In 1803, he was appointed as Resident of Malacca and remained as Resident there until the Dutch returned in 1818. His time in Malacca provided Farquhar with valuable Malayan experience and he gained an intimate knowledge of politics in the Riau-Lingga region. He was known as the 'Rajah of Malacca' and commanded respect with a combination of grace and authority. Farquhar was accessible to all, was ready to hear complaints and judge disputes and he had a reputation for being impartial towards rich and poor. He spoke fluent Malay and married a girl from Malacca. Farquhar had negotiated a treaty in 1818 to safeguard British trade against the revival of Dutch trading privileges. He urged the East India Company to set up a base there to protect British trade in the Straits of Malacca. He was a close colleague of Raffles and had his complete trust. In December 1818, the Dutch annulled Farquhar's treaty and established a garrison in Riau and installed a Resident with authority over the Riau region including Johore and the nearby islands. In December 1818, Raffles dispatched Farquhar to the Carimon Islands to see if the islands would provide a suitable site for a trading post. Raffles was not due to sail with Farquhar but when Raffles was prevented from sailing to Aceh, Raffles sailed south to find Farquhar. They found that the Carimons were rocky and unsuitable for a settlement.

On 28 January 1819, the fleet of 8 ships anchored off St John's Island near the mouth of the Singapore River. The following morning Raffles and Farquhar went ashore. The Temenggong trusted Farquhar and realised the material advantages of a British trading post in Singapore. On 6 February 1819, Raffles signed a formal agreement with Sultan Hussein and the Temenggong to establish a trading post subject to a payment of $5000 per year to Sultan Hussein and $300 to the Temenggong. The next day, Raffles appointed Farquhar as the first Resident of Singapore responsible to Raffles as Lieutenant Governor of Bencoolen. Apart from a brief visit by Raffles in May 1819, Farquhar ran the trading post for three years.

Under his leadership and direction, Singapore became a successful trading port. Farquahar sent to Malacca for settlers and suppliers and his reputation encouraged traders to come flocking to Singapore. Singapore's location and free trade policies encouraged the growth of trade. Within two and a half years, Singapore was able to attract 3000 trading vessels and the import/export trade was worth $8 million. Farquhar encouraged traders from all parts of the region and by 1821, Singapore became a cosmopolitan port of 5000 inhabitants including Bugis, Chinese, Indians, Armenians and Straits Chinese.

Raffles returned to Singapore in October 1822 and was delighted with the progress of the port. However, he disapproved of many of the measures taken by Farquhar. He set aside Farquhar's considerable achievements and removed him from office. Farquhar remained in Singapore for a few months before leaving for Scotland at the end of 1823. He was given a wonderful farewell by the people of Singapore who understood his achievements far better than did Raffles. He died in Perth, Scotland in 1839.

Restaurant, Revolving

Top of the 'M', 1973. The Top of the 'M' restaurant on the 39th Floor of the Meritus Mandarin Hotel opened in 1973. It is Singapore's first and highest revolving restaurant and is situated 173 metres above the ground. It has a seating capacity of 124 persons and takes about two hours and fifteen minutes to make a complete revolution. A full course dinner is almost perfectly timed to coincide with one full revolution, but it is also dependent on the pace at which guests consume and enjoy their meal.

Rhodes Scholar

See **Scholars**.

Rickshaw

1880. The first rickshaw arrived in Singapore in 1880. The first consignment came from Shanghai although most of the later rickshaws came from Japan. It was a small light-hooded cart with springs and two large diameter wheels was drawn by a man running between the shafts. It quickly superseded the gharry, a horse drawn carriage, and by 1910 the rickshaw reigned supreme. It was popular because it was cheap, effective and manoeuvrable. Before 1890, the rickshaw coolies were usually Hokkien or Cantonese. By 1898, the trade was dominated by Hockchia and Hengwah dialect-speaking Chinese from Foochow province in China.

By 1902, there were 22,000 rickshaw pullers and 15,000 of those were from Foochow. In 1904, a 1st class rickshaw was introduced into Singapore. They had rubber tyres and were designed for comfort and speed. A ride in a 1st class rickshaw cost nearly twice as much. By 1906, there were 1,226 1st class rickshaws and 6,138 2nd class rickshaws. The rickshaw pullers were hard-working, exploited and poor. They made less than $1.00 per day after paying rent on the rickshaw and it was almost impossible for the pullers to save to purchase their own rickshaw. The rickshaw pullers made their owners very rich. The pullers were mainly single and transient and lived in rickshaw coolie lodging houses. The Hockchia pullers tended to live in Lower Victoria Street and the Hengwah pullers lived in Queen Street. The rickshaw industry was controlled by the Rickshaw Department of the Municipality. It was set up in 1892 and the first Registrar was William Hooper. During the 1930s, the popularity of rickshaws began to decline. By 1939, there were less than 4,000 rickshaws down from a peak of 30,000 rickshaws in 1922.

Rifle Association

Rifle Association, 1873. The formation of the Singapore Volunteer Rifle Corps in 1854 encouraged an interest in shooting, and the introduction of the Snider carbine rifle stimulated the formation of a rifle association, named simply, The Rifle Association, in 1873. The Association used the rifle range at the Race Course but when it proved to be too short, it switched over to old Artillery Range at Balestier. In 1901, the Volunteer Corps was expanded to include a Chinese Company. This stimulated a new interest in rifle shooting. In 1903, Tay Soo Bin won the Individual Snap Shooting Competition organised by the Rifle Association. He won the General's Cup at the Rifle Association annual meeting in 1905. In October 1905, the Rifle Association introduced the first of the regular Monthly Handicap Shoots with about 50 competitors. Any member of the Volunteer Corps was entitled to take part in these competitions free of charge. In 1906, the annual competition was won by Sapper A Murray. Song Ong Siang came in sixth. The Association held regular inter-port rifle shooting matches with Ceylon and Calcutta on one hand and Perak and Selangor on the other. The last Inter-Port competition before the Great War was held in May 1914. Singapore won for the first time and the winning team consisted of Song Ong Siang, Tan Chow Kim and Miss B Kerr. This was the first time a lady participated in the Inter-Port Cup. Miss Kerr was Principal of Singapore Chinese Girls' School. She finished sixth in the competition. The Singapore Rifle Association continues to be active today.

Rifle Club

Swiss Rifle Shooting Club, 1871. In 1871, the Swiss community formed Singapore's first shooting club, the Swiss Rifle Shooting Club. In 1870, the Swiss were a small community mainly involved in the weaving industry. Otto Alder invited some of his friends over for tiffin at his house in Bunker Hill. He asked them to bring rifles and he made a Swiss style target. The affair was a great success and the Swiss shooters decided to form a shooting club. The members roamed the island on horseback looking for a site for a rifle range. In August 1871, about 30 members met at the newly-opened rifle shooting range at Balestier Road. In 1872, the **first shooting festival** was held and the **first shot** was fired by Miss Baenziger, who was from a famous Swiss shooting family. In 1875 a large clubhouse was built on the site. In 1901, the shooting club was given notice to quit. They bought a piece of land at Bukit Tinggi and in August 1902, the new clubhouse was opened on the site. In 1925, the name of the club was changed from the Swiss Rifle Shooting Club to the Swiss Club. The Swiss Club is still on Bukit Tinggi and now boasts a membership of 1,000 members from 40 nations.

Riots

Ghee Hok vs Ghee Hin Riots, 1854. The first major riots took place in Singapore in 1854. That year, the two leading Chinese secret societies – the Hokkien-dominated Ghee Hok and the Teochew controlled Ghee Hin – began fighting after their dispute over the weight of a bag of rice. The scale of violence soon escalated and nearly 5,000 men were fighting in the streets. It was a domestic dispute over the control of wealth sources within the Chinese community, rather than an anti-government riot. The government ordered the police not to use violence and military men were brought ashore from HM ships *Sybille, Lily* and *Rapid*. The government appealed to the Hokkien and Teochew leaders to stop the fighting. The town became quiet but the fighting spread to the rural areas. There were reports of atrocities in some areas and whole villages were wiped out. Local residents were sworn in as special constables and worked with the Captains and officers of the navy ships to keep peace in the town. After 8 days of fighting, 400 Chinese were dead. Chinese shops were looted but European business premises remained untouched. 81 men were arrested. 15 were transported, 64 imprisoned and 2 condemned to death. Following this riot, legislation was introduced in 1854 to register all Chinese societies. However, India did not ratify the Bill and it was never brought into law. The government had little or no control over the Chinese secret societies until the introduction of the Societies Act in 1890.

Risis Gold Orchid

1976. In 1976, the Singapore Institute of Standards and Research (SISIR) developed a process to capture the beauty of Singapore's orchids in 24 carat gold. The RISIS (SISIR in reverse) orchid proved to be very popular with locals and tourists alike and won the **first Best Tourism Souvenir Award**. Later, new precious metals such as rhodium were introduced to give the orchid a lustrous silvery finish. The orchid is lightly coated in copper which gives it sufficient body to accept the next stage of the process. It is then covered in 24 carat gold and hand-finished. If rhodium is to be used, the orchid is then overlaid with rhodium.

River Dredging, Singapore River

1903. The first successful dredging of the Singapore River was made in 1903 by the steam driven bucket dredge *Mudlark*. Some 2,000 tons of silt were removed from the river and 600 tons of rock were removed from the bar at the mouth of the Singapore River. The dredge removed 700 tons of mud every day, and by 1912, 482,000 tons of silt and waste material had been taken out of the river by the *Mudlark*.

There had been many previous unsuccessful attempts to dredge the river. As early as 1822, a committee appointed by Raffles found that a considerable amount of sand had started to silt up the river mouth due to the construction of jetties on the North side of Boat Quay. Despite numerous requests for a dredge, nothing was done until 1851. A dredge was built locally by Tivendale's and took over 2 years to complete. The machinery ordered from England was faulty. The dredge finally went into service in 1856 but was not able to function efficiently. It was too wide to fit under the Coleman Bridge and the upper reaches of the river could not be dredged. In 1857, the machinery was removed and the dredge was used as a Marine Police Station. In 1861, it was used as a floating chapel for seamen and in May 1875, the Municipality provided funds for the river in front of Boat Quay to be dredged by hand using buckets. Following a River Commission Report in 1899, the new steam bucket dredge, *Mudlark* was purchased and dredging operations began in 1903.

River Hongbao

1987. The first River Hongbao was held in 1987 on the banks of the Singapore River. The first programme director was Perng Peck Seng who had a budget of about $500,000. In 1987, it was more of a variety show featuring artistes from Singapore, Hong Kong, China and Taiwan. It was started by the Chinese newspaper *Lianhe Zaobao* but is now jointly supported by the Singapore Federation of Clan Associations, the Singapore Tourism Board, Chinese newspapers of Singapore Press Holdings, People's Association and the Singapore Chinese Chamber of Commerce and Industry. In 2005, the budget was nearly $2 million.

Road Pricing, Electronic (ERP)

See **Area Licensing Scheme**

Rowing Club

Singapore Rowing Club, 1883. Singapore's first rowing club was the Singapore Rowing Club, formed in 1883 on a site just above the Cavenagh Bridge on the banks of the Singapore River. FG Davidson was the Club's first Secretary.

Rubber

1876. The first five rubber saplings were planted in Singapore in 1876 at the Botanic Gardens. However, the commercial cultivation of rubber did not take off until Henry Nicholas Ridley, first Director of the Botanic Gardens discovered a way of tapping the rubber trees without sapping its yield. The **first rubber planter** in Singapore was Dr Lim Boon Keng who founded the Sembawang Rubber Plantation of 3,800 acres in 1898 in the northern part of the island.

Rubber Auction

1907. The first recorded rubber auction was held by Henry Coghlan of Coghlan & Co in 1907 on the ground floor of his premises in Raffles Place. So much rubber was sent to the auction that it spilled out onto the five-foot way. The success of the auction encouraged the Chamber of Commerce to form a Rubber Association to 'improve the conditions governing the trade in plantation rubber in Singapore' and to conduct Auction Sales governed by regulations laid down by the Chamber of Commerce. The Chamber of Commerce Rubber Association was established in June 1911. The Rubber Association auctions were held in the Exchange Building at the seaward end of Battery Road. The Exchange Building soon became known as the Rubber Exchange Building. The first auction was held on the 12 September 1911 with eleven lots going for auction. Ten were from Guthrie & Co. and one lot from Coghlan & Co. Gino, Pertile & Co. bought the first lot and the total amount sold was 24.32 pikuls. Prices were about $276 per pikul for crepe rubber, $266 for smoked rubber and $186 for bark crepe rubber. In 1912, 599 tons of rubber were offered at the Singapore auctions. In 1918, over 52,000 tons were offered. The auctions helped make Singapore the world centre of the rubber trade. The Exchange Building was pulled down in 1926 and replaced by the Fullerton Building. The new building housed the General Post Office as well as the Chamber of Commerce (1928).

Running Track, Tartan

National Stadium, 1973. The Tartan surface was developed by the 3M Company (Minnesota Mining and Manufacturing) in 1964. Originally developed for horse racing tracks to help horses avoid injury by having a smooth and cushioned surface on which to train. These surfaces substituted traditional bitumen and asphalt aggregates with polyurethane and crushed rubber, giving a pliable, shock-absorbing and springy surface. Tartan Track and Tartan Turf were two products 3M marketed, after discovering that most race-tracks could not afford the new material. Singapore's first tartan running track was installed in the National Stadium at Kallang in 1973.

S

Sailing Club

Singapore Yacht Club, 1826. Singapore's first sailing club, the Singapore Yacht Club, was established in 1826 by Dr William Montgomerie who was its first President. However, it became inactive a few years after that. In 1834, the Club was revived to organize the annual New Year Sports. William Henry Read was the Commodore of the Club in 1882. The club was again revived in 1919 with Walter Nutt as President, and on 1 July 1919 a new committee was formed. In 1922, the Singapore Yacht Club built a new clubhouse in Tanjong Pagar in Trafalgar Street. In 1922, the Prince of Wales visited the clubhouse and agreed to become the club's patron. The club then became the Royal Singapore Yacht Club. The Governor, Sir Laurence Guillemard was President of the Club from 1922 to 1927. In 1967, the club became the Republic of Singapore Yacht Club with first Head of State, President Yusof bin Ishak as Patron. See **Sailing Regatta**.

Sailing Regatta

New Year's Regatta, 1834. The New Year's Regatta was first held in 1834. The yacht races were organised by the Singapore Yacht Club. The main race was 6.5 miles around the harbour. The boats taking part were *Waterwitch, Maggie Lauder, Shamrock, Hawk's Hill* and *Jenny dang the Weaver*. The race was won by *Jenny dang the Weaver* in 2 hours and 19 minutes. An account of the race is to be found in Admiral Keppel's diary. Thereafter, it became a tradition to have shore and water sports on New Year's Day each year.

St. Andrew's Day Dinner and Dance

Reading Room, 1835. The first St Andrew's Day Dinner was held at the Reading Room in November 1835. Seventy people attended the dinner. Dr Montgomerie and William Napier presided and Messrs Spottiswoode, Lorrain, Carnie and Stephen were stewards. The following night a Ball and Supper was held in the upper apartments of the Courthouse (now Old Parliament House). The Malacca Band played and the ladies wore tartan sashes over their dresses and many of the men wore kilts.

Salvation Army

1935. In May 1935, the Salvation Army came to Singapore. It later spread to Penang (1938), Malacca and Ipoh (1940), Kuching (Sarawak) (1950), Kuala Lumpur (1966) and Kota Kinabalu (Sabah) (1996). They set up an Industrial Home in Singapore for waifs and stray boys. They were also involved in social relief, adoptions and after care for prison offenders. 'The General of The Salvation Army' is a 'corporation sole' under the Straits Settlements' Salvation Army Ordinance, 1939.

Satellite Imaging

Centre for Remote Imaging Sensing and Processing (CRISP), 1995. The first satellite imaging centre, Centre for Remote Imaging Sensing and Processing (CRISP) was set up in

1995 in the grounds of the National University of Singapore. It is used to download images taken by satellite cameras. These images can be anything on the earth's surface, for example fires in Sumatra, land use, surface temperatures and weather patterns. The images may also have military use.

Satellite Town

Tiong Bahru, 1936. The first public housing satellite town was Tiong Bahru. It was built by the Singapore Improvement Trust (SIT) between 1936 and 1941 and accommodated about 6,000 people. The estate was built by young architects working for the SIT and the design embraced contemporary European ideas. The estate was designed by James Milner Frazer who had previously worked with the London City Council Architectural Department. Design features of Tiong Bahru include planar white walls, horizontal windows, curved stair towers and excellent ventilation.

Scholars

Queen's Scholarship, 1886. The first government educational scholarship made available in Singapore was the Queen's Scholarship. It was introduced by Governor Cecil Clementi Smith 'in order to allow promising boys an opportunity of completing their studies in England, and to encourage a number of boys to remain in school and acquire a really useful education'. Students (actually, originally only boys) from the three Straits Settlements territories competed for this prestigious scholarship. The scheme was set up in 1885 but the first scholarships were not awarded until 1886. Between 1886 and 1911, 45 scholarhships were awarded, with 24 awarded to Eurasians. The **first Queen's Scholars** were CS Angus and James Aitken of Raffles Institution. The **first Chinese** to win the Queen's Scholarship was Lim Boon Keng (also Raffles Institution), who won the award in 1887. He became Singapore's first Western-trained Chinese doctor. Singapore's first Chinese lawyer, Song Ong Siang won the Queen's in 1888. The **first woman** to win the Queen's Scholarship was Maggie Tan who won the award in 1930.. Her brother, Tan Thoon Lip had won the Queen's Scholarship in 1929 and later became the **first Asian Registrar of the Supreme Court.** Maggie Tan later married another Queen's Scholar, Lim Hong Bee. The second woman winner was Thora Oehlers, who won the scholarship in 1932.

The Queen's Scholarship continued to be offered to students who completed their Standard VIII examinations (equivalent to the current GCE 'A' level examinations) up till 1940. Thereafter, selection of Queen's Scholars was transferred to a board of selection appointed by the Senate of Raffles College and were awarded to students of Raffles College. The **Anderson Scholarship** replaced the Queen's Scholarship at the Standard VIII level in 1940 and this was awarded to the top student in the Senior Cambridge examination for Malaya and Singapore. The **first Singapore winner** of this scholarship was Lee Kuan Yew.

In 1959, when Singapore achieved internal self-government, the Queen's scholarship was replaced by the Singapore State Scholarship. However, unlike the Queen's scholarship, it was tenable only at the local university. The **first three State Scholars** were: Leonard Tan Kim Tuan, Tony Tan Keng Yam (later to be Deputy Prime Minister) and Mah Puay Tim. In 1964, the scholarship was renamed the Yang di-Pertuan Scholarship. Five scholarships were awarded in 1965 and recipients included Lim Siong Guan and Lim Hng Kiang. In 1966, the Scholarship was renamed the President's Scholarship. The **first President's Scholars** were Chia Chee Liong, Barry Desker, Mark Hong Tat Soon, Koh Cher Siang, Lee Yock Suan, Lee Choon Huat, Leong Yu Kiang, Sim Yong Chan and Tan Leng Cheo. They received their scholarships from President Yusof Ishak at a special ceremony held at the Istana. The **first woman** to win the President's Scholarship was Suzanne Liau in 1968.

In 1971 the Public Service Commission awarded the **first Singapore Armed Forces Merit Scholarships** to develop the leadership cadre in the Singapore Armed Forces. They were awarded to students who attained high academic results and military performance. The first scholarship were awarded to Lee Hsien Loong (now Prime Minister of Singapore), Liu Tsun Kie, Boey Tak Hap, Lai Seck Khui and Sin Boon Wah.

The **Rhodes Scholarship**, first inaugurated in Britain in 1902, saw its first Singapore winner in 1961. He was Tan Eng Liang, who won the award to read for a doctorate in Chemistry at Oxford University. Tan, who was from Raffles Institution, was, besides being a top student, a very able sportsman as well, having represented Singapore in swimming and waterpolo. He later became a Senior Minister of State. At Oxford, Tan won a Half Blue at Water Polo and swimming. The first woman Rhodes Scholar was Jacqueline Chin in 1991.

In October 1991, the **Lee Kuan Yew Scholarship** for post-graduate studies was inaugurated. This prestigious scholarship was described as the 'Singapore Rhodes scholarship' and is awarded to outstanding Singaporeans to allow them to pursue postgraduate studies either overseas or locally. It is intended to allow the recipients the opportunity to develop their potential as leaders in their field. There are no restrictions on course and there is no bond. The first recipients were Martin Cher Soon Heng and Danielle Yew Woon Theng, both of whom applied to do Master's courses in the United States.

School

Singapore Institution, 1823. The first school in Singapore was the Singapore Institution, later renamed Raffles Institution. It was established by Sir Stamford Raffles, founder of modern Singapore. Originally, Raffles proposed to Sultan Hussein and the Temenggong that their sons be sent to Calcutta for their education, but they did not consent. Raffles then decided that he would establish a school in Singapore. A meeting was held at Raffles' house on Government Hill on 1 April 1823, it was decided that a school would be established to: (a) educate the sons of the higher order of natives and others; (b) afford means of instruction in the native languages to such of the Company's servants and others as may desire it; and (c) collect the scattered literature and traditions of the country with whatever may illustrate their laws and customs, and to publish and circulate in a correct form the most important of these, with such other works as may be calculated to raise the character of the institution and to be useful and instructive to the people.

Raffles' original plan was to transfer the Anglo-Chinese College from Malacca to Singapore and unite it with the proposed Malay College. He also wanted it to consist of three departments: a scientific department, a literary and moral department for the Chinese; and a similar one for the Siamese Malays and others. This proposal was never carried out. The first meeting of the Trustees of the Singapore Institution held their first meeting on 15 April 1823. JA Maxwell was the Honorary Secretary and AL Johnson & Co, the Honorary Treasurers. A total of $17,495 was collected for the Institution from subscribers, as well as from the proposed sale of the Anglo-Chinese College house in Malacca. Of this amount, $9,670 was designated for the Institution generally, $1,075 for the Scientific Department, and $6,750 for the Malayan College. The Government promised a monthly subscription of $300 for the schools, and $25 yearly for the library. Lieutenant Jackson made a plan and estimate of the proposed building, which he said could be constructed in twelve months. This was approved, and $15,000 was voted for the purpose. The first students were admitted soon after. The school's original campus was located at the junction of Bras Basah and Beach Roads, and it was to remain there for the next 149 years. The foundation stone was laid on 5 June 1823 by Raffles himself.

After Raffles left Singapore on 9 June 1823, the Trustees were left in a dilemma. Funds had run out and the new Resident John Crawfurd was silent on the grants promised by Raffles on behalf of the East India Company. Furthermore the Anglo-Chinese College had not been sold off. On 20 November, the Trustees held another meeting in an attempt to get the institution going, but the financial odds were heavily stacked against them. By 1830, the original building at Bras Basah was still uncompleted and in a derelict state. On 27 August 1835, a group of people met in the Court House under the chairmanship of Alexander Guthrie, a prominent merchant and resolved that Raffles' original scheme be modified to gain more support among the population. The meeting also decided that no one religion should form the basis of the education provided. It drew up salaries to be paid to teachers, and decided to invite the Governor and Resident of the Settlement to serve as patrons of the school to be established. This may have led to a promised monthly grant of $100 from the government. Subscription was also sought. Another factor that made it possible for the Institution building to be restored was the setting up of a monument fund on the death of Raffles, who had died in 1826. By the end of 1835, the fund stood at $3000. In the end of 1837, the original building was completed, and ready for use as a school. The Singapore Library was housed in the building for many years. The **first Headmaster** of the school was JH Moor who served from 1837 till his death in 1843. In 1868, the Singapore Institution was renamed Raffles Institution in honour of its founder.

Singapore's **first girls' school** was St Margaret's School. The school began as a shelter for young girls sold in the streets under the *mui tsai* system. It was begun by Mrs Maria Dyer, a missionary with the London Missionary Society who obtained permission from Governor Samuel Bonham to start a school and shelter for the girls. The school was started in 1842 in a shophouse in North Bridge Road and was then known as the Chinese Girls' School. The school gave girls from poor families the opportunity to have free education. Its primary school remained the shelter and education of destitute girls and orphans. In 1843, Dyer's husband died and she returned to Penang to run the Chinese Girls' School in Penang. She was replaced by Miss Grant who was a representative of the Society for the Promotion of Female Eduacation in the East. In 1850, the school moved to River Valley Road and then in 1861 to 134 Sophia Road. In 1853, Miss Sophia Cooke was appointed as Principal School. She remained at the school for 42 years. In 1900, the Society for the Promotion of Female Education in the East was taken over by the Church of England Zenana Missionary Society (CEZMS) and the school was renamed the CEZMS School. After World War II, the school came under the administration of the Diocese of Singapore and was renamed St Margaret's School. A separate secondary school was built in Farrer Road in 1957, while the primary school remained at Sophia Road.

The first **convent school** to be established was the Convent of the Holy Infant Jesus in Victoria Street which was founded in 1852. It was founded by Father Jean-Marie Beurel and the first teachers came from France to teach in Singapore under the leadership of Mother St Mathilde. The objectives of the school were to provide a proper education to the girls in the settlement, to provide a refuge and free education for orphans and to teach the dogmas of the Catholic faith. The school was located in a small house on the corner of Bras Basah Road and Victoria Street that had been built by George Dromgold Coleman.

The first **English-medium school for Chinese girls** was the Singapore Chinese Girls' School founded in 1899. The school opened in June 1899 with 7 girls enrolled. By 1923, 250 girls were enrolled in the school. The first **Chinese medium girls' school** was Chung Hua Girls School which was founded in 1911. The first **Anglo-Tamil School** was set up in 1873. The first **Chinese-medium secondary school** was the Chinese High School which opened in 1919 with 100 students. The **first principal** of the school was KY Doo and the first president was Tan Kah Kee with Lim Nee Soon as treasurer. The Chinese community raised nearly half a million dollars to start the school including $30,000 from Tan Kah Kee and $10,000 from Lim Nee Soon. It was the only institution offering a Chinese secondary education in Malaya. The first Tamil Secondary School opened on 30 March 1969. This was the Umar Pulavar Tamil High School in Maxwell Road. The school had 11 classrooms to cater to both primary and secondary classes.

School Health Service

1921. The first school medical service was offered in 1921. Dr Robert B Macgregor was appointed School Medical Officer in 1921, and he was assisted by Drs Pavillet and RB Hawes. During its first year of operations, 3,964 boys were given routine inspections. The medical officer pinpointed 558 cases out of the initial group for follow-up treatment. Medical service identified dental caries as the most serious problem. Another problem was the high rate of marked defective eyesight. 9.4% of Chinese boys examined were found to have marked defective vision. Dr L O'May, the Lady Schools Medical Officer examined the girls and found that 47% suffered dental caries and 32% had anaemia. Some 1,200 girls were examined at Methodist Girls' School, Singapore Chinese Girls' School, Raffles Girls' School and St Anthony's Convent. 77% of the girls at Raffles Girls School were found to be well nourished and in fair condition. Only 42% of the girls tested at Singapore Chinese Girls' School were classified as well-nourished. There was a surprising absence of malarial indicators such as an enlarged spleen. Pupils at Bukit Timah and Paya Lebar Schools were examined for malarial indicators, and 39.6% of the Bukit Timah children had enlarged spleens, and 26.3% of the Paya Lebar children tested. On the other hand, children at Pasir Panjang were only found to show indicators in 3.5% of cases. School buildings and their sanitary arrangements were also inspected. In his first report,

Dr Hawes admitted that a shortage of medical staff had prevented the scheme from being applied more widely. Dr Hawes also commented that the 'callous indifference of many parents in Singapore to the suffering of their children is appalling.' However, the introduction of the school medical service had done valuable work. Despite these earlier challenges, the school health service, introduced in 1921 soon became a vital part of the primary health care system in Singapore.

Scooter & Scooter Factory

The first motor scooter appeared in Singapore some time in 1920. The first scooter factory in Singapore was opened on 28 April 1965. Located in Jurong, the East Asiatic Company Ltd operated a Vespa Assembly Plant, making scooters for the Italian brand, Vespa.

Scout Troops

Maullefinch's Baden-Powell Corps, 1908. Calls to establish scout troops or Baden-Powell Corps were made as early as in 1908 by a chartered surveyor named KM Maullefinch, but Scouting officially started on 2 July 1910 with the establishment of the Boy Scouts Association. The meeting was chaired by Major Ernest Stephenson. The Committee, comprising TC Hay, TR Hill, Percy C Fenwick, Brother Stephen (Principal of St Joseph's Institution), OA Morris and Percy Gold. Major Stephenson was elected President of the Local Association, with Pierpont as Secretary. The first Scout Troop was Mauleffinch's First Singapore Troop which he first organized in 1908. Scouting really took off after August 1910 with the arrival of Nottingham scoutmaster Frank Cooper Sands. Sands, universally acknowledged as the Father of Malayan Scouting was instrumental in building up the movement and soon had two troops – the First and Second Singapore Troops – up and running under the sponsorship of the Young Men's Christian Association (YMCA). The **first Malay troop** in Singapore was the 5th Singapore Troop based at Victoria Bridge School. The **first school-based Scout Troop** was probably the 9th Singapore Troop of Outram Road School which was founded in February 1921, just a few months ahead of the 11th Singapore Troop of the Anglo-Chinese School. The **first Sea Scout Troop** was the First Trafalgar Sea Scout Troop established in 1938.

Scrabble

1956. The first record of scrabble being played in Singapore is in 1956. The Scrabble Association was set up in 1996 by a core group of enthusiasts. The **first Singapore National Scrabble Championship** was held in 1997 and was won by Austin Tan. In 1999, the **first World Masters competition** was held in Singapore at the Grand Hyatt Hotel.

Sculpture Show

National Library, 1967. Singapore's first sculpture show opened at the National Library in Stamford Road on 21 April 1967. A total of 117 clay figures, wood-carvings and metal works created by seven artists were on display. These included the busts of President Yusof Ishak and Prime Minister Lee Kuan Yew.

Seaman's Mission

Sailor's Home, 1851. In 1851, a public meeting was held to establish a Sailor's Home. One of the serious security problems in Singapore at that time was caused by the riotous behaviour of sailors on shore. Many of them were stranded in Singapore for months, waiting for another job. There was no provision for accommodation or entertainment for them and they could not afford to stay in cheap public houses and could find no other entertainment than beer shops and brothels. The residents hoped that a Sailor's Home would provide some alternative. A committee comprising James Guthrie, Captain Sparkes of the P&O Company, John Harvey and William Henry Read proposed that a fancy dress ball be organized to raise funds for the home. The ball was held on 15 May 1851 at the Assembly Rooms. Tickets were priced at $5.00 for individuals and $7.50 for families. The Sailor's Home was built in High Street. The Government paid 100 Indian rupees for the rent. Soon, the house became too small for its avowed purposes and Joseph Balestier's house was purchased in 1857 for the Home's use. The Government advanced 12,000 rupees and the building was given to the Government as security. It was extended in 1877, and Joseph Conrad stayed at the Sailor's Home during his visits to Singapore. Indeed, there are references to the Sailor's Home in many of his stories, including 'The End of the Tether'. The Home was pulled down in 1922 to make way for the Capitol Building and Theatre.

In 1882, two missionary workers, Miss Cooke and Mr Hocquard, started a Sailor's Rest House in Tanjong Pagar, near the Kreta Ayer Police Station. She collected donations from leading merchants and the premises were soon found to be too small. Edward Boustead of Boustead & Co bequeathed $55,000 to build an Institute for Seaman (later referred to as Boustead Institute). The Institute was for the use of seamen or seafaring men and dock employees frequenting or residing in Singapore and was to provide a place where they could be provided with means of shelter, rest and recreation, amusement or intellectual cultivation. The Tanjong Pagar Dock Company presented the building site and the Institute was opened in July 1892 by Governor Cecil Clementi Smith. Two adjoining shophouses were purchased in 1892 and four more in 1893. The Institute provided a well-supplied reading room and library, a billiard room and a bar where beer and light wines were sold. There was also accommodation for 14 persons. Thirty more temporary boarders could be accommodated in the hall. There was a church service at the Institute every Sunday night. The first manager of the Institute was a Mr Lee, who had been armourer on the *HMS Orion*. The Institute, which was situated at the corner of Tanjong Pagar Road and Neil Road, has since been demolished.

Sea Wall

Esplanade, 1847. In September 1847, the Government of India authorized the construction of a sea wall along the front of the Esplanade to prevent the sea from encroaching. In January 1851, the heavy rains caused the sea wall to collapse for a distance of about 80 feet. In three other places, the sea wall appeared on the verge of collapsing. The *Singapore Free Press* reported that it would have to be rebuilt. A second sea wall was built at what is now Collyer Quay. It ran from the old Fort Fullerton (the present Fullerton Hotel) to the old Telok Ayer Fish Market and was designed by Colonel George Chancellor Collyer in 1858 and built between 1861 and 1862. The ground behind the seawall was filled in during 1863–1864 and buildings were then erected along Collyer Quay. The first buildings were the offices of Nassim & Company, built in 1865.

Secret Societies

Ghee Hin & Ghee Hok. The first two secret societies operating in Singapore were the Ghee Hin and the Ghee Hok. The Ghee Hok was a Hokkien-dominated society and the Ghee Hin included branches from the other dialect groups. In 1819, the societies were already established in Penang and they were offshoots of large organisations based in Junk Ceylon (now called Phuket). There was also a secret society presence in Malacca at that time. It was estimated that there were at least 4,000 secret society members in Malacca in 1826. New branches were set up in Singapore in the early 1820s. The first indication of their presence was in November 1824 when several people were killed in secret society clashes. In 1854 there was serious rioting in Singapore between the two societies and the government took steps to control them. In 1869, an Ordinance for the Suppression of Dangerous Societies was introduced. Unfortunately, it was a toothless piece of legislation. In 1890, the government introduced a Societies Act. It did not lead to the suppression of secret societies but it did, for the first time, give the authorities the means to deal with them. Under the Societies Act, the government had the right to dissolve any organisation if it appeared necessary for public safety or welfare. The legislation encouraged the emergence of a whole range of ethnic, cultural and welfare orgnaisations within the Chinese community.

Securities Broker, Publicly Listed

Kim Eng Securities Holdings, 1990. In 1990, Kim Eng Securities Holdings became the first stockbroker to be listed on the Singapore Stock Exchange. The firm was founded in 1972 by Mrs Gloria Lee. Her son from her first marriage, Douglas Ooi was managing director in 1990 and steered the firm through the process of going public. Kim Eng is a member of the stock exchanges in five Asian markets, Singapore, Hong Kong, Indonesia, Thailand and the Philippines.

Seismic ship

Western Islander, 1972. In 1972, the first locally-built seismic ship was launched at Kallang Park Industrial Estate. The *Western Islander* was built by Weng Chan Engineering and weighed 500 tons. It was fully air-conditioned and fitted with modern electronic and satellite equipment. It cost more than $3 million and took nearly 6 months to build. It was built for the Western Geophysical Company, an American oil exploration company to be used for seismic operations and studies connected with oil surveys in Southeast Asian waters. Its maiden voyage was to West Irian.

Senior Counsel

1997. The Singapore Academy of Law Act, 1988 introduced created a new category of lawyers known as Senior Counsel. The Senate of the Academy was empowered to appoint an advocate, solicitor or legal officer as a Senior Counsel, the counterpart of the United Kingdom's Queen's Counsel. Appointment is considered a great honour and allows its bearers to wear silk gowns in court. The first Senior Counsels were appointed in January 1997. They were: KS Rajah, Michael Sydney Hwang, Tan Kok Quan, Woo Bh Li, VK Rajah, Kenneth Tan, Joseph Grimberg, Chan Sek Keong, Harry Elias, Giam Chin Toon, Michael Khoo, Wong Meng Meng and Davinder Singh.

Sex-change operation

1971. Singapore's first sex-change operation was performed at the Kandang Kebau Hopsital in 1971. It was performed by Professor SS Ratnam. Since then, over a thousand operations have been performed at the hospital. Operations were phased out in 1987 due to the risk of AIDS.

Sextuplets

1998. The first sextuplets were born in Singapore at Gleneagles Hospital on 27 November 1998. The babies were delivered by Dr Christopher Chen of the Centre of Reproductive Medicine at Gleneagles Hospital. The Indonesian parents, Madam Susan Tjokrosetio and Mr Andre S Prijono have named their daughter Deidre, and their five sons: Danny, Davis, Dylon, Douglas and Dominick.

Ship, Locally Built,

Sree Singapura, 1839. The first vessel built in Singapore was a 100-ton schooner, *Sree Singapura*, launched in May 1839 and built for an European firm called Shaw & Stephens.

Shipping Line, International

Pacific International Lines, 1968. On 2 January 1968, Pacific International Lines Ltd became the first international line to operate solely with Singapore registered ships and Singapore seamen. The shipping line had nine ships including 3 ocean-going 10,000-ton vessels on the Japan-China-Hong King-Malaysia-Singapore-India-Pakistan and East Africa route.

Siamese twin separation

Singapore General Hospital, 1961. Singapore's first conjoined twins (Karen and Kate) Yoon were born at the Kandang Kerbau Hospital and successfully separated at Singapore General Hospital by Professors Yeoh Ghim Seng and JE Choo on 18 December 1961. They were joined at the chest and abdomen. Unfortunately Kate Yoon died after the operation.

Sikh Temple (Gurdwara)

Sepoy Lines Gurdwara, 1870s. The first wave of immigrant Sikhs arrived in Singapore as sepoys (policemen) recruited to keep the peace, put down the Chinese gang wars, and to work for the Tanjong Pagar Dock Company. The first batch was recruited from Patiala, Ludhiana and Erozepur and arrived in Singapore in the late 1870s to form the first Sikh Police Contingent. They were stationed at Sepoy Lines (later known as Pearl's Hill). It was this group of Sepoys who built the first Sikh temple or *gurdwara* (Holy Place) at Sepoy Lines.

The Tanjong Pagar Dock Company also built a gurdwara in Anson Road for members of its Tanjong Pagar Dock Police Force. The Sikhs in the city area had their own gurdwara in Queen Street. This was established in 1920 when a wealthy Sindhi merchant donated his house for the temple. It was called *Wada Gurdwara* or 'Big Temple.' When members of the Sikh Contingent saw the new gurdwara, they petitioned the Government for the grant of a piece of land to build a new Gurdwara especially since their Pearl's Hill Gurdwara had become too small. In December 1922 the Singapore Harbour Board leased, for 20 years, to the Inspector-General of Police, the site of the present Silat Road Gurdwara comprising an area of 23,725 square feet. The Gurdwara building was completed in 1924 at a cost $54,000 of which 70% was raised by members of the police force in Singapore and Malaya and the balance was donated by Sikhs in neighbouring countries.

Silat World Champion

Sheik Alauddin, 1990. At the 1990 World Silat Championships in Holland, 23-year old Sheik Alauddin won the first world silat title for Singapore when he beat a field of 20 competitors in the 80-85 kg category. Four years on, Sheik repeated his gold medal performance at the 1994 World Silat Championships, this time in the Men's Open, the most coveted of all the categories. His win was all the more dramatic as he won it by unanimous 5-0 margins in all his bouts. A total of 22 competitors from 22 countries competed in this category. Sheik started learning silat in 1982 at the age of 15 and won his first national title three years later. From 1985 to 1997, Sheik won an unprecedented 13 successive national titles. He made his first international debut at 18 years of age and won his first SEA Games gold, six years later. He continued to win gold medals in two succeeding SEA Games. He was appointed national silat coach in 1998 when he retired from competition. In 2001, he was inducted into the Singapore Sports Council Hall of Fame.

Singapore Armed Forces Merit Scholarship,
See **Scholars**.

Singapore Idol

Taufik Batisah, 2004. The first Singapore idol contest was held in 2004. The contest was based on the same format as the highly-successful *American Idol*. The finals was held at the Singapore Indoor Stadium on 1 December 2004 and it was a needle-match between Sylvester Sim and Taufik Batisah. At the end of a nerve-wracking final, Taufik Batisah was pronounced the first *Singapore Idol*. They each sang three songs: one of their choice; one picked by the judges, and the last, a special composition 'I Dream' by Michael Fallon. A record 1.8 million television viewers tuned into the finals which was broadcast live on Channel 5 from the Singapore Indoor Stadium between 8.00 pm and 11.00 pm. The *Singapore Idol* series started on 9 August 2004 and it attracted over 3 million viewers and making it the highest-rated production in MediaCorp TV Channel 5's history. The Singapore Idol finalists were Sylvester Sim, Taufik Batisah, Olinda Cho, Daphne Khoo, Christopher Lee, Maia Lee, Beverly Morata, Jerry Ong, Leandra Rasiah, Jeassea Thyidor and David Yeo. In all, three million votes were cast throughout the six months since the start of the show in August.

Singapore Lecture

'The Invisible Hand in Economics & Politics' by Milton Friedman, 1980. The inaugural Singapore lecture was given by Milton Friedman at the Singapore Conference Hall on 14 October 1980. The title of the lecture was 'The Invisible Hand in Economics and Politics'. Friedman won the Nobel Prize for Economics in 1976. He was at that time, Senior Research Fellow at Hoover Institution at Stanford, California and also Professor of Economics at the University of Chicago. The lecture was organised by the Institute of South East Asian Studies and sponsored by the Monetary Authority of Singapore. The lecture was chaired by First Deputy Prime Minister Dr

Goh Keng Swee, and was attended by nearly 1,000 Singapore Government officials, university dons and business leaders. The aim of the lecture series is to allow young executives and decision makers in both the public and private sector to have the benefit of first hand contact with and exposure to leaders of thought.

Singapore Registered Vessel

Golden Wonder, 1966. On 23 September 1966, the Singapore merchant navy ensign was unfurled on the mast of the first Singapore-registered vessel, a 7,332-ton freighter *Golden Wonder*. The flag was unfurled by Deputy Prime Minister Dr Toh Chin Chye. The ship's owner, Guan Guan Shipping Ltd said that the company was proud that their ship was the first to fly the Singapore flag. The ship's Master was presented with a certificate from the Singapore Registry by the Marine Director. The ship was operating the Malaysia-Singapore-Malaysia run and has a crew of 54, of whom 48 were Singaporean.

Singapore State Scholarship

See **Scholars**.

Skating Rink, Ice

Taman Jurong, 1974. Singapore's first ice-skating rink was built in Taman Jurong in 1974. A few months later a new rink, the Ice Palace was set up in Kallang Leisure Park. Unfortunately , ice-skating proved unpopular and the two rinks were closed down in 1978. For the next decade, there were no functional rinks in Singapore. It was not till 1988 when the Fuji Ice Palace was built at the former Rex Theater in Magazine Road. In September 1994, the Fuji Ice Palace relocated to the current location in Jurong Entertainment Centre.

Skating Rink, Roller

Elite Skating Rink, 1896. Singapore's first roller skating rink was the Elite Skating Rink built by a Mr Marks on 30 January 1896. It was located at 30 Raffles Place in the premises of Messrs Meyer Brothers. At the opening, there was a festive atmosphere and the Santa Cecilia Band played. The admittance fee was 50 cents for the afternoon session from 5.00 to 7.00 pm and it was $1.00 for the evening session from 8.00 to 11.00 pm. It attracted enormous crowds and it was estimated that there were 300-400 people there on Saturday nights. They held specialty nights such as a Military Night, Dance Night and Race Night.

Skin Bank

Singapore General Hospital, 1991. The Singapore General Hospital established its Skin Bank/Skin Culture Laboratory in 1991 to meet the skin graft needs for the treatment of patients with severe burns. It is located within the hospital's Burns Centre and is run by the hospital's Department of Plastic Surgery.

Skyjacking

Singapore Airlines SQ 117, 1991. The first skyjacking of a Singapore Airlines airliner occurred on 26 March 1991. Four men took control of Flight SQ 117 from Kuala Lumpur to Singapore at 9.50 pm. it was allowed to land at Changi Airport. At 6.50 pm the next day, 4 specially-trained Commandoes from the Singapore Armed Forces took part in an assault on the plane. The four skyjackers were killed and all the crew and passengers were unharmed.

Skyscraper

Cathay Building, 1939. The Cathay Building was Singapore's first skyscraper. It was designed in 1939 by Frank Brewer. Brewer arrived in Singapore in 1919 with a degree in architecture from King's College in London. He set up his own practice in 1932 and his style is said to be a transition from Classicism to Modernism. The **first skyscraper complex** of low cost Housing Development Board flats was Selegie House, completed in June 1963. See HIGH RISE APARTMENTS AND HIGH RISE BUILDING.

Societies Act

1890. The Societies Ordinance first came into operation in 1890. In 1854, there were serious riots in Singapore between rival secret societies. The riots lasted 10 days and there were over 1000 casualties. The government felt that it needed to control the activities of the secret societies. The Peace Preservation Act gave the government some extra powers but did nothing to suppress these societies. In 1869, an Ordinance for the Suppression of Dangerous Societies was introduced. The title was misleading as it did not provide for their suppression but for the registration and control of all societies whether dangerous or not. It was a toothless piece of legislation and proved to be ineffective.

In 1890, the government introduced the Societies Act. The Act required every society of more than ten persons (except chartered companies and freemasons) to be registered under the Ordinance or else be declared unlawful. No society could be registered without approval from the Governor. It did not lead to the suppression of secret societies but it did, for the first time, give the authorities the means to deal with them. Under the Societies Act, the government had the right to dissolve any organisation if it appeared necessary for public safety or welfare. However, most organisations had nothing to fear from this Ordinance. The legislation encouraged the emergence of a whole range of ethnic, cultural and welfare orgnaisations within the Chinese community.

Sports Club

Billiards Club, 1829. The first sports club was the Billiards Club formed on 1 October 1829.

Sports Boy of the Year

Marc Tay, 1977. The Sports Boy of the Year of the Award was inaugurated in 1977. The first winner of this prestigious title was swimmer Marc Tay Tze-Hsin. Tay won 2 silver and 1 bronze medals at the 9th SEA Games. In the process, he broke the men's 9-year-old national 100m freestyle record and was the first person go under 56.0 seconds for the event.

Sports Girl of the Year

Junie Sng, 1977. The Sports Girl of the Year of the Award was inaugurated in 1977. The first winner of this prestigious title was swimmer Junie Sng Poh Leng, who won it a record three consecutive times from 1977 to 1979. In 1977, Sng won 5 gold and 1 silver medal at the 9th SEA Games. In the process, she broke 6 Games records as well as the Asian Games women's 200m and 400m freestyle records. That year, she also broke the women's 800m and 400m freestyle records at the Coca-Cola International Swimming Championship in

London, and won 8 gold medals at the First ASEAN Age-Group Swimming Meet. In 1978, Sng won 2 gold and 1 silver medals at the 8th Asian Games, the **first Singapore woman swimmer to win an Asian Games Gold medal**. In 1979, Sng won 5 gold, 2 silver and 1 bronze medals at the 10th SEA Games, breaking 3 games and 3 national records in the process. At the Tokyo Mini-Olympics that year, she won 2 gold and 1 silver medal as well as the Most Outstanding Swimmer award. She capped the year's achievement by winning 9 gold medals at the 3rd ASEAN Age-Group Swimming meet.

Sportsman of the Year

Tan Thuan Heng, 1968. In 1967, the Singapore National Olympic Council (SNOC) introduced awards to recognize outstanding sportsmen and sportswomen. In 1969, these awards were extended to teams and coaches. Then SNOC President, Othman Wok wanted to encourage Singapore's athletes at a time when there were few incentives and little recognition. The first Sportsman of the Year was swimmer Tan Thuan Heng who won 6 gold medals (4 individual and 2 team) at the 4th SEAP Games. In the process, Tan broke 4 Games records. Tan was also Singapore's second Rhodes Scholar.

Sportswoman of the Year

Patricia Chan Li-yin, 1967. See **Golden Girl**.

Sports School

Singapore Sports School, 2004. Singapore's first Sports School began classes on 5 January 2004. The Singapore Sports School is a specialized school providing an academic and training environment for youth athletes. The school is under the guidance of the Ministry for Community Development, Youth and Sports. The school is located in a specially designed 7-hectare complex in Woodlands that cost $75 million to build. The students live at the school for five days per week. Alongside their academic classes, they participate in two daily training sessions in their chosen sport. The school has selected 8 sports for the students to specialise in: badminton, bowling, football, netball, sailing, swimming, table tennis, track and field. The school has its own Sports Science Academy offering services such as Sports Psychology, Sports Physiotherapy and Nutrition to the students. The inaugural Awards night took place on 2 December 2004 and Bowler Gina Lim and sailor Glenn Sydney were named the School's Outstanding Students of the year.

Steamer

Van Der Capellan, 1827. The first steamship to call at Singapore was the *Van Der Capellan* which berthed on 17 April 1827. The 230-ton ship was built of teak by British merchants in Kerr's Yard in Java in 1825 with the object of establishing a regular service linking the ports on the north coast of the island. The paddle steamer was fitted with two 25hp engines manufactured by Fawcett & Co and was under the command of Captain Mackenzie. She was named in honour of Gordon Alexander Garard Philip, Baron van der Capellan (1778–1848), High Commissioner and Governor-General of the Netherlands East Indies from 1816 to 1826. The steamer started her maiden voyage on 23 December 1825 carrying 8 European passengers to Semarang and Batavia. She took 40 hours to steam the 250 miles from Semarang to Batavia. She called into Singapore from the 17 April to 19 April 1827 and was described by the *Singapore Chronicle* as being 127 feet long by 19 feet broad at the paddles. She was armed with 8 cannonades and four swivels astern for defence against pirates. She was registered in the name of Thompson, Roberts & Co and was used to transport troops and war supplies during the Java War. The steamer was sold to the King of Cochin China (now part of Vietnam) in May 1840 and never returned to Singapore.

The **first regular steamer service** was a monthly service between Singapore and Batavia. The service was provided by the paddle steamers *Bromo* and the *Koningen der Nderlanden* of the Netherlands India Steamboat Company. The **first government steamer** based in Singapore was the *Diana* in 1837. The 132-ton paddle steamer was built by JA Currie & Co in Calcutta in 1836 and was powered by two 15hp engines by Henry Maudslay & Co. The ship was built to government order in response to prolonged agitation from Singapore for a steamer to be used against the pirates operating in neighbouring waters. The steamer operated in the Straits Settlements from March 1837 to January 1846 under the command of Captain Samuel Congalton. In May 1838, the *HMS Wolf*, under the command of Captain Stanley, came across a junk being attacked by 6 pirate prows. Lack of wind prevented the *Wolf* from attacking, so Captain Stanley ordered the *Diana* to attack. Two hundred and forty pirates were killed or wounded by the *Diana* and 30 pirates taken prisoner. It was the **first successful action taken against pirates.** Captain Stanley was presented with a sword valued at 100 guineas for this action and honoured at a public dinner while Captain Congalton was not even publicly thanked. The *Diana* was replaced by the *PS Hoogly* in 1846. Captain Congalton commanded the *Hoogly* until his death in Penang in April 1850. The *Diana* returned to Bengal, the engines were removed and sold out of service.

The **first mail steamer**, *Lady Mary Wood*, arrived on 4 August 1845, just 41 days out of London. The service was operated by the P&O Shipping Lines. On her return voyage, the ship carried 4,757 letters from Singapore, mainly for London and Europe. Spottiswoode & Connolly were P&O's first agents in Singapore. The contract for the passage money shows that the company was awarded £160, including transit through Egypt. The monthly mail service had an enormous influence on Singapore's economic and social life and Singapore was plugged into the commercial and political events outside the Straits. In 1853, the services were increased to two a month. The first left London on the 8th of each month for Galle, Penang, Singapore and Hong Kong. The second left on the 24th of each month for Galle, Calcutta, Penang, Singapore and Hong Kong. They returned from Singapore on the 17th and 28th of each month, the first via Bombay and the second via Calcutta, reaching Marseilles in 44 days before sailing on to Southampton.

Stock Exchange

Stock Exchange of Singapore, 1973. The Stock Exchange of Singapore (SES) opened on Monday 4 June 1973. It replaced the joint Stock Exchange of Malaysia and Singapore which had served the investing public for 11 years. The SES was established under the Securities Industries Act of 1973. The chairman of the Stock Exchange of Malaysia and Singapore, Ng Soo Peng, was appointed the SES's **first Chairman**. The Deputy Chairman was Ong Tjin An and the other two committee members were Joseph Chin and Freddy Lee Thiam Yew. It was formally inaugurated by the

Minister for Finance Hon Sui Sen on 16 June 1973 at the SES offices in the Clifford Centre in Raffles Place. The Stock Exchange of Singapore dealing and Automated Quotation System or **Sesdaq** was launched on 18 February 1987. The **first local company to be listed on Sesdaq** was Creative Technologies.

Street Directory

Street Directory & Guide to Singapore, 1954. Singapore's first official street directory was issued by the Government Survey Department was in 1954. Costing $3.00, the Directory featured 115 detailed road maps, and also listed bus routes, taxi stands, post offices, police stations and even electoral district maps. It was issued under the authority of the Chief Surveyor and was released in November 1954.

Street lamps

1824. The streets were first lit by oil on 1 April 1824. The lighting was rather dim and the oil used was either coconut oil or animal oil. The **first gas lamps** were first used to light the streets on 24 May 1864. The occasion was part of the commemoration of the Queen's Birthday in 1864. The **first time electricity was used** to light the town was on 6 March 1906. Power was provided by the power station built by the Singapore Electric Tramways Company. The Municipality laid a system of mains for street and domestic lighting all over Singapore. The work was completed under the supervision of Municipal Electrical Engineer J Mackail. The electric lights were first demonstrated when they were used to illuminate the Birthday Ball at the newly completed Victoria Memorial Hall. It was lit up by a substation attached to the Adelphi Hotel. However, 6 March 1906 marked the first occasion on which a real and practical supply of electrical current was provided for private consumption. See ELECTRICITY INTRODUCED.

Street Party

Orchard Road, 1988. Singapore's first-ever street party was held in Orchard Road on 8 August 1988. More than 100,000 people turned up to dance, sing and join in the National Day festivities. It was organized by the Singapore Armed Forces Reservists Association (SAFRA) to celebrate Singapore's 23rd birthday. There was a large birthday cake with 23 candles and the party featured an hour-long variety show that began at 11.00 pm. At midnight, there was a countdown to National Day. First Deputy Prime Minister Goh Chok Tong opened a jeroboam of champagne at midnight. Orchard Road was closed from the Scotts Road junction right up to the traffic lights before Orchard Turn. The party ended at 2.00 am after which the road was cleared.

Strike

Rickshaw Pullers' Strike, 1897. The first major strike action taken in Singapore was by the rickshaw pullers in 1897. The first rickshaws arrived in Singapore in 1880 and rickshaws quickly became popular. By 1897, there were over 20,000 pullers trying to earn their living in the city. Rickshaws became indispensable especially among the colonial civil servants who usually resided some distance from their offices. The first strike began on the morning of 8 January 1897. It was unusual in that the pullers went on strike not on behalf of themselves but for the benefit of the rickshaw owners. The owners objected to government attempts to regulate the rickshaw trade through the Rickshaw Ordinance. They forced the pullers to stop work in protest against the government measures. The pullers stopped work and took action against anyone using other forms of transport such as bicycles and horse carts as well as pullers who refused to strike. Although this strike was for the benefit of the owners, it demonstrated quite clearly the strength of solidarity of action. The government held firm and after 4 days, the owners eventually instructed the pullers go back to work. The pullers went on strike again in 1901 and 1903 for similar reasons. In 1919, the pullers went on strike as part of an anti-Japanese boycott. In 1920, however, the pullers finally went on strike for their own benefit. They demanded an increase in fares to 15 cents per mile. The strike continued until the pullers achieved their objectives.

Submarine

Sjootmen Class Submarines, 1995. In 1995 and 1997 the Singapore Navy ordered its first 4 submarines. They were Type A12 Sjootmen class submarines and were built in Sweden.

Supermarket

Fitzpatrick's, 1958. Singapore's first supermarket was opened by Bill Fitzpatrick and his business partner George Holt in August 1958. It was called *Fitzpatrick's* and was located at 60 Orchard Road on what later became the Promenade (now an extension of The Paragon). Fitzpatrick and Holt established a ship chandlers and army tenders business in a small office Raffles Place in 1946. They ventured into the retail business and set up a grocery store called *Fitzpatrick's* in Oldham Lane in 1947. After Fitzpatrick was killed in an air crash in Malacca in 1951, Holt continued to develop the retail side and in 1958, he opened a large modern supermarket in Orchard Road. *Fitzpatrick's* was bought out by Cold Storage in 1985. Cold Storage opened its first supermarket in 1960 in Orchard Road.

Surveyor

John Turnbull Thomson. In October 1841, at the age of just 21, John Turnbull Thomson was appointed Singapore's first Government Surveyor for the Eastern Settlements. Thomson came to Singapore from Penang where he spent 5 years surveying many private estates, including the estates of Brown, Scott & Co. He learnt Malay and Hindi and his maps attracted the attention of Singapore's Governor Samuel Bonham and he was appointed Government Surveyor in October 1841. Thomson assumed his duties in November and for the next 12 years, he acted as both surveyor and engineer. As surveyor, he produced maps of Singapore Town, Singapore Island and the Straits of Singapore. His first map of the town and its environs was published in 1843. His survey of the Straits of Singapore in 1846 was an important work and was used by the Admiralty for its charts. For this survey, he used the Government steamer the *Diana* (see STEAMSHIP). In his capacity as engineer, Thomson designed and constructed many roads, bridges and buildings. Perhaps his greatest achievement was the building of Horsburgh Lighthouse on Pedra Branca, 54 km off the coast of Singapore (see LIGHTHOUSE). The two years he spent on Pedra Branca took a toll on his health and he had to leave Singapore and return to England on extended sick leave in May 1853. On his departure, he was presented with a silver epergne engraved with etchings of the Horsburgh Lighthouse. Thomson returned to Singapore briefly in 1855 but left for New Zealand in 1856 where he became Chief Surveyor. He died there in 1884. Thomson is best-known for his paintings of Singapore that form an important record of life in early Singapore. His book, *Some Glimpses into Life in the Far East* recount the adventures he experienced during his surveys.

Swimming Club

Singapore Swimming Club, 1894. In the early 1890s, a group of young European swimming enthusiasts found a 'splendid spot for swimming and recreation at Tanjong Rhu'. By October 1893, there was talk of forming a swimming club. On 7 February 1894, the Singapore Swimming Club was born. It was Singapore's first swimming club. To access the Club, members had to row from Johnston's Pier (renamed Clifford Pier in 1933) to the Club. However, Meyer Road was built just after World War I, followed by Tanjong Rhu Road which led right to the Club. Swimming was once confined to the sea and thus dependent on the tide, not to mention the hazards of a shark attack. In 1931, a swimming pool was constructed.

Swimming Pool, Public

Mount Emily Swimming Complex, 1930. Singapore's very first public swimming complex in Singapore was the Mt Emily Swimming Complex, which opened sometime in 1930s. This Complex was converted from an old reservoir which supplied water to Kandang Kerbau Hospital by the PWD. However, the swimming complex was demolished in 1983

Synagogue

Synagogue Street, 1841. In 1841, under the Jewish Synagogue Ordinance, a piece of land was leased for peppercorn rent to Joseph Dwek Cohen, Nassim Joseph Ezra and Exra Ezekiel, as Trustees for the purpose of providing a synagogue for the Jewish community. The land was 5,414 square feet and was located on what is now Synagogue Street, in the centre of what was then the Jewish quarter. The Synagogue was built in the same design as a shophouse and was later sold as a shophouse. It held 40 persons and soon proved to be too small. By 1879, there were 172 members in the Jewish community and the community moved to the new residential area around Waterloo Street (formerly Church Street). In 1873, Manesseh Meyer, a leading member of the Jewish community approached the Attorney-General for a piece of land and was granted a plot at 24 Waterloo Street. The new synagogue, named Maghain Aboth (Shield of our Fathers) was opened on 4 April 1878. It was a single-storey building and a second storey was added later. The synagogue remains in use today.

T

Tanker

Murex, 1892. The first tanker to arrive in Singapore was the 5,010-ton *Murex* which arrived on 16 September 1892, with a cargo of 4,720 tons of kerosene.

Teacher Training

The Teachers' Training College, 1951. Singapore's first formal teachers' training institution, the Teachers' Training College (TTC) opened on 8 June 1951 at Cairnhill Road. Up till then, there was only an informal training programme through the Singapore Free Schools. In September, the Singapore Free Schools Society was formed to manage the affairs of the Singapore Free Schools. The schools were not free in the sense that they were free of fees but were free in the sense that they were open to children of all races. They later became known as the Singapore Institution Free Schools. After 1857, this became known as the Singapore Institution (see SCHOOLS). A monitorial system was introduced to assist with training local teachers. This was replaced in 1864 by the pupil-teacher system to produce teachers familiar with methods of instruction in the school.

In 1906, training classes for teachers were introduced at Raffles Institution to provide training for teachers who taught at the school. In 1907, Normal classes were introduced to train local teachers who were already engaged in teaching. Classes were held at Raffles Institution outside school hours by competent school teachers attached to Government or Aided schools. This system was reasonably satisfactory but was no substitute for a teachers' training school.

In the inter-war years, the Sultan Idris Training College in Tanjong Malim provided training for men and the Malay Women's Teachers' College trained women for the Malay schools. The formation of Raffles College (see UNIVERSITY) proved to be an important source of graduate teachers. Graduates intending to become teachers were given a fourth year course in education.

As part of the post-war Ten-Year Education Plan, a training college for teachers was set up in Singapore. The TTC opened in March 1950 and all existing training courses were brought under its jurisdiction. Women made up more than half of those admitted to the TTC. It was originally housed in the old Anglo-Chinese School building in Cairnhill Road, but moved to its new campus on Paterson Road in 1956. The TTC initially only offered training for teachers in the English medium. This was expanded and extended to teachers in the Chinese medium (1956); and Malaya medium (1957). In 1960, the full-time classes were dropped in favour of part-time teacher-training. A part time Certificate in Education in the Tamil medium was introduced in 1962. It also provided special in-service courses for professional development. The TTC was maintained and controlled by the Ministry of Education. In 1971, Dr Ruth Wong became the **first woman Principal** of the TTC. She was later appointed **first Director of the Institute of Education** (now the National Institute of Education).

Telegraph

Singapore–Batavia, 1860. The first telegraph was sent in 1860 following the laying of a submarine telegraph cable between Singapore and Batavia by the Netherlands Government. The Singapore merchants sent the Batavia merchants a congratulatory message and the Batavia merchants replied. A congratulatory message was also sent by the Governor-General of Netherlands India to Governor Orfeur Cavenagh of the Straits Settlements. After the second message, the line was cut. It was repaired many times but never worked properly. Eventually, a new cable had to be laid. In 1870 the British Australian Telegraph Company was given permission to provide a cable service between Singapore, Java and Australia. In 1872, this was opened.

Telephone

1879. In Singapore, the telephone was introduced for the first time in 1879, just three years after its inventor, Alexander Graham Bell, patented his invention. A trial of the instrument was made on a telegraph line between Raffles Square and Tanjong Pagar. The local telephone service was operated by the Oriental Telephone and Electric Co Ltd under licence from the Government from 1881 to 1955. The Oriental Telephone and Electric Company Ltd. was established in 1882 with 38 subscribers. The exchange was situated on the first floor of Messrs Paterson, Simon & Co in Prince's Street. It comprised a 50-line standard plug switchboard without cords. The Exchange was moved to Robinson Road in 1898. Its first manager was JB Saunders. In 1882, its subscribers included most of the major companies including Behn, Meyer & Co, Boustead & Co, Tanjong Pagar Dock Company, Guthrie & Co and P&O Steam Navigation Co.

Telephone, 3G

2003. Singapore's first public 3G video calls were made on 16 January 2003. SingTel announced that it had successfully completed the first 3G (third generation) public video calls, confirming its position as a leading mobile communications operator. SingTel conducted the person-to-person mobile video calls in Singapore, with support from a trial system supplied by Ericsson.

Television Broadcast

1963. Singapore's first television broadcast took place on 15 February 1963. Television Singapura telecast a pilot monochrome service at Victoria Memorial Hall where 500 VIPs had been invited to watch. The broadcast lasted 1 hour and 45 minutes and was also viewed by the 2,400 families who owned TV sets and also at 52 community centres. Only 1 in 12 homes had TV at that time. When regular transmission began on 2 April 1963, the **first television channel** was Channel 5. The **first Chinese channel**, Channel 8 was introduced in 1968. The first stereophonic television programmes were transmitted on 1 August 1990.

The first programme to be shown on TV Singapura was a 15-minute documentary entitled, *TV Looks at Singapore*. It was produced by Television Singapura and introduced viewers to the world of television broadcasting and the role it would play in the lives of Singaporeans. It also included a cartoon, the news and an episode of 'Hancock's Half Hour'. The **first colour transmission** was carried in May 1974. The World Cup finals between Germany and

Holland was the **first 'live' colour telecast** on 7 July 1974. This stimulated a huge surge of interest in colour TV and 2,000 thousand sets were sold on the day before the match. On 11 November 1974 the news service was televised in colour.

Tennis Club & Championship

Lawn tennis was first played at Esplanade 1862. Singapore's first tennis club was the Ladies' Lawn Tennis Club, formed in 1884. They were given a piece of land at Dhoby Ghaut. There were around 100 members. The club built a pavilion that cost $632. Men played tennis at the Singapore Cricket Club. The **first tennis championship for men** was organised by the Singapore Cricket Club in 1875. It was won by JR Almeida. The **first tennis championship for women** was that of the Ladies Lawn Tennis Club in 1884. It was won by Miss Dennys.

Test-Tube Baby

See **In-Vitro Birth**

Theatre

Cross Street, Telok Ayer, 1833. According to Buckley the first theatre in Singapore was in Cross St. in Telok Ayer. See PLAY. Little else is known about this theatre. Choa Chong Long's house in Kampong Glam was also used as a theatre in 1834. In 1844, Gaston Dutronquoy (see HOTEL) converted part of his London Hotel in Coleman Street into the Theatre Royal. This theatre was apparently quite successful, but closed down when Dutronquoy's hotel moved in 1845 to a new location. A new Theatre Royal was established as part of the Assembly Rooms in Hill Street, the first performance taking place in November 1845. By 1854, the Assembly Rooms were in a bad state of disrepair and it was closed. In 1856, it was demolished and a temporary theatre established on the site. A new Town Hall (now Victoria Concert Hall) was built in 1862.

Theme Park

Haw Par Villa, 1937. Haw Par Villa was Singapore's first theme park. It was built in 1937 by Aw Boon Haw as a residence for his brother Boon Par who had helped create the analgesic balm, *Tiger Balm* that made them both wealthy. It was originally known as the Tiger Balm Gardens. It was later turned into a theme park to teach and preserve Chinese values. It contained 1,000 statues and 150 giant tableaux from Chinese folklore. The features included a 7,000 kg gorilla and the popular Ten Courts of Hell. There was a tribute to the pugilist Wu Song who tamed a ferocious tiger with his hands. Admission was free. By the early 1980s, it had fallen into disrepair and was taken over by the Government in 1988. It was remodeled at a cost of $80 million and it reopened in October 1990. Its static sculptures were brought to life using the latest technology and various new features were added such as a boat ride and indoor theatre. It attracted large crowds in the first two years but eventually lost money and closed in 2001. In 2003, the gardens were reopened and the public can once again enter without charge. See also **Amusement Parks**.

Thomas Cup Championship Win

1948. In 1948, preparations were made for Malaya (including Singapore) to compete for the first time in the Thomas Cup to be held in 1949. At that time, all matches organised by the

Singapore Badminton Association (SBA) were played at the Clerical Union Hall (one court), where conditions were far from ideal; the ceilings were too low and the lighting insufficient. Players had to be content with practices mostly in open-air courts. In November 1948, when the Thomas Cup team made their final preparations by playing at the Happy World covered stadium, the *Malaya Tribune* voiced the strong opinion that Singapore should have its own badminton hall. In 1948, the Malayan Thomas Cup team of Wong Peng Soon, Ooi Teik Hock, Law Teik Hock, Teoh Seng Khoon, Chan Kon Leong, Yeoh Teck Chye, Lim Kee Fong and Ong Poh Lim, left to play in the inaugural Thomas Cup Championship in London. The team manager was Lim Chuan Geok. Against all odds, the Malayan team beat Denmark 8-1 in a spectacular final.

Tiger Cup

1996. The first ever Tiger Cup soccer competition was held in Singapore in September 1996. Ten teams took part and it was a huge success. Thailand won the first cup by beating Malaysia 1-0 in the final. Singapore first won the Tiger Cup in 1998 when the team defeated the host nation Vietnam by 1-0. The goal was scored by R Sasikumar.

Tigers, sighted or shot

1831. The first mention of tigers sighted near the road leading to New Harbour not far from Sepoy Lines appeared in *The Singapore Chronicle* of 8 September 1831. John Cameron, in his book, *Out Tropical Possessions in Malayan India*, relates a story about the **first tiger attack** on the island of Singapore in 1835:

Mr Coleman, the surveyor accompanied by a large party of Indian convicts was laying out a new road about 4 miles from town. He was in the act of taking an observation using his theodolite when a huge tiger leaped into the middle of the party of men. The tiger landed right on top of the theodolite. The theodolite was overturned and broken and the noise and chaos caused the tiger to flee. The convicts fled back to town and Mr Coleman followed quickly behind.

The last tiger to be shot in Singapore was shot in Lim Chu Kang in 1932.

Time, Standard

1905. The first time standard time was established in Singapore was in 1905 when Singapore Standard Time was set at 7 hours ahead of GMT. On 1 January 1982, Singapore's time was brought forward by half-an-hour to synchronise with the time-zone adjustment in Malaysia.

Time Ball

Fort Canning, 1849. In 1849, a time ball was fixed to the Fort Canning flagpole for the use of shipping. The time ball was dropped at a predetermined time to enable sailors to set their chronometers. This enabled mariners determine their longitude at sea. The Fort Canning time ball was dropped at 9.00 am daily. On 1 June 1905, the mean time of the 105th Meridian (Longitude 105 deg East) was adopted by the Straits Settlements and the Federated Malay States as the new Standard Time. This decision was made way back in February, 1904. The mean time of the 105th meridian is 7 hours ahead of Greenwich Mean Time. This Standard Time went into effect when the Time Ball on Fort Canning was completed and became operational on the same day. The old time ball has been dismantled and has been replaced by a replica at a lower level area known as Raffles Terrace.

Tin Smelter

Straits Tin Company. In the mid-nineteenth century, there was a world wide demand for tin. Tin had been discovered in significant quantities in Perak in Malaya in the 19th century and the ore was smelted on site by the Chinese who dominated the industry. The smelting process was very primitive and wasteful, and in 1873, Samuel Gilfillan attempted to set up a smelter in Singapore. However, as the export of ore from Malaya was strictly forbidden he was forced to give up the venture. In 1886, the rules were changed and tin ore from Selangor and Sungei Ujong was permitted to be exported. James Sword and Herman Muhlinghaus took advantage of this to set up a new smelting business. They formed The Straits Trading Company with the declared purpose to 'purchase, crush, win, get, quarry, smelt, calcine, refine, dress, amalgamate, manipulate and prepare for market, ore, metal and ineral substance of all kinds'. With a capital of $150,000 from 1500 shares of $100 each, 7 people became major shareholders: Sword and Muhlinghaus, Samuel Gilfillan, TE Earle, James Miller, W Adamson and HH Wood. The company was incorporated in 1887. They bought the disused Bon Accord Dry Dock on Pulau Brani that had been built in 1866. This provided them with buildings that could be adapted to be a smelter and provided them with access to the deep water and coal supplies at the Tanjong Pagar Docks. In 1890, the first 3-ton reverberatory furnace began smelting tin from Malaya. The product was marketed as Straits Tin, and Straits Tin was stamped on every ingot of tin. The company gained an international reputation for its product and it was regarded as the purest quality tin. They developed a close relationship with the Straits Steamship Company who shipped all their tin from Malaya and transhipped it overseas. See JOINT EUROPEAN AND CHINESE BUSINESSES.

Topless Revue

Tropicana Club, 1968. The first establishment to bring in a topless revue was Tropicana Club on Scotts Road in 1968. The Club was well-known for its family-oriented *dim sum* lunches and its adult-oriented topless revues in the evenings. Attracting full-houses in the 1970s and 1980s, the Tropicana went out of business in 1989. The Golden Million Deluxe Nightclub in Peninsula Hotel also introduced topless revues when it opened in the 1970s. It closed down in the mid-1990s.

Toto

1968. The first Toto tickets were sold in June 1968 by the Government-owned Singapore Pools (Private) Limited. The state-run betting system was introduced by the Bulgarians and the Chief Advisor to the company was Vassil Popov, former Director-General of the Bulgarian sports totalisator. The games was very popular in many European countries and was loosely based on Lotto or Bingo. In Bulgaria, the betting system raises over $100 million annually.

Tourism Awards

Lien Ying Chow, 1985. In December 1985, the first awards for outstanding contributions to tourism in Singapore was jointly awarded to

Lien Ying Chow for creating the Mandarin Hotel; Singapore Airlines; and Tan I-Tong for his role as Chairman of the Singapore Tourist Promotion Board. The awards were presented by Dr Wong Kwei Cheong, Minister of State for Trade and Industry at a ball at the Neptune Theatre Restaurant.

Town Hall

Assembly Rooms, 1861. The first town hall was known as the Assembly Rooms. It was situated at the foot of Fort Canning at the corner of Hill Street and River Valley Road (where the current MICA Building is). It was a modest structure with an attap roof. It lasted for ten years and then had to be demolished. It was replaced by the new Town Hall building, which later became the Victoria Memorial Theatre. The foundation stone was laid by Governor Colonel Butterworth in 1855 but the building was not completed until 1861. It was used as assembly rooms, municipal offices and a library for many years. The Municipal offices remained in the Town Hall until 1893 when they moved to the Borneo Company office in Finlayson Green.

Trade Unions

The early Chinese guilds acted in many respects like a trade union. However, the guild usually represented the interests of both employers and employees. The employers' interests were defended by the *Tong Ka* section of the Guild. The members of the *Tong Ka* were extremely powerful and controlled the economic life of the Chinese community. The *Sai Ka* represented the employees and was considerably less powerful. However, in time the *Sai Ka* grew stronger and eventually used the guild as a power base from which to promote employee interests in the same way as a trade union. The Societies Ordinance was introduced in 1889, and in 1890, the first guild was registered. It was the *Pak Seng Hong* and represented Cantonese carpenters, masons and painters. Skilled mechanics were among the earliest workers to develop associations along trade union lines. The Singapore Chinese Engineering Association Union was established in the 1930s to represent skilled shipyard workers, and the Singapore Harbour Board Employees Union represented wharf and stevedore workers. Together these two unions had a membership of between eight and nine thousand men. Employee guilds began to become more popular and by 1941, 163 guilds were registered. Of these, 90 were employee guilds that performed the tasks of a trade union. The emergence of organisations representing workers' interests was assisted by two important factors. One was the influence of communism and the second was the more settled character of the work force. Chinese nationalism and the growth of communist influence in Malaya and Singapore led to an interest in collective action. The establishment of the first left wing union, the Nanyang or South Seas General Union in 1925 encouraged workers to take action to protect their interests. The Singapore Traction Company strike in 1927 was probably influenced by the new union. During the 1930s, the workforce became more settled and permanent. The need for skilled and semi-skilled workers led to demands for improved wages and conditions. In 1937, the pineapple workers went on strike. They were joined by Municipal workers and later by rubber tappers. Attempts to use police and military force to break the strike were ineffective and the employers were forced to grant substantial concessions. The Colonial Office in London recognised that the emergence of trade unions was inevitable, and compulsory registration of trade unions under the Trade Unions Ordinance began in 1939. The establishment of a wide range of organisations representing the interests of a range of workers provided a springboard for the rapid development of the trade union activities following the end of the Japanese Occupation.

Tram

Singapore Tramway Company, 1886. In 1882, the Singapore Tramway Company was given permission under the Tramways Ordinance of 1882, to operate up to 5 tramlines in Singapore. The first rails were laid on 7 April 1885. The trams originally operated on steam. The first tram service started on 3 May 1886 and ran from Tanjong Pagar to Johnston's Pier. The tram service appeared to be successful at first but ran into financial difficulties. The main problem was that the fares charged were high in order to cover the costs of imported machinery and fuel, but the rickshaw pullers operated at a fraction of the cost. The company refused to lower the fares and in 1889, the tramway was sold to the Tanjong Pagar Docks Company. In 1901 a new tram company was registered. Singapore Tramways were given permission to operate 5 services within the municipal boundary. In addition they were given permission to build a power station to generate power for its own use, and for the use of the Municipality. In July 1905 the electric trams began to operate. However the tram service faced the same problems as the steam tram and eventually the service came to an end in September 1927. The trams were replaced by trolleybuses, and in 1927, the first motor bus service began. See **Trolleys and Buses.**

Tram company

See **Trams.**

Trials

1828. The first criminal sessions were held in June 1828. There were 27 indictments, of which six were for murder, one for manslaughter, ten for burglary and six for assaults. In the six murder cases, two were convicted and hanged on June 26. They were the first executions in Singapore.

Transsexual Fashion Show

2004. Singapore's first major transsexual beauty pageant was held over the weekend of 25 September to raise money for the poor. The event's organisers hailed it as a ground-breaking, sell-out success as an audience of 1,350 people watched 13 finalists compete for the title of Miss Tiffany Singapore. It is based on the famous Thai contest of the same name.

Transfusion

See **Blood Transfusion.**

Triathlon

1982. Singapore's first triathlon took place at National Univeristy of Singapore in 1982. It was restricted to the campus grounds and 34 contestants took part. The first International Triathlon was held at Changi Beach in 1984. In 1992, the first triathlon association, the Triathlon Association of Singapore was formed with Alex Kuok as its first President.

Trolley Buses

Singapore Traction Company, 1926. In 1923, the government drafted an agreement to allow the operation of the first trolley buses in Singapore. Three years later, the newly-formed Singapore Traction Company slowly began taking over routes from the tram company. By 1927, the takeover was complete and the trolley bus company was given a monopoly to provide trolley and bus transport to the municipality. The service was extensive and would eventually cover 24.23 miles. It was claimed to be the 'largest trolley bus system in the world'. The company gradually began to introduce buses in 1929 but the trolley bus service continued until the Japanese occupation in 1942. The trial run, which took place on 4 March 1929, ran from Johnston's Pier to Geylang. The service operated during the Japanese Military Administration period under the name of *Syonan-Si Siden*. At the end of the Occupation, the trolley buses continued to operate until 1964.

Tuberculosis, Mobile Treatment Vans

1955. In 1955, the Singapore Anti-Tuberculosis Association (SATA) launched its first mobile Treatment Van to help fight tuberculosis (TB) in Singapore. Tuberculosis had become a serious menace during the Japanese Occupation. Medical facilities to combat the disease were inadequate. In 1947, a group of doctors and laymen decided to form SATA to try and bring TB under control. The charity was registered on 23 August 1947 and its first Chairman was was SH Peck. Founder members of the organisation included Lee Kong Chian, Tan Chin Tuan and Lien Ying Chow. A temporary diagnostic clinic was set up at the St Andrew's Mission Hospital in Tanjong Pagar. Dr Garlick was recruited as the first radiologist and administrator. In 1952, the Royal Tuberculosis Clinic at Shenton Way was opened. One of the early doctors at the clinic was Dr Elizabeth Comber, better known as Han Suyin (of *Love is a Many Splendoured Thing* fame). In 1955, SATA launched its Mobile Treatment Service. On 14 March 1955, the specially-prepared van made its first trip into the outlying areas. A qualified nurse accompanied the van and administered drugs and advised families on procedures and helped out with welfare problems. The van played an important role in the fight against TB in Singapore. When the Mass X-ray Service was begun, SATA took responsibility for the management of the programme on the west side of the Singapore River. By 1960, over 140,000 people had been X-rayed.

Turf Club

See **Race Course**

U

Underground Shopping Mall

Citilink Mall, 2000. Singapore's first underground shopping mall, CityLink Mall, opened on 1 July 2000. It is located between City Hall MRT and One Raffles Link. There are over 50 shops in the mall which has an area of 60,000 sq ft of retail space. The Mall was designed by world-renowned New York architects, Kohn Pedersen Fox.

United Nations Agency Head

1994. Dr. Noeleen Heyzer was appointed Executive Director of the United Nations Development Fund for Women (UNIFEM) in 1994. Dr. Heyzer was born and educated in Singapore. She was awarded a BA and MA from the University of Singapore and she received a PhD in Social Sciences from Cambridge University. She was formerly the head of the Gender and Development Programme of the Asia Development Centre in Kuala Lumpur, Malaysia where she was a key figure in the formulation of national development policies, strategies and programmes with a gender perspective. She was founding member of a number of women's networks including Development Alternatives with Women for a New Era (DAWN). In 1994-5, she played a major role in the preparation for the Fourth World Conference on Women in Beijing. She was appointed to her new role at the UNIFEM in 1994. Her work has been recognised with a number of awards including the UNA-Harvard Leadership Award and the Dag Hammarksjold Medal in 2004. Her work at UNIFEM has focussed on strengthening women's economic security and rights, and promoting women's leadership in conflict resolution, ending violence against women and combating AIDS amongst women. Her books include *The Trade in Domestic Workers* and *Working Women in Southeast Asia*.

United Nations Peacekeeping Force

Namibia, 1989. In 1989, Singapore sent its first contingent to form part of the United Nations Peacekeeping Force in Namibia. The 21 policemen-strong contingent was sent to help oversee Namibia's transition to independence. The force consisted of volunteers led by Acting Superintendent Lee Kok Leong. The team came under the command of UN Special Representative Martii Ahtisaari who headed the United Nations Transition Assistance Group (UNTAG). The request for Singapore's help came from UN Secretary General Javier Perez de Cuellar. The Singapore policemen were joined by contingents from Barbados, Egypt, Ghana, Hungary, Ireland, Jamaica, Holland, Nigeria, Sweden and Tunisia. Namibia was the last colony in Africa and had been under colonial rule for 105 years. It was a German colony until 1915 when it came under South Africa's control.

University

University of Malaya, 1949. The first full-fledged university in Singapore (and Malaya) was the University of Malaya in Singapore. It was established in 1949 through an amalgam of two earlier higher institutes of learning: the King Edward VII Medical College (originally founded in 1905), and Raffles College (1928). It was declared open in a very grand ceremony on Foundation Day, 8 October 1949, and its first Vice-Chancellor was Sir George V Allen. In its first year, 645 students were enrolled, including 168 Arts students, 310 medical students, 82 science students and 85 dentistry students. In 1962, the University of Malaya was renamed the University of Singapore. In August 1980, it merged with the Nanyang University to become the National University of Singapore.

The **first Chinese-medium university** to be established in Southeast Asia was Nanyang University which was founded in March 1956. In 1953, Hokkien rubber tycoon Tan Lark Sye proposed establishing a Chinese-medium university in Singapore. The Singapore Hokkien Huay Kuan donated 500 acres of land in Jurong for the university. Under the leadership of the Chinese Chamber of Commerce, a Preparatory Committee was set up to examine the proposal. Its four founding objectives were to: (a) provide high-school graduates with opportunities for higher education; (b) train teachers for high schools; (c) develop specialists of Singapore; and (d) meet the needs of Singapore's growing population. The response from the Chinese community was overwhelming and people from all walks of life donated generously to the new University. In July 1953, a ground-breaking ceremony was performed by Tan Lark Sye at the site of the University. In 1955, pre-university classes were started to prepare high-school students for university studies. An opening ceremony was held on 15 March 1956 with Governor Sir William Goode as Guest-of-Honour, and classes began on 30 March 1956. A total of 584 students enrolled: 239 in the Faculty of Arts; 256 in the Faculty of Science; and 89 in the Faculty of Commerce. The early years of Nanyang University (popularly referred to as Nantah) were beset by problems. For 12 years, the Singapore Government refused to recognise Nantah degrees and it was not till May 1968 that the Government agreed that they were satisfied with Nantah's standards. In 1979, a new inquiry recommended that the university merge with the University of Singapore to form a single university, the National University of Singapore. In April 1980, the Nanyang University Council accepted the proposal and the last Nantah graduation ceremony took place in August 1980.

The **first open university** was the Singapore Open University which opened in 1993, offering two degree programmes in the sciences and the humanities. A total of 1,000 students were admitted. The Open University Programme is run by the Singapore Institute of Management (SIM) on behalf of the Ministry of Education. The programme is affiliated with the Open University in the United Kingdom in a programme that allows adults to acquire a degree through self-paced learning. The degrees are recognised and accepted as being on par with those of other British universities. The first graduation ceremony was held on 29 May 1998 at the Westin Stamford Hotel. The University moved its campus from Namly Avenue to Clementi Road in 2001.

Singapore's **first private university** funded by the Government is the Singapore Management University (SMU) which was incorporated on 12 January 2000. The SMU's educational and administrative practices are modelled after American institutions, in particular the Wharton School of the University of Pennsylvania. It comprises four schools: Lee Kong Chian School of Business; School of Accountancy; School of Economics & Social

Sciences; and School of Information Systems. The SMU bachelor's degree programmes in Business Management, Accountancy, Economics, Information Systems Management and Social Science. The university offers master's degree programmes in Wealth Management, Applied Finance, Professional Accountancy, Applied Economics and in Economics and Finance (by research). The University of New South Wales (UNSW), Australia will be **the first foreign university based in Singapore.** It is estimated that the University will open in 2007. The UNSW, Singapore will be wholly-owned independently governed and run by the University of New South Wales in Australia. Its campus will be located at Changi South near Changi Business Park and will offer places to 15,000 students to read Science, Engineering, Information Technology, Commerce and Economics, Humanities and Social Sciences.

V

Vaccination programme

Smallpox, 1819. In 1819, the first Western-trained doctor in Singapore, Sub-assistant Thomas Prendergast was directed to undertake a smallpox vaccination programme. He remained in charge of the programme until he left Singapore in 1823. In order to encourage families to participate, free rice was given to any child vaccinated. Vaccination was made compulsory in 1868.

Vehicle Quota System

1990. The Singapore Government announced the nation's first vehicle quota system on 26 February 1990. The system, which came into operation on 1 May 1990, aims to control the number of vehicles on the roads and to ease traffic congestion. Anyone wishing to purchase a new vehicle from that date had to take part in a public tender to buy a licence (Certificate of Entitlement) to buy a vehicle.

Veterinary Surgeon

Charles Emmerson, 1860. In October 1860, Charles Emmerson arrived in Singapore and advertised that he had commenced practice as a veterinary surgeon. He was an American and became the first veterinary surgeon to practise in Singapore. Emmerson is perhaps better remembered today for his famous Emmerson's Tiffin Rooms which first opened in Battery Road. Later, he was forced to relocate the eatery and situated it beside Cavenagh Bridge. Well-known plant collector, Frederick Burbidge visited Singapore in 1877, and recommended that other travellers visit Emmerson's for tiffin and glance at the European papers and telegrams. Charles Emmerson was nicknamed 'The Colonel' and was an admirable host. He was full of stories and jokes and provided convivial company. He was also a keen amateur actor and participated in many plays. Emmerson also ran the Clarendon Hotel on the corner of Middle Road and Beach Road. He remained in Singapore till his death in 1883.

Volunteer Corps

Singapore Volunteers Rifle Corps, 1854. The first volunteer force was formed in 1854. The idea of a voluntary force was first raised in 1846 following serious rioting in Singapore. However, a force was not considered viable and the idea was abandoned. During the riots of 1854, 70 Europeans volunteered to be sworn in as special constables to assist the police in controlling riots. This led to the formation of a volunteer corps. On 22 July 1854, the residents held a public meeting to discuss the issue and decided that a Volunteer Rifle Corps would be a 'manifest advantage to the Settlement'. The men who volunteered as special constables during the riots formed the core of the new Singapore Volunteers Rifle Corps. Over the years, the force made substantial contributions to the restoration of internal security. Dwindling membership led to its disbandment in 1887.

In 1888, a volunteer artillery unit was established to act as a local reserve to the

Garrison. This became known as the Singapore Volunteer Artillery. Eurasians became involved in the force from the beginning and a Eurasian company was set up. In 1901, the Straits Chinese enrolled as volunteers and formed the 2nd Company (Chinese) of the Singapore Voluntary Infantry. The Malay Company was formed in February 1910. During World War I, the presence of the volunteer corps allowed the European battalion on active duty in Singapore to be withdrawn for active service in Europe. They also contributed to the suppression of the Singapore Mutiny of 1915 and to the restoration of law and order. In that instance, they were joined by 190 special constables from two Japanese cruisers anchored in the harbour, and by 150 men of the Johore Military Force. In the period leading up to the Japanese Occupation, the Straits Settlements Volunteer Force of Singapore (as it had become known), contributed towards the overall defence preparations of the island. Many of the volunteers were taken prisoners of war.

During Confrontation (1963-1966), the volunteers played a vital role in the defence of Singapore through their guard duties at vital installations such as gas, water and electrical works. Following Singapore's separation from Malaysia in 1965, the Government needed qualified people to provide the foundation of a credible defence force. The volunteers contributed to the building of the Singapore Defence Force by their work in establishing the Singapore Armed Forces Training Institute (SAFTI) and the School of Basic Military Training (SBMT). Many were co-opted into service with the Singapore Armed Forces and they contributed to the defence and security of Singapore during the post-Independence period. The emergence of a professional army in Singapore led to dwindling membership in the volunteer units, and in March 1984, the historical volunteer force was disbanded after 130 years of service.

Voting, Compulsory

1958. Although elections were introduced into Singapore from as early as 1948, voting was not made compulsory till 1958 when a new State Constitution was enacted. In the 1959 general, voting was, for the first time, made compulsory. Nomination Day was on 25 April 1959 and Polling Day on 30 May 1959. A total of 586,098 voters turned up to vote. This was 92.9% of the total number of eligible voters.

War Memorial

Cenotaph, 1922. The first war memorial in Singapore was the Cenotaph, built in March 1922. It was dedicated to the memory of those who had died in the First World War (1914-1918) and was designed by Swann & Maclaren. The foundation stone was laid in November 1922 by the Governor of the Straits Settlements, Sir Laurence Guillemard. The completed memorial was unveiled by the Prince of Wales, who later became King Edward VIII. The memorial was later altered to additionally recognise those who sacrificed their lives in the Second World War. The side facing the Padang commemorates those who died in the First World War and the side facing the sea commemorates those who died in the Second World War.

Watch Factory

United Precision Instruments, 1968. Singapore's first watch factory opened in Jurong on 17 May 1968. The factory was owned by Swiss firm United Precision Instruments and was a joint venture between the European company and local entrepreneurs. The factory was declared open by Finance Minister Goh Keng Swee.

Water Agreement

1961. In 1961, Singapore signed the first water agreement with the State of Johor. These were known as the Tebrau and Scudai Water Agreements. The following year, another agreement, called the Johor River Water Agreement, was signed. These two water agreements were confirmed and guaranteed under the 1965 Separation Agreement with Malaysia. Under these agreements, Singapore built and maintains the waterworks in Johor (dams, pipelines, reservoirs) and has 'sole and absolute right' to a fixed amount of raw water until 2011 and 2061 respectively. Under the 1961 agreement, Singapore can draw up to 86 million gallons of water per day (mgd) from the Pontian and Gunung Pulai Reservoirs, as well as the Tebrau and Skudai Rivers, while the 1962 agreement allows up to 250 mgd of water to be drawn from the Johor River. In total, these agreements allow Singapore to draw up to 250.4 mgd (1.55 million m^3 per day). Singapore buys this raw water from Malaysia at 3 sen (Malaysian cents) per 1,000 gallons and Johor pays 50 sen for every 1,000 gallons of treated water Singapore is obliged to sell back to the state. Both agreements give Malaysia the right to review the price of water after 25 years. Malaysia did not revise the price of water in 1986 and 1987 due to financial considerations because that would have made treated water dearer for them as well. In June 1988, a Memorandum of Understanding on water and gas was signed between Singapore's Prime Minister Lee Kuan Yew and Malaysia's Prime Minister Mahathir Mohamad to give Singapore the right to construct more reservoirs and to draw more than what has been presently set for an additional one hundred years. By the 1990s, Singapore had already spent more then $1 billion on the water projects between Singapore and Johore. To cement the relationship and to build the Linggiu Dam, Singapore signed the 1990 Agreement with Johore on 24 November 1990.

Water, Aerated

1836. In January 1836, the Singapore Dispensary advertised that 'soda water of superior quality' was available. The **first large scale commercial a**erated water company was started in 1882 by John Fraser and David Neave. The Singapore and Straits Water Company started in a small way in Battery Road and moved 5 times in those early years. it manufactured soda water, lemonade, tonic and ginger beer. It became a public company in 1889 and was renamed Fraser & Neave (F&N). In 1931, the company diversified into the brewing business through a joint venture with Heineken to form Malayan Breweries. The brewery made Tiger Beer, perhaps the most well-known brand in Singapore.

Water, Supply to Ships

1863. In 1863, W Hammer and one Mr Hansen formed a partnership, Hammer & Co. to supply water to the ships in the port. They acquired a site on Blakang Mati and constructed a reservoir. They owned 2 wooden steam driven water boats with steam pumps and a sailing boat with a hand pump. All the boats were 30-ton vessels. The offices of Hammer & Co were situated at the mouth of the Singapore River. They supplied all the water to the Tanjong Pagar Dock Company. In 1891, the company built a pier at Finlayson Green.

Weather Readings

1820–1825. Between 1820 and 1825, Singapore's first Resident, Colonel William Farquhar took meteorological readings from an attap shed on Fort Canning. Between 1841 and 1845, Lieutenant Charles Morgan Elliot (see Observatory) took weather readings from the Observatory at the Kallang River. Elliot also kept a tide guage. The first official weather readings were made by Jonas Daniel Vaughan in 1862. In 1856, he was appointed the Master Attendant in Singapore. He was also Assistant Resident Councillor and a Police Magistrate. Between 1862 and 1866 he made observations on rainfall and temperature. After he left, the readings were made by Arthur Knight. From 1869, weather records were kept by the Medical Department and there is a complete series of weather readings from that time. Between 1869 and 1873, the readings were taken at the Convict Gaol Hospital and after 1874, at the Kandang Kerbau Hospital. The records showed December and January to be the wettest months and February and March the driest. The wettest year was 1913 when the annual rainfall was 135.92 inches. The driest year was 1877 with only 58.37 inches. The lowest recorded temperature was recorded on 31 January 1934 when it was 19.4 C. The maximum recorded temperature was 35.8 C (no date given).

Wine Merchant

Caldbeck, Macgregor & Co, 1905. The first wine and spirits merchant was Caldbeck, Macgregor & Co. The Singapore branch of this London firm was established in 1905, and held agencies for the best wine and champagne firms of France and the Continent. They provided wine for the Navy and the Army in Singapore and was also patronised by Government House. The firm had large cellars on Finlayson Green that were filled with the choicest wines from Europe. The company was run by Kenneth Stevens, a Municipal Commissioner, Justice of the Peace, and originator of the Straits Settlements Automobile Club.

Woman Air Traffic Controller in RSAF

Vasanti Durai, Ting Nguk Ing & Wee Puay Cheng, 1979. In June 1979, the first women to train as air traffic controllers in the Republic of Singapore Air Force assumed duty at the Changi, Sembawang and Tengah air bases. They were Officer Cadets Vasanti Durai, Ting Nguk Ing and Second Lieutenant Wee Puay Cheng.

Woman Ambassador

Chan Heng Chee, 1989. In January 1989, the Ministry of Foreign Affairs announced the appointment of Associate Professor Chan Heng Chee as Singapore's permanent representative to the United Nations. She took up her post in New York in February that year, replacing Kishore Mahbubani who returned to the Ministry of Foreign Affairs. In 1996, she was appointed Singapore's Ambassador to the United States of America, the first woman to be appointed to an ambassadorial post.

Woman Army Colonel

Karen Tan, 2005. The first woman army officer to be promoted to the rank of full colonel was Karen Tan, Commander of the Central Manpower Base. At a ceremony held on 28 June 2005, Tan, aged 42, was promoted to full colonel, making her the highest-ranking woman among 300 officers and 800 warrant officers and specialists.

Woman Doctor

See **Doctor**

Woman Legislative Assembly Members

In 1959, 5 women were elected as members of the Legislative Assembly. Four were from the PAP and one from the SPA. They were Chan Choy Siong, Che Sahora bte Ahmat, Fung Yin Ching, Ho Puay Choo. and Seow Peck Leng.

Woman Legislative Councillor

Vilasini Menon, 1951. In 1951, Mrs Vilasini Menon was elected to the Legislative Council as the Member for the Seletar district. She stood as an Independent candidate.

Woman Municipal Councillor

Mrs Robert Eu 1949. Mrs Robert Eu (1914-2004) was the first woman to win a seat in the City Council in the 1949 elections. Born Phyllis Chia, Eu was a former principal of Paya Lebar Methodist Gorls School (1958-1965). In 1949, she entered politics as one of the three candidates put up by the Progressive Party, and won the seat in Tanglin constituency. Her daughter Bernice Eu was the **first Singapore-born woman to become an Australian Member of Parliament** (1990-1996).

Woman Naval Combat officer

Tay Poh Ling & Phiu Chiu Yoke, 1991. In December 1991, two women graduated from the Midshipman Training School and became the first two women combat officers in the Republic of Singapore Navy. Tay Poh Ling and

Phiu Chiu Yoke were part of a pilot scheme to attract young women to become naval officers. They had completed a 12-month training course and would be later be posted to the Fleet.

Woman of the Year

Chan Heng Chee, 1991. The first *Her World* Woman of the Year award was given in 1991 to Associate Professor Chan Heng Chee, who was then Director of the Singapore International Foundation and the Institute of South East Asian Studies. She has also written 5 books on politics, two of which have won the National Book Awards for non-fiction. In 1989, Chan became the first woman to become Singapore's Permanent Representative to the United Nations. In July 1996, she was appointed Singapore's Ambassador to the United States of America.

Woman Pilot

The first women to qualify as **air force pilots** were Koh Chai Hong and Tan Bee Har. On 16 June 1978, Koh and Tan completed their training as air force pilots with the Republic of Singapore Air Force. Both Koh and Tan had already clocked over 100 hours flying time each in light aircraft before starting their training as members of the Junior Flying Club (JFC). Koh joined the JFC while doing her pre-university at Raffles Institution and had obtained her private pilot's licence while Tan gained her pilot's licence while completing her Polytechnic course in electronics and communications.

Mary O'Brien was the **first woman commercial pilot** working in Singapore. She completed her commercial pilot's licence and instructor's rating in Australia. In 1970, she came to Singapore to work as an instructor with Singapore General Aviation Services. As there were no other women commercial pilots in Southeast Asia at that time, O'Brien needed persistence, hard work and a sense of humour to overcome considerable resistance by the Singapore aviation authorities to grant her a local licence. Anastasia Gan, a flight instructor in the Republic of Singapore Air Force, became the **first woman pilot to be employed by the Singapore Airlines** group in 2001.

The **first woman helicopter pilot** in the Republic of Singapore Air Force was Lieutenant Christine Sim who graduated at the 76th Wings Presentation Ceremony in 1994.

Woman Police Officer

See **Policewoman**

Woman Taxi Driver

Wong Ai Moi, 1958. Singapore's first woman taxi driver was Miss Wong Ai Moi, who was granted a taxi licence on 23 May 1958. She was 32 years old at the time and became the first woman to join the ranks of over 2,000 male taxi drivers.

Woman Weapon System Officer

Doris Ng, 1994. Lieutenant Doris Ng became Singapore's first female Weapon System Officer (WSO) the Republic of Singapore Air Force in September 1994.

Women's Charter

1961. In May 1961, Singapore introduced the first Women's Charter. The Singapore Legislative Assembly passed the Women's Charter Bill on 24 May 1961. This important piece of legislation protected many of the important rights of women. It incorporated the principle of one man, one wife for non-Muslims. All marriages had to be legally registered. It gave married women a separate legal entity and the right to use their own surname, engage in any trade or profession or social activity, and to acquire or dispose of property in their own right. It gave married women the same rights as her husband in caring and providing for the children and protected her right to have the custody of her children. The Charter was amended in 1980 to recognise the non-monetary role of women and to protect women from domestic violence.

Working Mother of the Year Award

Geraldine Tay, 1988. In 1988, the first Working Mother of the Year Award went to Mrs Geraldine Tay, Director of Physiotherapy at Mt Elizabeth Hospital.

Writer-in-Residence

Ho Minfong, 1984. In 1984, Ho Minfong became the first Writer-in-Residence at the National University of Singapore. A well-known children's writer, Ho's books include *Sing to the Dawn* (which is being made into Singapore's first animated film); *Tanjong Rhu and Other Stories, The Clay Marble, Hush! A Thai Lullaby, Gathering the Dew*, and *Peek! A Thai Hide-and-Seek*.

X

X-Ray Machine

1898. On the 3 January 1898, Dr WRD Middleton, Singapore's first Municipal Health Officer, gave the first demonstration of the first X-ray machine in Singapore in the Municipal Offices. There were some 30 or 40 people there including Sir Lionel Cox, Mr Justice Leach, the Municipal President and the US Consul-General. The X-ray machine had been paid for by generous donations from a few gentlemen. Middleton was invited to take charge of the machine with the intention that he would place it at the service of any of the recognised medical practitioners when they needed it. It was hoped that fees paid for the maintenance of the machine. During the evening, Middleton gave an exhibition of the use of X-rays. He had previously put some items in a box and taken some photographs. These clearly showed what the items were. He also took some X-rays of the hands of a number of Ladies present during the evening although they had to wait until the next day to see the photographs. The X-ray machine was soon put to good use. On 11 January 1898, a coolie who had been shot in the back was examined in hospital and brought to the Offices for an X-ray. The bullet was not found and it was believed that it had splintered on entry. The man recovered.

X-Ray, Mass Programme

1958. The first Mass Xray programme took place in 1958 in four selected areas; two city areas, Jalan Sultan and Chinatown; and two rural areas, Geylang Serai and Bukit Panjang. Tuberculosis (TB) was a serious problem in post-war Singapore, and in 1950, nearly 1,200 people died of the disease. In May 1955, the government invited Sir Henry Wunderley, the Director of the Division of Tuberculosis at the Australian Commonwealth Department of Health to visit Singapore to advise on setting up a mass-screening programme to help identify TB cases. At the end of 1957 the Tuberculosis Control Unit was set up at Tan Tock Seng Hospital. A Tuberculosis Culture laboratory capable of testing 200 cultures per day was set up at the hospital's old mortuary. The Government Tuberculosis Case Finding programme initiated an intensive publicity campaign before commencing the mass-screening programme in July 1958. The 2 objectives of the scheme were to ascertain the incidence of tuberculosis in Singapore so as to be able to formulate plans for its eventual control, and to discover and treat all cases with active disease, especially those who were infectious. The survey was carried with the help of Australia under a Colombo Plan initiative. Australia provided a team of 5 experts under the leadership of Dr. Cotter Harvey. The survey team used high quality Watson-Odelca Mirror Camera X-Ray units. By October 1958, more than 50,000 residents and 4,000 non-residents had been screened. In Chinatown and Jalan Sultan and Geylang Serai about 84% of the eligible population were X-rayed, while in Bukit Panjang about 74% were X-rayed. The programme was completed on schedule. The people who screened as negative were given BCG injections, and the ones showing positive were investigated further. The programme showed that the incidence of active tuberculosis in the crowded city areas was about 3.5% and the incidence in the rural areas was about 1.5%. The results apurred a national TB control programme by government and the private chariity Singapore Anti-Tuberculosis Association (SATA). Susceptible people were vaccinated, a mass X-ray scheme was launched for all people over 14 years old, and the diseased were adequately treated. In 1959, nearly 17,000 residents of Tanjong Pagar were screened. By 1963, over 100,000 had been X-rayed under the Community Mass X-ray Scheme.

X-Ray Training

School of Radiography, 1963. The first School of Radiography was opened in 1963. Radiographers in Singapore had previously been sent on scholarships to train in the United Kingdom. The School was built next to the Department of Radiology at the Outram General Hospital (Singapore General Hospital). The first students were enrolled in 1963 and they completed their training in December 1965. The following students were the first locally trained radiographers: Ruth Low Sow Yuen; Ng Ek Heong; Ng Yock Chun; Alan Pang Wah Hing; Thomas C Row, Paul; Lee-Tan Bee Neio; Seah-Yeo Joo Geok and V George de Silva.

Y

YMCA

1902. In 1902, Robert Pringle arrived in Singapore from London to help set up a Young Men's Christian Association (YMCA) in Singapore. The YMCA began operating in June 1903 out of a building in Armenian Street that had been formerly used as Whitfield's Guest House. There were reading rooms for educational and religious meetings, and boarding accommodation. The organisation expanded rapidly and within 12 months, the membership had grown to 180 members. They soon ran out of room. In August 1909, Sir John Anderson, the Governor of the Straits Settlements laid the cornerstone of a new permanent building. The building was at the corner of Fort Canning Road and Stamford Road and had a 999 year lease. The building was opened by Sir John Anderson on the 16 February 1911. It cost $81,000 for the buildings and furnishings and was paid for by donations from Great Britain, Straits Settlements and Australia. The YMCA offered a wide variety of educational and recreational classes such as singing, mathematics, shorthand and typing. It offered 6-month courses in architecture and building construction that prepared recruits for government service in the Straits Settlements and the Federated Malay States. It also offered classes for entrance to Oxford and Cambridge. The organisation offered a wide range of sporting facilities including the use of the saltwater tanks on Fort Canning as a swimming pool. The tanks were used to store sea water to clean the streets and drains. In 1932, the YMCA bought the Ladies Lawn Tennis Club at Bras Basah Road for $5,000. This provided them with 12 tennis courts. There was an active drama group called The Sceneshifters. The YMCA building was used by the Japanese Kempitei during the Japanese Occupation. It was re-opened in December 1946 and the current building was completed in November 1984 and officially opened by Minister for Law, EW Barker on 24 November 1984. The first meeting of the **Chinese YMCA** was held on 10 April 1946. Dr Chen Su Lan, a member of the Advisory Council of the British Military Administration was elected Chairman.

YWCA

1875. The Young Women's Christian Association was established in Singapore by Miss Sophia Cooke (1814–1895) who came to Singapore in 1853 as a missionary of the Society for the Promotion of Female Education in the East. She organized self-improvement classes for a group of 11 Chinese young women and from these classes, founded the YWCA. She not only established a school for Chinese girls (see SCHOOL), but over the next 42 years, did much to better the lives of young women in Singapore. She died in September 1895 in Singapore. The YWCA of Singapore is affiliated to the World YWCA which originated in London in 1855 with the purpose of providing secured housing for young women.

Z

Zoo

Botanic Gardens, 1870s. The first proper zoo in Singapore was started at the Botanic Gardens in the early 1870s. The zoo's collection grew quickly and by 1902, it had all the important animals of the region. Although many tourists visited the zoo, it was forced to close down in 1903 because of financial difficulties. During the 1920s and 1930s, many 'Great White Hunters' came to Southeast Asia to collect wild animals and sell them to foreign zoos. One of the most famous was Frank Buck who starred in his own films about his collecting trips. Buck once boasted that he safely exported over 5,000 monkeys, 500 small mammals, 60 tigers, 60 bears, 60 leopards, 52 orang utans, 49 elephants and 100,000 birds in his 35 years of collecting. Soon shops started selling wild animals in Singapore. Many of them were in Rochor Road. Some animal dealers also started 'zoos' which were actually wholesale centres for their trade. Some time around 1925, an animal-lover named William Lawrence Soma Basapa started a zoo in Ponggol. It featured over 200 wild animals, including orang utans, a tame tiger named Apay (which was kept on a leash) and non-Asian animals such as chimpanzees. Admission charge was 40 cents. The zoo survived most of the Japanese Occupation, but in the end it was burnt down in 1945 before the war was over. The next zoo was started in 1954 off Tampines Road by a LF de Jong. A newspaper report says that it contained 100 cassowaries, tapirs, leopards, gibbons, crocodiles and snakes. In 1963, the Chan Brothers chose Ponggol as the site for their zoo in 1963. Their collection featured a lion, tigers, tapirs, monkeys, kangaroos, seals and a large number of crocodiles and snakes. This zoo, like those before it, went out of business and was forced to auction off its animals in 1970. However, less than a year later, in January 1971, the Singapore Zoological Gardens had already been planned and was being laid out in Mandai next to Seletar Reservoir. Today, it is one of the most famous zoos in the world.